Carthage Conspiracy

Carthage Conspiracy

The Trial of
the Accused Assassins
of Joseph Smith

DALLIN H. OAKS

and

MARVIN S. HILL

University of Illinois Press

Urbana and Chicago

Illini Books edition, 1979

© 1975 by the Board of Trustees of the University of Illinois
Manufactured in the United States of America
P   9   8   7

LIBRARY OF CONGRESS CATALOGING IN PUBLICATION DATA

Oaks, Dallin H
    Carthage conspiracy.

    Includes bibliographical references and index.
    1. Williams, Levi, d. 1858. 2. Smith, Joseph,
1805-1844. 3. Smith, Hyrum, 1800-1844.   I. Hill,
Marvin S., joint author.   II. Title.
KF223.W5302   345'.73'02524   75-20126
ISBN 0-252-00554-6

⁓ Contents ⁓

75931

❧ Preface ❧

This study of the trial of the accused assassins of Joseph Smith dates from the authors' student days at the University of Chicago. As a potential historian and a young lawyer, we stood on a street corner discussing some problems in Mormon legal history and wondering whether there were enough sources on the trial for a joint scholarly article. A preliminary search disclosed many original documents in the courthouse at Carthage, Illinois, and we began the long process of investigation that has resulted in this book.

Our book is intended to have significance for both scholar and layman. We have tried to look at the trial as a significant legal event in Mormon and American history. But we have tried not to lose sight of the fact that good history is good narrative. Our introduction and concluding chapter may be of special significance for the scholar, but for most readers the point of interest will be the story between.

Scores of persons have assisted the authors during their work of more than a decade on this book. None can properly be charged with any of its deficiencies, but singly and as a group they must enjoy a substantial share of the credit for its merits, since the book would not have been possible without them.

Our first indebtedness is to the scores of named and anonymous persons who recorded and preserved the manuscripts, articles, and books comprising our source material. Only the most prominent could be acknowledged in the Bibliographical Note, but our gratitude extends to all.

We obtained access to essential library and records resources through the generous cooperation of Leonard J. Arrington, historian of the Church of Jesus Christ of Latter-day Saints, and his associates, K. Haybron Adams, Dean C. Jessee, and Earl E. Olson; Roscoe L. McDaniel, clerk of Hancock County; Lillian Woodbury Wood, custodian of the Wilford C. Wood Collection; Wayne C. Temple of the Illinois State Archives; F. Mark McKiernan, director of the Mormon History Manuscripts Collection at Graceland College, Lamoni, Iowa; Chad J. Flake, curator of special collections, and Marvin E. Wiggins, general reference librarian at the Harold B. Lee Library, Brigham Young University; Richard J. Bowler, law librarian at the University of Chicago Law School; and Rowena J. Miller of Nauvoo Restoration, Inc. Librarians at the Chicago Historical Society, the Huntington Library of San Marino, California, the University of Chicago, and Yale University have also been especially helpful.

Research assistance on individual aspects of the book was performed over a period of years by Brigham Young University history students Richard E. Bennett and Terry Butler, by University of Chicago law student Danny J. Boggs, by Brigham Young University law student Lynn W. Davis, and by secretaries Judith Burke and Janet Lloyd.

Countless hours of typing and retyping on scores of drafts were performed capably by Mariel Budd, Judith Burke, Janet Calder, Juanita Evans, Ann Ferguson, Lila Hill, Janet Lloyd, Marcia Sayer, and Lesley Stein.

Valuable suggestions on portions of our drafts were provided by Richard L. Bushman of Boston University, Robert B. Flanders of Southwest Missouri State University, Hans Zeisel of the University of Chicago Law School, Frank W. Fox of the history department and Noel B. Reynolds of the philosophy department at Brigham Young University, and Joseph H. Groberg, Esq., of the Colorado Bar. Our penultimate draft was read by three colleagues, each of whom gave us valuable guidance in his own discipline: Leonard J. Arrington, church historian and director of the Brigham Young University Charles Redd Center for Western Studies; Woodruff J. Deem of the Brigham Young University J. Reuben Clark Law School and for many years district attorney of Ventura County, California; and Byron W. Gassman of the Brigham Young University English department.

The released time and research assistance granted to one of the authors by the Brigham Young University history department and to the other by the University of Chicago Law School at various stages in the preparation of this book are gratefully acknowledged.

Brigham Young University   DALLIN H. OAKS
May 1, 1975   MARVIN S. HILL

∾ Introduction ∾

Like today's citizens struggling with the legitimacy of civil disobedience, pre–Civil War Americans debated a fundamental question: What is the ultimate source of authority in a democratic society — who should have the final say? Nineteenth-century Americans as diverse in their social backgrounds as Henry David Thoreau, John C. Calhoun, and Abraham Lincoln spoke on this issue: Thoreau argued that a moral man must rely solely upon individual conscience to define the extent of his obligation to man-made governments; Calhoun maintained that the Constitution gave certain constituent groups in a state the sovereign authority and final say on all political issues; Lincoln held that a numerical majority, ever changing in its constituency, is the "only true sovereign of a free people."[1]

Before the revolution Americans sometimes discussed the issue of ultimate authority in terms of "higher law," but they were not agreed on its source. Some said it was based upon the will of God.[2] This was the view of William Blackstone, the English jurist whose text was used by the American legal profession as the most authoritative statement of the common law in early nineteenth-century America: "This law of nature, being coeval with mankind and dictated by God himself, is of course superior in obligation to any other. It is binding over all the globe in all countries, and at all times; no human laws are of any validity, if contrary to this."[3]

In contrast, some Americans maintained that God's role was remote and that the higher law was based upon a self-sustaining order of nature.[4] Patriots like Thomas Jefferson relied confidently on "the Laws of Nature and of Nature's God" as the final claim to legitimacy in their political controversy with England. While this seemingly gave credence to both a secular and a religious higher law, the trend was toward the secular. Thus, when Jefferson supported the separation of church and state in Virginia, he argued that Christianity was not part of the inherited common law;[5] this position contributed to the demise of established churches in various states. The American legal profession, increasingly active in the law-making process after 1787, promoted a secular view of the law that was a potent force in American life and contributed to the diminishing influence of a higher law based upon religious assumptions.[6]

During the American Revolution the idea grew that the people were sovereign[7] — they made and unmade governments and fundamental law, acting to be sure out of self-interest and natural human desires, but nonetheless ultimate in their authority and responsible to no one but themselves. Their representatives wrote the United States Constitution, and their votes ratified it in 1787. In the scheme of government they created, the Constitution was a higher law. As its supremacy became secure by popular acceptance and judicial review, the Constitution tended to displace the idea of a higher law in any religious or other transcendental sense. Issues once discussed in terms of a transcendental higher law now tended to be posed in terms of sovereignty — not what was in accord with "the Laws of Nature and of Nature's God," but who had the final right to decide. Thus, de Tocqueville did not exaggerate greatly when he observed in the 1830's, "The people reign in the American political world as the Deity does in the Universe."[8]

The question of the ultimate source of authority was at issue in western Illinois during the 1840's. While the rest of the American people were moving toward a secularization of the higher law, with consequent preoccupation with popular sovereignty, the people who were called Mormons,[9] who founded a community at Nauvoo, Illinois, established a society whose every institution was infused with religious values and religious purpose, and whose higher law was given through their prophet-leader by divine revelation. That law was embodied in their sacred books, the Bible, the Book of Mormon, and the Doctrine and Covenants, but was also embodied in what they called their "Living Constitution," the Council of Fifty of the Kingdom of God, with the prophet at its head.

Despite great fidelity to their prophet, the Mormons were also committed to obeying the laws of the land, a commitment reinforced by religious principles.[10] Nevertheless, the Mormons met with bitter opposition from Illinois citizens who charged that they followed their prophet implicitly and had little respect for man-made law. In advancing their opposition to the increasing political power of the Mormons, the anti-Mormons appealed to two versions of the higher law — the right of self-preservation, and popular sovereignty. When a group of anti-Mormons pressed these concepts to their extreme and assassinated Joseph Smith, the Mormon prophet, and his brother, Hyrum, the state intervened and sought to bring the guilty parties to justice. A trial was held at Carthage, Hancock County, in May, 1845, involving many of the most prominent citizens of Illinois.

Although formally concerned with the guilt or innocence of the accused assassins, the trial tested a more fundamental question: would the jurors, as spokesmen for the community, enforce the law against murder, which was based on religious-moral principles, or would they excuse the crime by recourse to a supposed higher law of popular approval?

1. The views of Thoreau, Calhoun, and Lincoln on this issue are generally well known. In his essay treating civil disobedience, Thoreau inquired: "Must the citizen even for a moment, or in the least degree, resign his conscience to the legislator? . . . It is not desirable to cultivate a respect for the law, so much as for the right. The only obligation which I have a right to assume, is to do at any time what I think right." Calhoun's thesis of concurrent majority (that is, the necessity of granting interest groups in a state veto power over the national numerical majority) was argued in his *Disquisition on Government*, his thesis of state sovereignty in his *Discourse on the Constitution*. Lincoln best expressed his thesis in his first inaugural address, March 4, 1861. These works are available in many places. We have made use of Owen Thomas, ed., *Walden and Civil Disobedience* (New York: W. W. Norton, 1966), p. 225; C. Gordon Post, ed., *John C. Calhoun, A Disquisition on Government* (New York: Liberal Arts Press, 1953), 22-23, 28, 87-88; and Roy P. Bassler, ed., *Abraham Lincoln: His Speeches and Writings* (New York: World, 1969), 585.

2. Clinton Rossiter, *The Political Thought of the American Revolution* (New York: Harvest Books, 1963), 87-88.

3. William Blackstone, *Commentaries on the Laws of England*, I, St. George Tucker, ed. (Philadelphia: William Young Birch & Abraham Small, 1803), 41.

4. Rossiter, *Political Thought*, 88-89.

5. Perry Miller, *The Life of the Mind in America* (New York: Harvest Books, 1965), 192.

6. *Ibid.*, 99-108.

7. See "The American Revolution: The People as Constituent Power," in R. R. Palmer, *The Challenge*, vol. I of *The Age of the Democratic Revolution* (Princeton: Princeton University Press, 1959), 213-35.

8. Alexis de Tocqueville, *Democracy in America*, ed. Phillips Bradley (New York: Vintage Books, 1955), 60.

9. The term "Mormon" is a nickname based upon the Book of Mormon. The actual name of the Church that is based in Utah is the Church of Jesus Christ of Latter-day Saints.

10. Observance of "the laws of the land" is commanded in the Mormon Doctrine and Covenants 58:21, and the "Articles of Faith," 12.

◈ 1 ◈

Court Week in Carthage

The Circuit Court came to Carthage, Illinois, twice each year, on the third Mondays of May and October. Its two-week sessions were better than a traveling circus. By wagon, on horseback, or on foot, the farmers of Hancock County gathered at the county seat for court week. This was the natural time for men to swap stories, make trades, learn the news, hear the speeches, and decide who would have their votes for the legislature. Though its 22,559 inhabitants made Hancock the most populous county in Illinois in 1845, Carthage, the county seat, had only a few hundred inhabitants — except during court week. Then it was impossible to find sleeping space on a floor. The judge and visiting lawyers took rooms in the Hamilton House, the leading local tavern or hotel. But the citizens of the county, the participants and spectators in this frontier exhibition of democracy in action, made their beds on haystacks and in wagon-boxes.[1]

The central attractions of court week were the judge and his party. This dusty, congenial cavalcade followed a circuit, crisscrossing the prairie land of the ten western Illinois counties in the fifth judicial circuit. Their baggage was limited to what they could carry behind a saddle or in a light buggy — not more than a change of shirt and underwear. They wore the rest of their wardrobe: "tall black hats, 'tailcoats' . . . and 'biled shirts,' with limp cotton collars rolling over black neckerchiefs tied in single bows."[2] The circuit rider's traveling law library was a worn volume of the *Revised Statutes of Illinois*, perhaps supplemented by a copy of *Blackstone's Commentaries*. Formal learning and court opinions were less important than common sense, plain talk, a good memory, a persuasive manner, and a shrewd judgment of situations and people. Relations with the judge and among opposing lawyers were friendly and informal. Men would not remain strangers when they rode the prairie together and slept four or five to a room. To amuse themselves in the long evenings between court sessions, the circuit riders and local citizens occupied the porches or common rooms of the taverns in casual conversation or used the courtroom or the tavern for frontier drama, impromptu debates, or political speeches.[3]

One of the most exciting events of court week was the arrival of the circuit riders. At the first cry of recognition, loungers ran for the Hamilton House to get there before the cavalcade of buggies and riders. Potential litigants had to make a speedy evaluation of the dusty and saddle-sore advocates and engage their champions before they were committed to the opposition. A popular lawyer could not swing out of the saddle and brush the dust from his tailcoat before he was surrounded by a noisy chorus of litigants shouting descriptions of their controversies and seeking his services.[4]

The great men of the Illinois bar passed through Carthage on these circuits, so the regular spectators at court week had seen and judged the performance of such luminaries as E. D. Baker, Stephen A. Douglas, O. H. Browning, Archibald Williams, and Abraham Lincoln. These and others like them were the present and future leaders of the state. Thomas Ford was an example — only a few years earlier he had been riding circuit as states attorney of the fifth circuit, and now he was governor of the state.

The courtrooms of frontier settlements like Carthage filled the place of the theater, concert hall, and opera. The judges and lawyers were the stars; the drama, wit, pathos, and eloquence of their calling always had appreciative audiences. The episodes viewed in the courtroom during these brief weeks of May and October were told again and again in the cabins, schoolhouses, and social gatherings of the county in the following months. The leading advocates had their partisans, personal and political, and their respective merits were argued with fervor.[5]

As court week drew near in May, 1845, the night crowd at the Hamilton House must have looked across the darkened square to their new courthouse, anticipating the extraordinary events of the coming weeks. Hancock citizens were proud of their new courthouse, completed in 1839. It was a far cry from the private cabins or other log structures used for court in other counties. A two-story brick building, it had four rooms on the first floor for the offices of the county sheriff, treasurer, and the clerks of the circuit court and the county commissioners' court. The second floor consisted of a large courtroom and two jury rooms.[6]

In the first court term in the new courthouse Carthage visitors had seen the trial of the only man ever hanged for murder in Hancock County. William Fraim, a twenty-one-year-old Irishman employed as a deckhand on an Illinois steamer, had killed a man in a drunken brawl in Schuyler County just east of Hancock. He was defended by Abraham Lincoln of Sangamon County, who was riding circuit that spring. After a one-day trial, the jury found him guilty, and the judge sentenced him to hang. Lincoln tried to have the judgment set aside, but the judge denied the motion and the hanging went forward about three weeks after the trial.[7]

The people of Carthage attended to this hanging as though they would never have another. They built a gallows in the center of a natural amphitheater in a field about a mile southeast of Carthage, where they could accommodate a large crowd. School was dismissed, and many of the spectators brought their families and dinners and made a sort of picnic of the occasion. Many of the children of Carthage had gotten acquainted with Fraim between the time of the trial and the hanging. Since Carthage had no jail at this time, the condemned man was confined and guarded in the second-floor jury room in the southwest corner of the new courthouse. His windows looked out on the adjoining schoolyard, and Fraim passed the long hours by talking to the children who were playing at recess. He was a pleasant and engaging youth, and the children were sorry to see him hang.[8]

Carthage hadn't had a murder trial since the Fraim hanging. The grand jury had brought in about a dozen indictments in every term of court, but they included no really serious crimes. Stealing of livestock or household effects were the most common crimes, followed by riot, adultery, and fornication, and then a smattering of others like perjury, kidnapping, false imprisonment, and assault. Few of these indictments ever came to trial; usually they were postponed from one term of court to the next, and finally disposed of by some technicality or by the states attorney's refusal to prosecute. The men who served as judge and states attorney often changed

3

from one term to another, and many crimes that had appeared worth prosecuting six months or a year earlier didn't seem worth the effort to a different prosecutor in the crowded schedule of a new term. About two-thirds of the Hancock County grand jury indictments in this period were dismissed by states attorneys without trial. In May, 1844, the court had had the most criminal trials that anyone could remember in a single term: six jury trials, including two appeals from minor cases in the justice of the peace court, a perjury trial, and three trials for selling liquor without a license. Juries found the defendants not guilty in all cases. In contrast, in October, 1844, there had been no criminal trials.[9]

Spectators, characteristically impatient with legal maneuvers, preferred trials, but there weren't many. Over half of the court's business involved civil cases, which included a few trials. But among the criminal cases on the docket there were no more than one or two jury trials in a single term of court, and these usually involved only a few witnesses and were concluded in an hour or two.

Compared with past experiences, the May, 1845, term would be unforgettable. As the time drew near, the attention of the entire county — indeed, the attention of the whole state of Illinois — focused on the case of *People* v. *Levi Williams,* set for trial in Carthage. The charge was murder. The defendants were among the most prominent men in western Illinois: a state senator; a colonel, major, and two captains in the local militia; and one of the region's most prominent newspaper editors. The governor's personal choice as prosecutor was Josiah Lamborn, recently attorney general of the state and renowned as one of the most able and merciless prosecutors of his time. The defendants were to be represented by a group of the finest lawyers in Illinois. Deputy sheriffs, busy serving subpoenas for the trial, let it be known that there were almost thirty subpoenas for prosecution witnesses and half that many for the defense. This trial could take as much as a week.

Tensions grew as spectators filtered into Carthage and gathered to speculate about events of the coming week and as riders galloped out across the prairie to summon witnesses and prospective jurors. Each day brought new rumors on trial strategy. Carthage was becoming important, despite its size. In June, 1844, a little less than a year before, a large mob had shot and killed two of the most influential men in Illinois in the Carthage jail out on the northwest edge of town. Their bodies had lain overnight in the Hamilton House. Now the men indicted for that murder were to be tried in the Carthage courthouse. This was the setting for the trial of the indicted assassins of the Mormon prophet, Joseph Smith.

1. Augustus S. Mitchell as quoted in Maurice G. Baxter, *Orville H. Browning, Lincoln's Friend and Critic* (Bloomington: Indiana University Press, 1957), 9; Orville F. Berry, "The Mormon Settlement in Illinois," *Transactions of the Illinois State Historical Society* (1906), 88, 98; Charles J. Scofield, ed., *History of Hancock County,* in Newton Bateman, J. Seymour Currey, and Paul Selby, eds., *Historical Encyclopedia of Illinois and History of Hancock County* (Chicago: Munsell, 1921), II, 1103, hereafter cited as Scofield, *History of Hancock County.* Vol. I will be cited hereafter as Bateman, *Historical Encyclopedia of Illinois.*

2. These are novelist Joseph Kirkland's recollections, quoted in J. C. Furnas, *The Americans* (New York: G. P. Putnam's Sons, 1972), 257.

3. This description of the circuit riders and their activities is drawn from Isaac N. Arnold, "Recollections of Early Chicago and the Illinois Bar," *Chicago Bar Association Lectures,* Fergus Historical Series, no. 22 (Chicago, 1880), 11-12; Furnas, *The Americans,* 257; Eudocia Baldwin Marsh, "Mormons in Hancock County: A Reminiscence," *Journal of the Illinois State Historical Society* 64 (Spring, 1971), 31-32. The judicial circuit was prescribed by law. *Revised Statutes of Illinois* (1845), 143-46, 628.

4. John Dean Caton, *The Early Bench and Bar of Illinois* (Chicago: Chicago News Company, 1893), 223.

5. Arnold, "Recollections," 12.

6. Scofield, *History of Hancock County,* 692-94.

7. *Ibid.,* 761-66; Carl Sandburg, *Abraham Lincoln: The Prairie Years* (New York: Harcourt, Brace, 1926), 222.

8. Scofield, *History of Hancock County,* 761-66.

9. These generalizations are based on a careful study of the docket entries in the five court terms in Hancock County from May, 1844, through May, 1846. *Circuit Court Record, Hancock County, Book D,* 64-451, hereafter cited as *Circuit Court Record.*

～2～

"Murder... by a Respectable Set of Men"

The murder of Joseph and Hyrum Smith at Carthage, Illinois, was not a spontaneous, impulsive act by a few personal enemies of the Mormon leaders, but a deliberate political assassination, committed or condoned by some of the leading citizens in Hancock County. As such it falls within the brutal but familiar American tradition of vigilante activity,[1] and formed but one episode in a long series of anti-Mormon depredations in New York, Ohio, Missouri, and Illinois. According to Joseph Smith, he was the object of controversy and persecution from the beginning of his prophetic career in 1820. He said that when he received his first vision, in which God had informed him that the existing Christian churches were all apostate and that he was called to restore the true church, a local minister in Palmyra, New York, treated him with "great contempt," insisting that revelations had ceased with the death of the Apostles.[2] Nine years later, in 1829, Joseph Smith stirred more controversy when he announced the forthcoming publication of a new scripture, the Book of Mormon, a record of God's teachings to ancient Americans. One of his followers said that the clergy in Wayne County "tried their best to have him indicted for blasphemy," believing that his book was an affront to the Bible and a source of false doctrine.[3] From its inception the Mormon movement seemed to run contrary to prevailing Protestant values.

In South Bainbridge in Chenango County, New York, where a few were converted to the new faith from among the Presbyterians, the town fathers determined to stop the movement by having Smith brought to trial as a "disorderly person." To escape further harassment and violence, the Mormons began to hold meetings in secret, but this gave rise to the charge that Smith planned the subversion of the government.[4] The charge may also have stemmed from the fact that the Book of Mormon depicted a theocratic social order in America which encompassed religious, social, economic, and political life.[5] As opposition mounted in New York, the prophet received a revelation which said that the enemy was combined against the Saints and they should flee to the West. After they took asylum in Kirtland, Ohio, in 1831, the "laws of the kingdom" were revealed.[6]

The Mormons who fled New York were refugees from religious pluralism who found sectarian conflict disorienting and disillusioning. Joseph Smith said his initial vision came when he could not decide which, if any, of the contending sects in Palmyra was right. But Mormonism was more than a dissatisfaction with sectarianism. The prophet, members of his family, and his early converts spoke with contempt of a deference to social rank among the churches, of wealthy church members built up in pride, and of a "hireling clergy" who served the Lord for pay and competed with other ministers for converts at revivals rather than unselfishly bringing men to Christ. The Mormons deplored the multiplying voluntary associations and societies that were agitating for reform and political preferment. Above all, they feared that America might become governed by corrupt men whose primary purpose was the acquisition of profits and power.[7] Running deep within Mormon consciousness was a fear that a society once built upon moral integrity and religious commitment was now in decline and that mass democracy could not preserve a just and lasting government. The prophet himself said in 1842 that man's attempt to establish government had failed and that God must take the reins of power.[8] Only when the Kingdom of God was established upon earth would justice and mercy prevail.

Such a kingdom would fully come only during the millennium, an event the Mormons took to be imminent. In the meantime, they sought to implement some of its elements and to find refuge from the disintegrating forces of pluralism around them. Their refuge was to be a holy city, a Zion, with locations in Kirtland and in Jackson County, Missouri. Here the Saints would have all things in common, as in the days of the Apostles, and God's laws would be fully revealed and fully practiced. But when the political nature of the kingdom and some of its anti-pluralistic tendencies became manifest, the Mormons again found themselves the object of vigilante activity.[9]

In Missouri during the 1830's, the Mormons initiated a communitarian experiment, and hundreds of poor flocked into the new economic order. Although the Mormons did not become involved in local politics during their first year there, many Missourians feared that the immigrants would soon monopolize political offices. As Mormons occupied public lands, the old settlers perceived them as economic rivals. Still more perilous, it seemed, was the likelihood that free Negro converts might have a subversive influence upon Missouri slaves. When the Mormon newspaper in Independence published an editorial that appeared to encourage the immigration of free blacks into the state, the mood of the leading Missourians became violent. They formed a "vigilance committee" which destroyed the Mormon press and forced the exodus of the Latter-day Saints from Jackson County.[10] In the spring of 1834 the prophet raised a volunteer army in Ohio to march to Missouri and restore the exiles to their lands; but despite promises of support from the governor of the state, none was forthcoming, and the expedition failed in its apparent purpose.[11] Afterward, the Saints who had taken refuge in Clay County to the north lived on borrowed time, as their basic cultural differences with the Missourians remained.

At Kirtland, Ohio, the movement flourished for a time, as more than two thousand converts gathered to hear the gospel message of restoration and millennium. With great energy Joseph Smith organized a lay priesthood who were to preach the gospel without monetary compensation. He also received and published a book of revelations to guide the infant church, and initiated the building of a temple where the Saints were to receive special ordinances preparatory to the coming of Christ.[12]

Increasing in potential political power with each convert, Mormons in Ohio began to publish a newspaper in support of Andrew Jackson and the Democratic party, thus initiating an effort to exert political influence in county affairs.[13] It is uncertain, however, whether their political activities were the result of their apocalyptic political expectations or a by-product of their gathering and a natural inclination to use the political potential of their people to promote their own security and welfare. One factor in their political activities was the typically American view that citizens could exercise their votes as they saw fit, whether individually or collectively.[14] Whatever their intention, they soon quarreled with other Ohio Democrats, who affirmed that the Mormons planned to monopolize all political offices.[15]

Despite these difficulties, Kirtland enjoyed a modest industrial output and well-developed family farming, so that by 1836 the Mormons had a viable economy. Joseph Smith acquired considerable wealth in land and borrowed on this to initiate a mercantile business. But too many Saints took advantage of his good will and made more promises than payments for their purchases. To promote Kirtland's economy Smith initiated a banking experiment in the fall of 1836, but he was unable to acquire a banking charter from the state legislature, which was dominated by an anti-banking faction of the Democratic party. Advised by legal counsel, he pursued the evasive tactic of attempting to transform his banking firm into a joint stock company with note-issuing powers, but the effort failed when relatively few Mormons or non-Mormons would accept the bank's notes, fearful that in so doing they would violate an 1816 Ohio law against unauthorized banking. Smith himself was later fined $1,000 in a civil action for having violated the act. Within a few weeks after the bank was launched, he was unable to redeem the outstanding notes in specie; in June, 1837, he completely withdrew his support.[16]

Since the Mormon people held high hopes for the bank, its demise shook their confidence in the economic policies of their leader. Some apostles and other church leaders became open critics, affirming that Joseph had no right to involve the church in the economic life of Kirtland and charging that he had too much power concentrated in his hands. Before the turmoil at Kirtland had run its course, a series of lawsuits were initiated against Smith which he was only partially able to settle. Fearful of violence and imprisonment for failure to pay his debts, he fled in January, 1838, to take refuge in Missouri, where a new Mormon community was being established in Caldwell County.[17]

The Mormons had been forced out of Clay County, Missouri, in 1836, but had reached a tacit agreement with the Missourians that they could occupy a region north of Clay, to be organized as a separate county, provided they would confine themselves to that area.[18] Soon another gathering was underway in new Caldwell County, with Far West becoming the county seat. But by 1838 the Mormons had occupied much of Caldwell and were spilling over into Daviess County to the north, to the dismay of land speculators, squatters, and politicians. In the fall the Mormons, still Democrats from their Kirtland days, made preparations to vote at Gallatin, the Daviess County seat; the Whigs reacted by organizing to keep them from the polls. The resulting fight between the Whigs and the Mormons at Gallatin initiated a series of belligerent acts by both parties and brought on armed conflict that verged on civil war.[19]

Soon after this, armed Missourians by the hundreds laid siege to two outlying Mormon communities, demanding that the inhabitants withdraw to Far West in Caldwell County. Joseph Smith made an appeal to Governor Lilburn Boggs to relieve the siege at one of these towns, DeWitt, but was told that Mormons must fight their own battles.[20] Angry at this, and tired of legal harassments, dissent, and persecution, the prophet told his people that he would endure no more. A Mormon army rode into Daviess County and drove the mobbers out, finding sustenance by sacking dwellings and stores in two or three towns.[21] The governor immediately declared the Mormons in rebellion and called the militia to arms. Thousands from surrounding counties seized their muskets and hastened toward Far West.[22]

At Haun's Mill, a nearby Mormon village, an army of two hundred angry Missourians, encouraged by the governor's proclamation to drive out the Mormons or exterminate them, massacred eighteen unarmed men and a boy who had not followed the prophet's urging to gather at Far West. Before another bloody battle ensued Joseph made peace with the Missouri militia, surrendering himself for trial under a charge of treason against the state. After a preliminary hearing found probable cause for holding him and other Mormon leaders for the grand jury (after allowing only a few defense witnesses to be heard), the Missouri authorities remanded them to jail at Liberty, Missouri. Six months passed without another hearing before they escaped and fled to Illinois.[23]

While Joseph Smith was incarcerated in Missouri, the Mormons had begun to gather around the town of Commerce, Illinois, on the upper Mississippi. By the time he reached them in April, 1839, the settlement was already established. Joseph negotiated with several landowners to purchase large tracts of land on both sides of the river. He then invited the Saints to seek refuge by gathering once more, warning them that "the time is coming, when no man will have any peace but in Zion and her stakes."[24] Soon the city of Nauvoo was booming as thousands of new converts immigrated from the eastern United States, Canada, and England. Under the prophet's energetic leadership construction was begun on another temple high upon the bluffs overlooking the river, and a bimonthly newspaper was published to inform the Saints in America of the progress of the work and to encourage the gathering. Before long the Mormons made up half the population of Hancock County, and Nauvoo had become the largest city in the state.[25]

Once more Mormon collectivist ways ran counter to the prevailing culture, and hostility toward them began to mount. The old citizens in Hancock County were increasingly apprehensive about the size of the Mormon gathering and its purposes, fearing that non-Mormons would be relegated to second-class citizens politically if the Mormon population continued to increase.[26] Assuming leadership of the anti-Mormon movement was Thomas C. Sharp, a youthful citizen of Warsaw, a town of about 500, several miles down the river from Nauvoo; he edited the influential *Warsaw Signal*. To counter Mormon political power Sharp organized an anti-Mormon political party in 1841, urging Whigs and Democrats to come to his support.[27] Searching for issues upon which to challenge Mormon power, Sharp criticized the establishment of the Nauvoo Legion (a semi-independent army of Mormon militia), the city charter which authorized it, the prophet's expansive land transactions, and the solid Mormon vote. Sharp bitterly denounced Joseph Smith's excessive power, manifest in his role as mayor, lieutenant-general of the legion, presiding judge of the highest city court, land speculator, and political boss. He warned that Smith, by extending his influence into so many areas of life, had stepped beyond the sanctuary of religion and would be held accountable, thus voicing a traditional American antipathy for the undue concentration of economic and political power. Above all, Sharp protested that the powerful prophet was exempt from civil law. When the city council passed an ordinance allowing for review of all state arrest orders, Sharp exploded. "Now we ask our citizens; what think you of this barefaced defiance of our laws by the City Council of Nauvoo, and if persisted in what must be the final result?"[28]

Despite Sharp's efforts, the Mormons were also becoming a factor in state politics by 1842. No election could occur without the opposing Whig and Democratic candidates courting or denouncing the Mormon vote. Although initially supporting the Whig party, Mormons voted consistently for the Democrats after 1841, causing the Whigs to drift into the anti-Mormon camp.[29] Two Whig newspapers, the *Quincy Whig* and the *Sangamo Journal,* thereafter regularly voiced their irritation with Mormon principles and Mormon politics,[30] reaching a large number of highly literate and news-hungry citizens whose long and often uneventful evenings were filled with reflections upon the Mormon question.

The question became inflammatory in mid-1842 when John C. Bennett, church leader and the first mayor of Nauvoo, had a falling out with the prophet. Speaking through the Whig newspapers and in a book, he published charges that Smith and some of his leading men were practicing polygamy. Emphatic denials by Mormon editors and missionaries did not completely persuade Illinoisans, and from this point onward Mormons were on trial with church-going people in Hancock County and in the state.[31]

Mormon–non-Mormon relations reached a point of impending hostility in June, 1843, when the prophet was arrested at some distance from Nauvoo by two deputies who sought to return him to Missouri. He was saved by a segment of the Nauvoo Legion, which intercepted the deputies and brought him triumphantly back to Nauvoo. But this act seemed high-handed to non-Mormons, who said that no legal process could be served on the Mormon leader. They became more hostile when the Nauvoo city council subsequently passed a law authorizing a review by the mayor of any "foreign" legal process issuing from outside the city.[32]

Fearful of another round of armed conflict, the Mormons sought political protection. Early in 1844 Smith wrote to several of the candidates for the United States presidency, inquiring about their willingness to sustain Mormon rights with federal power.[33] Disappointed at receiving negative or ambiguous responses, he announced his own candidacy — a move which did much to alienate even the Democrats, who were still anxious for the Mormon vote.[34] If elected, he pledged sufficient protection for all minorities.[35] In the meantime, he petitioned Congress for territorial status for Nauvoo,[36] hoping to gain freedom from interference by state authorities and to secure a guarantee of federal protection should Nauvoo come under attack. Expecting that these measures might fail, Joseph fully organized the "Kingdom of God" by establishing the Council of Fifty, the executive and legislative arm of a theocratic government.[37] He sent emissaries to Texas seeking permission to settle in the Southwest and petitioned Congress to allow him to raise an army of 100,000 to secure American rights to Oregon, thinking that the Saints might emigrate to that area.[38] With some of his advisers urging him to set up an independent empire in the Rockies, he also made plans to send an expedition to that area as a possible central gathering place for his people.[39]

But before any of these programs could come to fruition, the prophet was confronted with another dissenting movement within the ranks of the church. Headed by one of his former counselors, William Law, the dissenters opposed polygamy and the political Kingdom of God. By mid-May a small but determined group of three hundred seceders was holding regular meetings and demanding the repeal of the Nauvoo Charter. To solicit support for their cause, they visited surrounding towns and represented the prophet as "pretty much a rough character, especially in relation to the 'spiritual wife' doctrine." One local historian indicated that they "left no opportunity unimproved to influence the public mind to the highest pitch" against Joseph and Hyrum.[40] The anti-Mormons at Warsaw, recognizing allies, worked closely with the dissenters. In April, when the prophet brought to the city council charges that two of the dissenters had conspired to take his life, the editor of the *Warsaw Signal* warned, "Let Joe dare to harm one of them, and he will awaken a spirit to which resistance will be useless."[41]

In May the anti-Mormons moved to bring Smith before the court in Carthage. One of the dissenters sought to have him arrested on the basis of a civil damage action, but he was released on a Nauvoo writ of habeas corpus.[42] Thomas Sharp reacted angrily in the *Warsaw Signal,* charging what many in the county had come to believe, that "Joe Smith is *above the law. He cannot be punished* for any crime."[43] Other dissenters gave the grand jury evidence on which it indicted Joseph Smith for adultery and perjury. At this, Smith rode to the county seat and demanded an immediate trial, but his enemies countered by having the cases held over until the following term of court.[44] While Smith was at Carthage, Thomas Sharp warned in the *Warsaw Signal:* "We have seen and heard enough to convince us that Joe Smith is not safe out of Nauvoo, and we would not be surprised to hear of his death by violent means in a short time. He has deadly enemies — men whose wrongs have maddened them. . . . The feeling of this country is now lashed to its utmost pitch, and will break forth in fury upon the slightest provocation."[45]

The anti-Mormons in Hancock were readying themselves in vigilante style to take the law into their own hands. Thomas Sharp wrote in the June 5 issue of the *Warsaw Signal:* "If one portion of the community sets the law at defiance, are we bound to respect the laws in our reaction to it? . . . if we do not mistake the people in this vicinity will solve . . . [the issue] practically unless there is speedy and effective reform at Nauvoo."

To contribute their share to the heightening anti-Mormon feeling, on June 7 the Mormon seceders published the first issue of the *Nauvoo Expositor,* charging Smith with bringing innocent females to Nauvoo under the pretext of religion to add to his harem. They declared that their purpose was to "explode the vicious principles of Joseph Smith, and those who practice the same abominations and whoredoms which we verily know are not accordant and consonant with the principles of Jesus Christ and the Apostles." Castigating Smith's candidacy for the presidency, they informed the Saints, "You are voting for a man who contends all governments are to be put down and the *one* established upon its ruins," and added, "we cannot believe that God ever raised up a prophet to christianize [*sic*] a world by political schemes and intrigue."[46]

On the Saturday morning following the publication of the *Expositor* the Nauvoo city council met to consider the threat to the city which the newspaper posed. After a lengthy discussion Joseph Smith said that such men and newspapers "are calculated to destroy the peace of the city, and it is not safe that such things should exist, on account of the mob spirit which they tend to produce." Following the hearing of some further testimony, he said he "would rather die tomorrow and have the thing smashed, than live and have it go on, for it was exciting the spirit of mobocracy . . . and bringing death and destruction upon us."[47]

On Monday the discussion of the council continued. Councilor Warrington, a non-Mormon, urged that rather than destroy the press the city fathers should impose a fine of $3,000 for every libel published; if that did not curb its slanders, then it could be declared a public nuisance. Smith objected to this, saying Mormons would have to journey to the county seat at Carthage to prosecute these cases and that their lives would be in danger. He urged that the newspaper be declared a nuisance and destroyed without judicial process, a procedure supported by Blackstone.[48] John Taylor, a city councilman and high-ranking church leader, agreed, saying that the *Expositor* "stinks in the nose of every honest man." The Monday meeting lasted until 6:30 in the evening, by which time Joseph had won over most of the council. They passed an ordinance declaring the newspaper a public nuisance and issued an order to the mayor to have it abated. Joseph Smith, acting as mayor, ordered the city marshal to destroy the newspaper and press without delay and instructed the major general of the Nauvoo Legion to have the militia assist. Shortly after eight o'clock that evening, citizens and legionnaires marched to the *Expositor* office and smashed the press, scattering the type as they did so.[49]

This act infuriated the non-Mormons of Hancock County, who saw it as a final act of contempt for their laws. The *Quincy Whig* denounced the "HIGH-HANDED OUTRAGE" and said that if this was a specimen of "Mormon attitude toward law and rights it is not surprising that the Missourians were raised to madness and drove them from the state."[50] H. H. Bliss of La Harpe expressed the prevailing view when he said the issue was whether the law "should have its corse [*sic*] on Smith or not."[51]

At Warsaw Thomas Sharp said, "We hold ourselves at all times in readyness to co-operate with our fellow citizens . . . to exterminate, utterly exterminate, the wicked and abominable Mormon leaders." Advocating an attack upon the Mormon city, he screamed in his headlines, "Strike them! for the time has fully come."[52]

To provide legal justification for a march on Nauvoo, charges of promoting a riot were made against Smith and several Mormon leaders, and Constable David Bettisworth was sent to Nauvoo on

June 12 to apprehend them. When Bettisworth reached Nauvoo, Smith refused to go to Carthage, fearing his life would be endangered. He said he would stand trial before any judge in Nauvoo. To prevent Bettisworth from taking him, he secured a writ of habeas corpus from a city court and later was tried and acquitted before a non-Mormon judge.[53] When Bettisworth came back to Carthage without his prisoner, the reaction of the old citizens was nearly hysterical. Samuel Otho Williams, a member of the Carthage militia, observed, "Such an excitement I have never witnessed in my life."[54] One citizen remarked, "Joe has tried the game too often."[55] The Carthaginians sent messengers as far as three hundred miles urging armed men to come to Carthage to take Smith into custody. Emissaries were sent to Governor Ford, charging that Smith had defied the law and asking Ford to bring the state militia.[56]

Everywhere the old citizens readied for war. At Warsaw they voted $1,000 for arms and ammunition, and at several other towns in the county smaller amounts were raised. In Rushville, Illinois, northeast of Quincy, 3,000 men prepared, and in Iowa and Missouri the prophet's old enemies took up arms.[57]

In the face of an imminent attack on his city, Smith declared Nauvoo under martial law and called out the legion, a defensive action which later led to treason charges being levied against him at Carthage.[58] Meanwhile, Governor Ford had learned of the excitement in Hancock and decided to intervene, arriving at Carthage by June 21. There he wrote the Mormon leader requesting that evidence be shown to justify the actions taken against the *Expositor*. After reviewing this and counter-evidence from the anti-Mormons, Ford wrote Joseph Smith on the next day, denouncing the city's proceedings as unlawful and demanding that those involved in the move against the *Expositor* submit to the processes of the law at Carthage. Ford warned that an attack upon Nauvoo seemed imminent if the Mormon response was not prompt.[59]

Remembering the warning of the *Warsaw Signal* that his life was in jeopardy outside Nauvoo, the prophet weighed his chances. He wrote to Ford on June 22 that he dared not come to Carthage until the mob had been dispersed, and that he was considering appealing to the federal government in Washington.[60] Quickly despairing of this course, he and his brother, Hyrum, crossed the river into Iowa and hid themselves near a community of Saints at Montrose.[61] The next day Joseph wrote to his wife, Emma, and urged her to bring the family and join him, intending to flee west beyond the reach of his enemies.[62] At Nauvoo, however, there was fear that if the prophet did not surrender himself, the Carthaginians would attack as Ford had warned. Helen Mar Whitney, a young girl at Nauvoo, recalled that many were "dreadfully tried in their faith to think Joseph would leave them in the hour of danger."[63] Some elders persuaded Emma to write her husband, asking him to return. Upon delivering her letter on June 23, one cuttingly remarked: "You always said if the Church would stick to you, you would stick to the Church, now trouble comes you are the first to run."[64]

The charges of betrayal and cowardice stung the prophet. He said, "If my life is of no value to my friends it is of none to myself,"[65] adding, "if they had let me alone there would have been no bloodshed but now I expect to be butchered." Hyrum said, "We had better go back and die like men."[66] Before nightfall the brothers returned to Nauvoo and made arrangements through a lawyer to give themselves up, relying on a pledge from the governor that he would protect them at Carthage.[67] On the morning of June 24 the prophet and a party of fifteen set out for Carthage, only to meet Captain Dunn of the militia with an order from Governor Ford to repossess the state arms at Nauvoo. The Smiths rode back to the city to urge their people to surrender these arms peacefully, and in the evening they started once more on the fifteen-mile ride to Carthage. The prophet remarked as he rode out of Nauvoo, "I go as a lamb to the slaughter."[68]

When Captain Dunn and his companions rode into Carthage at midnight, they went to the Hamilton House, where Governor Ford was lodged. After Joseph and Hyrum were taken inside to be quartered for the night, citizens swarmed around the hotel demanding to see the prisoners. Ford came to the window and promised that, come morning, all would meet them.[69]

In the morning General James Singleton ordered the Carthage troops to stand for review by Governor Ford. When Ford appeared, he was accompanied by Joseph and Hyrum Smith and General Minor Deming, who commanded the Hancock County militia units.

Deming began to introduce the prisoners to the two columns of troops on the south side of the town square. When the entourage reached the line of Carthage Greys, violent protests began. Bitterly resentful of Joseph Smith's military pretensions, the Greys exclaimed, "No, no, no introductions for us," and followed with loud hisses and cries of "down with all impostors." The officer in charge tried to silence them but, in his words, "had no more command over them than I would have had over a pack of wild Indians." Joseph and Hyrum, fearful for their safety, urged the governor to return them to the hotel.[70] Ford, angry at what appeared to be mutinous behavior, is reported to have ordered the Greys under arrest for insubordination in loading their guns and refusing to surrender them, but General Deming later denied that such an order was issued.[71] The Greys' behavior at least confirmed that they were among the prophet's most bitter enemies, and led to criticism of Ford when he later assigned them to guard the jail where Joseph and Hyrum were held.[72]

Following this episode Joseph and Hyrum voluntarily surrendered themselves to the constable on the original warrant for riot. That afternoon the prisoners were taken before Justice of the Peace Robert Smith, captain of the Carthage Greys, their bitter enemy, instead of before the justice who issued the original writ. Justice Smith fixed bail at $500 each on the riot charges. The bail was quickly posted by the Mormons, so Joseph and Hyrum might have gone free. But in the meantime they had been arrested on another writ for treason against the state for declaring martial law at Nauvoo. The latter charge was apparently initiated by the anti-Mormons at Carthage so there would be less likelihood of release on bail. Since treason was a capital crime, bail could only be fixed by a circuit judge, and the nearest such officer was a day's ride away. The question of bail was not raised, however, because Justice Smith adjourned the proceedings without calling the treason case, thus leaving the prisoners in the custody of the constable. Then, without any hearing on the treason charge, the justice issued an order to have the prisoners committed, without bail, until June 29, when a material witness, Francis M. Higbee, could appear.[73] So it was that Joseph and Hyrum Smith were scheduled to be incarcerated for four days in the prisoners' quarters on the second floor of Carthage jail, a small,

two-story building in the northwest corner of town, near the Warsaw road.

On June 26, during the whole day and into the evening, great
excitement prevailed at Carthage. George T. M. Davis, editor of
the *Alton Telegraph,* wrote a contemporary account: "No one could
close his ears against the murmurs that ran throughout the entire
community. Little squads could be seen at the taverns, at the tents
of the soldiers, and in every part of the town . . . expressions falling
from the lips of numbers, there assembled, could leave no other impression upon any sane mind, than that they were determined the
Smiths should not escape summary punishment."[74]

During the evening the troops urged Governor Ford to lead them
to Nauvoo, ostensibly to search for bogus money allegedly minted
in the Mormon city.[75] Eudocia Baldwin Marsh, a girl in her teens,
reported that the troops looked with great anticipation toward the
march on the Mormon stronghold. For days their women had been
preparing supplies for the men sufficient to allow for a siege.[76] Minor
Deming, the brigade commander, had already ordered the regiment
of Warsaw troops to march north to Golden's Point, a few miles
short of Nauvoo.[77] Late in the evening Ford learned that once in
Nauvoo the troops would seek a pretext to begin hostilities. During
the morning of June 27 Ford went to his officers in Carthage and
discussed the possibility of this development and the desirability of
disbanding the troops, a measure that Thomas Sharp strongly opposed.[78] Despite some objections, Ford dismissed the twelve or thirteen hundred men at Carthage and sent a messenger to the men at
Golden's Point, discharging them and telling them to return to their
homes. He would go to Nauvoo with only a small force.

When the Warsaw troops en route to Golden's Point received
word of dismissal, they voiced bitter protests. About two hundred of
them refused to return home, saying that the governor had trifled
with them in promising to lead them into Nauvoo. Many felt that
the old citizens must act now or surrender their rights to the Mormons.[79] At about noon a majority of these men took the road to
Carthage.[80]

Prior to his departure, Governor Ford was warned by one of his
aides that a plot was developing to kill the prophet.[81] One of Joseph
Smith's lawyers told Ford to place a guard on the Warsaw road to

prevent an attack on the jail from that direction.[82] Ford said he gave these warnings little consideration because he believed them based on rumor. He later told the members of the legislature that he made plans to hurry back from Nauvoo to forestall any attempt on the prophet's life.[83]

In the Carthage jail on the morning of June 27 Joseph Smith wrote a letter to his wife, reassuring her that, if there was an attack, some of the militia would remain loyal.[84] Later he and Hyrum entertained several visitors, including Cyrus H. Wheelock, who, fearing an attack on the jail, slipped a pistol into Joseph's pocket.[85]

At about four o'clock William R. Hamilton, a young boy who had been stationed as a lookout on the courthouse roof by Captain Robert Smith of the Greys, hurried down from his perch to inform the captain that a large group of men were coming from the west. Captain Smith told him to tell no one, but to let him know should these men head directly toward the jail.[86]

At the jail Franklin Worrell commanded a seven-man detail of guards. The main company of Greys was nearly a half mile away, in or near their tents on the southeast corner of the town square. Eudocia Marsh, visiting her sister in Carthage, reported that toward evening her brother-in-law, an officer of the Greys, burst into the house to announce that "a party of men are coming to take Joe Smith from jail and to hang him on the public square."

On the square the Greys were formed up in front of their tents by Captain Smith, who had difficulty getting them into line as some had been sleeping and were slow to react to the captain's commands. Tom Marsh, Eudocia's brother, wanted to run to the jail without any military formality; he shouted, "Come on you cowards damn you, come on, those boys [the Greys on guard at the jail] will all be killed."[87] Tom broke away from the rest of the troops and ran toward the jail, but the remainder delayed, executing a slow, disciplined march, "with guns properly at shoulder and flag flying, as if on dress parade."[88] By this time the mob, grotesquely disguised by blackened faces, had already reached the jail.

"While there were guards around the jail," eyewitness William Hamilton recalled later, "they were guards that did not guard and in fact I think understood the whole matter."[89] The guards fired directly into the attackers from a distance of twenty feet, but no one fell. Scuffling briefly with the guards, the mob tossed them aside and stormed up the stairs toward the room where the prisoners were held. Upon hearing the guns firing below, Joseph and Hyrum seized their pistols and ran to the door to hold it shut against the attackers. Some of the mob fired shots through the wooden door, hitting Hyrum in the face. He fell upon his back, dead, his head toward an open window on the east. Joseph, seeing his fallen brother at his feet, stepped up beside the door and began firing his pistol at the men in the hallway. After attempting to fire all six barrels (three misfired) he ran to the window. Outside were more of the mob, who fired at him from below as bullets struck him from behind.[90] He teetered on the sill, with one leg and an arm out the window, and then fell to the ground, landing on his left side.[91] An examination of his body showed that he had been hit four times, once in the right collar bone, once in the breast, and twice in the back.[92] Accounts differ as to whether he was dead before he hit the ground,[93] but Thomas Dixon, who was standing near the jail, said that while there was blood on his pants when he came to the window, "he was not dead when he fell — he raised himself up against the well curb."[94] He then "drew up one leg and stretched out the other and died immediately."[95] William R. Hamilton confirmed Dixon's statement that the body was not molested after it hit the ground.[96]

Hamilton was able to go upstairs, view the body of Hyrum, and return in time to see the Carthage Greys just arriving at the jail. According to another witness, when the Greys reached the jail members of the fleeing mob were still in sight, only three hundred yards away, but none of the Greys gave pursuit. Before sunrise of the next day most of the Greys had "broke for the tall timber," expecting retaliation by the Mormons for their ineptitude at the jail.[97]

Upon hearing of the murder, Artois Hamilton, William's father and the proprietor of the Hamilton House, drove a team and wagon to the jail to secure the bodies, taking them to his hotel, where coffins were subsequently made. The next day he took Hyrum's body in his wagon, while Samuel Smith drove another wagon with Joseph's body. As they departed for Nauvoo, they saw a few Carthaginians beginning to return to their homes after fleeing so quickly during the night that some had left their windows and doors wide open. Three or four days passed before all the townspeople mustered enough courage to return home. In the interim, many lived in dread that the Nauvoo Legion would burn their community to the ground.[98]

At Nauvoo the people were too stunned to react when they learned of the prophet's death on the evening of the murder. The following morning at ten o'clock Major General Dunham addressed the legion on the parade ground, urging them to keep the peace. At noon a council of officers met and then assembled to greet the procession coming from Carthage with the bodies. At 2:30 the procession arrived at Mulholland Street and proceeded toward Joseph's home, the Mansion House.[99]

Vilate Kimball said that the "very streets of Nauvoo seem[ed] to mourn." The tears and groans of the remaining members of the Smith family "were enough to rend the hearts of the adamant."[100] Eight to ten thousand Mormons were on hand to resolve "to trust in the law for a remedy of such a high handed assassination and when that failed to call upon God to avenge [them] of [their] wrongs."[101] For six months following the murders the bodies were hidden and carefully guarded for fear marauders would come to desecrate the graves.[102]

For several days following the funeral there was speculation throughout Hancock County as to who had committed the murders.[103] Rumors circulated that Missourians had done the killing; one rumor even affirmed that Mormons had tried to free the prophet and that he had been killed in the exchange of gunfire.[104] William R. Hamilton said the murders were committed "by a respectable set of men."[105] Thomas Sharp said that the killing constituted "summary execution," and admitted that the anti-Mormons had agreed in early June to exterminate the Mormon leaders.[106] George Davis said the decision was made by the "Vigilance Committee of Safety," who maintained that the Smiths must be killed or Nauvoo destroyed.[107] George Rockwell, a member of the Warsaw militia, wrote to a friend that the militia decided they were "unwilling to be trifled with any longer" and "determined to take the matter into their own hands." Rockwell said he regretted the necessity of murder but did not doubt that the Smiths deserved it.[108]

Within the state generally there was a denunciation of the brutal execution of helpless men who had been given a pledge of safety from the state. Nonetheless, according to Minor Deming, most of the citizens in Hancock County and those downstate were satisfied to see the brothers dead.[109] Many hoped that the Mormons would now disperse. The editor of the *Quincy Whig* spoke for the non-Mormon community when he warned: "So long as they are banded together under the direction of one head . . . so long will they be looked upon by the people of the State with mistrust and suspicion."[110]

1. See Richard Maxwell Brown, "The American Vigilante Tradition," *The History of Violence in America,* ed. Hugh Davis Graham and Ted Robert Gurr (New York: Praeger, 1969), 154-208. For an insightful interpretation of anti-Mormon activity in Illinois within the context of American vigilantism, see Robert Bruce Flanders, "Dream and Nightmare: Nauvoo Revisited," in *The Restoration Movement: Essays in Mormon History,* ed. F. Mark McKiernan, Alma R. Blair, and Paul M. Edwards (Lawrence, Kans.: Coronada Press, 1973), 141-66.

2. Joseph Smith, *History of the Church of Jesus Christ of Latter-day Saints,* ed. B. H. Roberts (Salt Lake City: Deseret Book Company, 1971), I, 6-7.

3. These are the recollections of W. W. Phelps in a letter to Brigham Young, August 6, 1863, located in the Archives of the Church of Jesus Christ of Latter-day Saints in Salt Lake City, Utah, hereafter referred to as Church Archives.

4. On the sectarian motives for the disorderly charges brought against Smith, see the admissions of A. W. B. in *Evangelical Magazine and Gospel Advocate* 2 (April 9, 1831). The Reverend John Sherer of Coleville, N.Y., noted the initial missionary successes of the Mormons in Broom County in his letter to the American Home Missionary Society, November 30, 1830, located in the library of the Chicago Theological Seminary. For the recollections of Sidney Rigdon on the accusation of subversion, see his sermon in *The Prophet,* June, 1844, 2.

5. See 4th Nephi in the 1920 edition of the Book of Mormon.

6. See *Book of Commandments for the Government of the Church of Christ* (Independence, Mo.: W. W. Phelps, 1833), 81; and "Journal History," February 22, 1831, for Joseph Smith's acknowledgment to Martin Harris that the laws of the kingdom had been revealed. "Journal History" is a large collection of unpublished, chronologically arranged sources which date from 1830. These are located in the Church Archives.

7. Mario S. DePillis, "The Quest for Religious Authority and the Rise of Mormonism," *Dialogue: A Journal of Mormon Thought* 1 (Spring, 1966), 68-88; Marvin S. Hill, "The Role of Christian Primitivism in the Origin and Development of the Mormon Kingdom, 1830-1844" (Ph.D. dissertation, University of Chicago, 1968), 56-64; see also Alma 46, Helaman 2:35, and Helaman 6 for examples of this fear expressed in the Book of Mormon.

8. One of the recurring themes in the Book of Mormon is that a nation prospers only when the people are governed by religious men and religious principles. When the people become worldly and permit power-hungry leaders to seize control of the government, decline and destruction follow. The citations in note 7 illustrate the point, as do Mormon 8:37-41, Moroni 9:9-22. For Joseph Smith's lamentations upon man's abortive attempts to govern himself and the need for a theocratic government, see "The Government of God," *Times and Seasons* 3 (July 15, 1842), 855-56.

9. *Book of Commandments,* 74, 78, 89-96, 105-10, 119, 159. For a persuasive

argument that the key issue between Mormons and non-Mormons was political, see Klaus Hansen, "The Political Kingdom as a Source of Conflict," *Brigham Young University Studies* (Spring-Summer, 1960), 241-60.

10. On Mormon communitarianism in Missouri, see Leonard J. Arrington, "Early Mormon Communitarianism: The Law of Consecration and Stewardship," *Western Humanities Review* 7 (Autumn, 1953), 341-69. The best study of the Mormons in Missouri and the social conflict is Warren Abner Jennings, "Zion Is Fled: The Expulsion of the Mormons from Jackson County, Missouri" (Ph.D. dissertation, University of Florida, 1962), 36-312. Jennings indicates on p. 120 that the Mormons did not get involved in politics during the first year.

11. Hill, "Role of Christian Primitivism," 143-48; Peter Crawley and Richard L. Anderson, "The Political and Social Realities of Zion's Camp," *Brigham Young University Studies* 14 (Summer, 1974), 406-20.

12. Hill, "Role of Christian Primitivism," 183, 158-61; Robert Kent Fielding, "Growth of the Mormon Church in Kirtland, Ohio" (Ph.D. dissertation, Indiana University, 1957), 69-108.

13. Hill, "Role of Christian Primitivism," 179-81.

14. Robert Bruce Flanders in "The Kingdom of God in Illinois: Politics in Utopia," *Dialogue: A Journal of Mormon Thought* 5 (Spring, 1970), 26-36, argues the prevailing view that Mormon apocalyptic expectations precipitated their quest for political power. While there is some truth in this, Marvin S. Hill has suggested that the kingdom of God was more a quest for refuge than a quest for empire. See "Religion in Nauvoo: Some Reflections," an address delivered before the Mormon History Association, April 20, 1974, to be published in a slightly revised form in *Utah Historical Quarterly* (Spring, 1976). That the Mormons considered their bloc voting defensive in nature is apparent from Joseph Smith's remark to Governor Thomas Ford that the Mormons "were driven to union in their elections by persecution, and not by my influence; and that the 'Mormons' acted on the most perfect principle of liberty in all their movements." See Smith, *History of the Church,* V, 232. Mormon belief that the right to vote to protect their interests (whether in a bloc or not) was an American right is reflected in Elias Higbee's letter to Joseph Smith written from Washington, D.C., in January, 1840. Smith, *History of the Church,* IV, 85-86.

15. *Painesville Telegraph,* April 17, 1835.

16. Larry T. Wimmer, econometric historian at Brigham Young University, Keith Rooker, associate professor in the J. Reuben Clark Law School, and Marvin S. Hill have argued these points in "The Kirtland Economy Revisited: A Market Critique of Sectarian Economics," a lecture presented at Brigham Young University on January 15, 1975, to be published in the Charles Redd Monographs in Western History in 1975-76.

17. *Ibid.;* Hill, "Role of Christian Primitivism," 169-71.

18. "Journal History," January 8, 1837; cf. "Letter to the Editors," *Missouri Argus,* November 5, 1838; *Saint Louis Commercial Bulletin,* September 27, 1838.

19. Hill, "Role of Christian Primitivism," 205-10.

20. Smith, *History of the Church,* III, 153, 157.

21. See the letter of Phineas Richards to Wealthy Richards, January 21, 1839, in the Coe Collection at Yale University. See the testimonies of Apostles Hyde and Marsh in *Senate Document 189.* Cf. "Book of John Whitmer," 22, a typewritten manuscript in the Church Archives; and Benjamin F. Johnson, *My Life's Review* (Independence, Mo.: Zion's Printing and Publishing Co., 1947), 38-39, 42.

22. Smith, *History of the Church,* III, 175-76.

23. See *Senate Document 189* for the disparity in the number of witnesses for and against the Mormons. Forty-two appeared for the state, and only seven

for the Saints. On the intimidation of the Mormon witnesses, see Smith, *History of the Church,* III, 210-11, and the statement of prosecution witness W. W. Phelps in *Nauvoo Neighbor,* June 12, 1844. On Smith's imprisonment, see Smith, *History of the Church,* III, 251, 254-56, 261-63, 284, 308-9, 319, 322-23, 327.

24. Smith, *History of the Church,* III, 341-42, 390-91.

25. *Ibid.,* IV, 23, 186-87, and Thomas Gregg, *History of Hancock County* (Chicago: Chas. C. Chapman & Co., 1880), 638. Nauvoo's population was 11,036, while Springfield had less than 7,500 and Chicago only 7,580 by 1845. See John P. Frank, *Lincoln as a Lawyer* (Urbana: University of Illinois Press, 1961), 2; and Bessie Louise Pierce, *A History of Chicago* (New York: Alfred A. Knopf, 1937), I, 415.

26. *Warsaw Signal,* June 9, 1841. The editor asked the Hancock County citizens, "Are you prepared to see the important offices of sheriff and county commissioner selected by an unparalleled knave, and thus have power to select your jurymen, who are to set and try our rights of life, liberty and property?"

27. *Warsaw Signal,* June 9, 16, 1841. See the notice of a "Public Meeting" (July 9, p. 3), where Sharp and others vowed to vote as a unit at election time regardless of party loyalties. Gregg, *History of Hancock County,* 638, gives the 1845 population as 472.

28. *Ibid.,* July 7, December 8, 1841, and January 26, August 20, 1842.

29. At election time from 1842 onward the *Sangamo Journal* and the *Quincy Whig* on the Whig side, and the *Illinois State Register* for the Democrats, kept close watch on Nauvoo and the Mormon vote. The gubernatorial election of 1842 and the 1843 election to the House of Representatives were bitterly contested, with both parties courting Mormon favor. See Hill, "Role of Christian Primitivism," 257-62, 264, 271-73; and Robert Bruce Flanders, *Nauvoo: Kingdom on the Mississippi* (Urbana: University of Illinois Press, 1965), 229-41.

30. See Thomas Ford, *A History of Illinois* (Chicago: S. C. Greggs & Co., 1854), 269; *Quincy Whig,* July 25, September 12, 1840, September 25, 1841. Compare the *Whig* for January 22, 1842; *Sangamo Journal* June 18, 1841, January 21 and June 10, 1842, which mark decided changes in attitude toward the Mormons by both these strongly partisan editors.

31. Flanders, *Nauvoo,* 260-77; John C. Bennett, *History of the Saints, or an Expose of Joe Smith and the Mormons* (Boston: Leland and Whiting, 1842).

32. On the arrest at Dixon, see Hill, "Role of Christian Primitivism," 269-72. For the legislation against foreign processes, see *Nauvoo Neighbor,* December 27, 1843; Smith, *History of the Church,* VI, 105-6, 124; Hill, "Role of Christian Primitivism," 277-78.

33. Smith, *History of the Church,* VI, 64-65.

34. *Ibid.,* 156-60, 188; Ford, *History of Illinois,* 321.

35. Smith, *History of the Church,* 188.

36. *Ibid.,* 130-32.

37. See the recollections of Bishop George Miller in H. W. Mills, ed., *A Mormon Bishop and His Son* (London: H. W. Mills, 1917), 48. Cf. Juanita Brooks, *John D. Lee, Zealot — Pioneer Builder — Scapegoat* (Glendale, Calif.: Arthur H. Clark, 1962), 56; and Klaus Hansen, *Quest for Empire: The Political Kingdom of God and the Council of Fifty in Mormon History* (East Lansing: Michigan State University Press, 1967), 52, 60.

38. Hansen, *Quest for Empire,* 82-86.

39. Flanders, *Nauvoo,* 289-90, 331-36, has argued that Smith made no final commitment to abandoning Nauvoo for the Rocky Mountains in his lifetime but proposed many settlements rather than one. According to Flanders, the decision to abandon Nauvoo was not made by Brigham Young until the fall of 1845. The evidence is ambiguous, but there is some support for the traditional Utah view

that it was Joseph Smith who planned a major exodus to the Rockies. Willard Richards wrote for Joseph Smith in his manuscript journal on February 20, 1844, that the prophet instructed the Twelve to send a delegation to California and Oregon to "find a good location where we can remove after the temple is completed — and build a city in a day — and have a government of our own in a healthy climate." James Monroe, who taught Joseph's children, wrote in his journal on April 25, 1844, that the elders in the presence of the Twelve were singing songs which "incline me to the belief that it is the intention to go to that country [upper California] when we remove from here." James Arlington Bennett advised the prophet in April to abandon Nauvoo and settle outside the United States, possibly in California, Texas, or Mexico. See his letter of April 14, 1844, in the James Arlington Bennett file in the Church Archives.

40. "Journal of Wilford Woodruff," May 5, 1844; *Warsaw Signal,* May 8, 1844; *Quincy Whig,* May 22, 1844; George T. M. Davis, *An Authentic Account of the Massacre of Joseph Smith* (St. Louis: Chambers and Knapp, 1844), 19.

41. *Warsaw Signal,* April 25, 1844; cf. Smith, *History of the Church,* VI, 333.

42. Smith, *History of the Church,* VI, 356-61.

43. *Warsaw Signal,* May 15, 1844.

44. Smith, *History of the Church,* VI, 405, 412-13; *Warsaw Signal,* May 29, 1844; *Nauvoo Expositor,* June 7, 1844, p. 3.

45. *Warsaw Signal,* May 29, 1844.

46. The only issue of the *Expositor* was published on June 7, 1844.

47. Smith, *History of the Church,* VI, 438, 442.

48. Dallin H. Oaks, "The Suppression of the *Nauvoo Expositor,*" *Utah Law Review* 9 (Winter, 1965), 890-91. Oaks indicates that while there was "considerable basis in the law of their day for their action in characterizing the published issues of the *Nauvoo Expositor* as a nuisance . . . there was no legal justification in 1844 for the destruction of the *Expositor* press."

49. *Ibid.,* 876; Smith, *History of the Church,* VI, 432-45, 448.

50. *Quincy Whig,* June 19, 1844.

51. Letter from H. H. Bliss to Franklin Bliss, June 8, 1844, Indiana University Library.

52. *Warsaw Signal,* June 19, 1844.

53. Smith, *History of the Church,* VI, 454, 485-91.

54. Letter from Samuel Otho Williams to John A. Pricket, July 10, 1844, Mormon Collection, Chicago Historical Society.

55. See the letter from an old citizen in the *Missouri Republican,* June 21, 1844.

56. George Rockwell to Thomas H. Rockwell, June 22, 1844. Rockwell's letters are on film in the Stanley B. Kimball Collection, Southern Illinois University. See also *North Western Gazette and Galena Advertizer,* June 21, 1844.

57. *Warsaw Signal,* June 19, 1844; Marsh, "Mormons in Hancock County," 45.

58. Smith, *History of the Church,* VI, 497. Governor Ford, formerly a justice of the state supreme court, maintained that if the legion was called out to resist a legal posse from Carthage this might constitute treason. But if (as subsequent events proved) the posse was actually intent upon the murder of the Smiths, the charge was doubtful. See Ford, *History of Illinois,* 337.

59. Smith, *History of the Church,* VI, 521, 533-37.

60. *Ibid.,* 538-41.

61. *Ibid.,* 540, 545-46; see "Journal History," June 27, 1844, for the recollections of James W. Wood.

62. Smith, *History of the Church,* VI, 545-50; Joseph Smith's Journal kept

by Willard Richards, June 23, 1844, Church Archives; cf. Helen Mar Whitney, "Scenes in Nauvoo after the Martyrdom of the Prophet and Patriarch," *Woman's Exponent* 11 (December 15, 1882), 106.

63. Whitney, "Scenes in Nauvoo," *Woman's Exponent* 11:106.

64. "Journal of Wandle Mace," 144. This is a typewritten journal in Brigham Young University Library.

65. Smith, *History of the Church*, VI, 549. Emma Smith claimed Joseph said, "I will die before I will be called a coward." See Elder Edmund C. Briggs, "A Visit to Nauvoo in 1856," *Journal of History* [Reorganized] 9 (October, 1916), 453-54.

66. "Journal of Wandle Mace," 144.

67. "Journal History," June 27, 1844, for the testimony of James W. Wood.

68. Quoted in an editorial in *Times and Seasons* 5 (July 15, 1844), 585, as being a remark to a friend. Mary B. Smith, daughter of Samuel Smith, the prophet's brother, in a letter to Ina Smith Coolbrith in 1908 recounts that Smith made a similar comment to his mother, adding, "If my death will atone for any fault I have committed during my life time I am willing to die." The letter is in the library of the Reorganized Church of Jesus Christ of Latter-day Saints at Independence, Mo.

69. Smith, *History of the Church*, VI, 560; Marsh, "Mormons in Hancock County," 46-47.

70. Smith, *History of the Church*, VI, 563-64; Marsh, "Mormons in Hancock County," 47; Samuel Otho Williams to John A. Pricket, July 10, 1844.

71. *Warsaw Signal*, July 10, 1844; *Times and Seasons* 5 (July 1, 1844), 563 for the statement of H. T. Reid; Samuel Otho Williams to John A. Pricket, July 10, 1844.

72. *Times and Seasons* 5 (July 1, 1844), 563 for reflections of H. T. Reid.

73. Oaks, "Suppression of the *Nauvoo Expositor*," 866-67; Smith, *History of the Church*, VI, 567-70.

74. G. Davis, *An Authentic Account*, 17.

75. Ford, *History of Illinois*, 339.

76. Marsh, "Mormons in Hancock County," 48.

77. Brigade Order of June 25, 1844, Mormon Collection, Chicago Historical Society. Golden's Point was located on Larry's Creek in the southern part of Sonora Township, where the timber projected farthest into the prairie. Robert M. Cochran *et al., History of Hancock County, Illinois* (Carthage: Journal Printing Co., 1968), 554.

78. "Minutes of Trial of Members of Mob Who Helped Kill Joseph Smith, the Prophet," 82 (testimony of John W. Williams). For additional information on this source, see Bibliographical Note. Hereafter referred to as "Minutes of Trial."

79. Marsh, "Mormons in Hancock County," 48; Smith, *History of the Church*, VI, 606; *Warsaw Signal*, July 10, 1844 (account of the murder by Thomas Sharp).

80. "Minutes of Trial," 38 (testimony of John Peyton).

81. See Ford's address to the Legislature of Illinois, *Nauvoo Neighbor*, January 1, 1845, p. 2.

82. *Times and Seasons* 5 (July 1, 1844), 564 (testimony of James W. Wood).

83. *Nauvoo Neighbor*, January 1, 1845, p. 2. For a sympathetic treatment of Ford's conduct on the eve of the murder, see Keith Huntress, "Governor Ford and the Murderers of Joseph Smith," *Dialogue: A Journal of Mormon Thought* 4 (Summer, 1969), 41-52. This piece has been reprinted in Marvin S. Hill and James B. Allen, eds., *Mormonism and American Culture* (New York: Harper and Row, 1972), 74-86.

84. Smith, *History of the Church*, VI, 605. If the prophet had any misgivings about this arrangement, he concealed them from his wife, writing her that the dismissal of the militia was "right as I suppose." "Manuscript History of Joseph Smith," June 27, 1844, Church Archives.

85. Smith, *History of the Church*, 607.

86. Scofield, *History of Hancock County*, 845 (testimony of Hamilton). H. H. Bliss of La Harpe wrote on the day after the murder that the mob had come "from toward Warsaw." His letter is reproduced by Jan Shipps in *B.Y.U. Studies* 14 (Spring, 1974), 392.

87. Marsh, "Mormons in Hancock County," 51.

88. According to William R. Hamilton in Scofield, *History of Hancock County*, 845.

89. Quoted in Berry, "The Mormon Settlement in Illinois," 88, 89.

90. This account is based on the recollections of eyewitnesses Willard Richards, John Taylor, and John H. Sherman. Joseph Smith's Journal kept by Willard Richards, June 27, 1844; *Times and Seasons* 5 (August 1, 1844), 598; Smith, *History of the Church*, VII, 102-4; VI, 617-19; Scofield, *History of Hancock County*, 846-47.

91. Hamilton and Sherman agree on this. See also testimony of Thomas Dixon in "Minutes of Trial," 60.

92. See Willard Richards to Brigham Young, June 30, 1844, Richards Papers, Church Archives.

93. Cf. Ford, *History of Illinois*, 354, and Marsh, "Mormons in Hancock County," 53, with the recollection of William H. Hamilton in Scofield, *History of Hancock County*, 845.

94. "Minutes of Trial," 60.

95. This recollection is attributed to Thomas Dixon in "Documents Relating to the Mormon Troubles," 26, handwritten notes on the trial testimony, Chicago Historical Society. Hereafter referred to as "Documents." For additional information on this source, see Bibliographical Note.

96. Scofield, *History of Hancock County*, 845; "Minutes of Trial," 60. Another eyewitness states that Joseph was stabbed with a bayonet while on the ground. Samuel Otho Williams to John A. Pricket, July 10, 1844.

97. Scofield, *History of Hancock County*, 845; and handwritten manuscript of George D. Watt's original minutes of the trial, p. 24, for the testimony of Eli H. Wilson, who is actually Eli H. Williams. This source will be referred to hereafter as Watt Manuscript. For additional information on this source, see Bibliographical Note.

98. Scofield, *History of Hancock County*, 845-46; letter of William Weston to George Weston, July 1, 1844, Manuscript Collection, Newberry Library, Chicago.

99. Smith, *History of the Church*, VII, 133-34.

100. Letter of June 30, 1844, quoted by Helen Mar Whitney, "Life Incidents," *Woman's Exponent* 11 (January, 1883), 114.

101. *Times and Seasons* 6 (July 1, 1844), 561.

102. Whitney, "Scenes in Nauvoo," *Woman's Exponent* 12 (June, 1883), 6-7.

103. Ford, *History of Illinois*, 353.

104. See Willard Richards's June 27 note from the jail at Carthage, which charged the killing to the Missourians. Smith, *History of the Church*, VII, 110; *Davenport Gazette*, July 17, August 22, 1844; cf. *Quincy Whig*, July 3, 1844, for three different accounts of the murder, one of which was that the Mormons had tried to free the Smiths.

105. Quoted by Berry, "The Mormon Settlement in Illinois," 97.

106. *Warsaw Signal,* July 10, July 31, 1844.

107. George T. M. Davis, *Autobiography of the Late Col. Geo. T. M. Davis* (New York: Published by His Legal Representatives, 1891), 80-81.

108. George Rockwell to Thomas H. Rockwell, August 3, 1844, in Kansas Historical Society. Thomas Gregg in his *Prophet of Palmyra* (New York: John B. Alden, 1890), 283, concluded that the mobbers were mostly from the Warsaw militia.

109. Deming to his parents, July 1, 1844, Minor Deming Letters, Illinois Historical Survey, Urbana. Deming said there are "but a few in the state that do not feel that a violent death was but their [the Smiths] *retributive justice.*"

110. July 3, 1844.

‚Ä£ 3 ‚Ä£

"To Vindicate the...
Broken Pledge of the State"

Governor Ford had just left Nauvoo on June 27 when he learned that Joseph and Hyrum Smith had been murdered. Fearing Mormon wrath like that of the Romans against their Carthage, he rode "bad scared" to Carthage to warn the people that the town would be in ashes by morning.[1] Riding out after midnight, he paused nine miles south of the city to water his horses and found Eudocia Marsh and her family at a roadside inn to which they had fled in terror. Ford was "storming, scolding and impatient to be off," and ordered the Marsh family to "get up at once and go to Augusta — declaring that the Mormon avenger would come before daylight."[2]

Hurrying to Quincy, Ford set up temporary headquarters and then issued a proclamation "to the people of Illinois," describing the bloody events at Carthage and affirming his determination to "preserve the peace against all breakers of the same, at all hazards."[3] He called to active duty several companies of state militia (deliberately excluding Hancock County troops), believing that the Mormons and anti-Mormons would momentarily wage war on each other.[4] To discourage war Ford instructed General Minor Deming to request all citizens to remain in their homes.[5] By June 30 the governor wrote to General Deming that he did not think there would be a Mormon outbreak and that Deming should disband his troops, but Ford warned that he should first order all Iowans and Missourians out of the area and make sure that there would be no attack on Nauvoo.[6] Despite his confident note to Deming, Ford sent two emissaries to Nauvoo on the same day to determine whether the Mormons had any militant intentions. Apparently in response to Ford's inquiry, the Nauvoo city council on July 1 resolved to discourage "private revenge on the assassinators of General Joseph Smith."[7]

The governor said nothing in his official pronouncements about finding and prosecuting the murderers, but he told the people of Carthage that there would be an investigation.[8] Three months would pass before the harassed governor would be able to bring those accused of the murder before a judge for their preliminary hearing. In the meantime, he had to wait for the results of his appeal to St. Louis for federal troops to be stationed in Hancock. He did not receive a negative answer to this request until August.[9] Even more crucial, he had to wait for the election returns of early August to determine whether there would be any officials in Hancock County willing to prosecute the murderers.[10]

While Ford waited, he had to keep the peace. Armed men were still gathering at Warsaw and Carthage and talking of attacking Nauvoo. When Ford instructed Deming to disperse all those anti-Mormons who had collected from Iowa and Missouri, the "Warsaw Committee of Safety" wrote Ford an open letter on July 3. Reviewing the history of social conflict in Hancock, they insisted that they had left no method untried to counter Mormon political solidarity.

When we approach the ballot box we find we are virtually disfranchised; for the Mormons greatly outnumber us; if we appeal to the laws the process of our justices are disregarded in Nauvoo. . . . [W]hen our court is placed completely under the control of an unprincipled faction at Nauvoo, with Mormon officers, Mormon jurors, and Mormon witnesses, we ask, sir, with serious concern what can the anti-Mormon citizens of Hancock County expect? They have rendered themselves highly obnoxious to their troublesome neighbors, by their determined and manly efforts to preserve their rights. Many of them are already marked as fit subjects for vengeance and they expect Mormon *Justice.*

The committee concluded by urging, "There can be no compromise between the two parties. It is out of the question: they are greatly our superior in numbers and we cannot confide in their faith. They must leave or we must leave."[11] The governor replied to the committee on the same day, saying that their action at Carthage had destroyed his influence with the Mormons and thereby any hope that he might persuade them to leave Illinois voluntarily: "If you mean to request me to exercise a forcible influence to expel them

31

from the state, I answer you now, as I have uniformly done, that the law is my guide, and I know of no law authorizing their expulsion. . . . I am informed that a design is still entertained at Warsaw of attacking Nauvoo. In this you will not be sustained by myself or the people."[12]

The anti-Mormons reacted by organizing a campaign to win the support of the uncommitted in Hancock County and the state. As part of their strategy they charged the Mormons at Nauvoo with general lawlessness, with counterfeiting and thievery, and with an immunity from judicial process. They stressed again and again the major points of their position: that the Mormons were a disruptive force in the community, and that opposition to them was not based on politics or religious prejudice.[13] On July 10 Thomas Sharp argued on the basis of Lockean revolutionary theory that the old citizens had called upon their reserved rights to life, liberty, and property. When these were threatened by the Mormon leaders, they had taken the law into their own hands.[14]

But the anti-Mormons encountered increasing criticism in the press with respect to the murdering of the Smiths. Many saw it as cowardly to attack these men while they were in the custody of the state and virtually helpless.[15] Fearful of a possible general swing of sentiment in the Mormons' favor, the anti-Mormons intensified their campaign. A resident of Adams County wrote to the *Quincy Whig* that Mormons had precipitated social strife wherever they had gone. The difficulties arose from the claim that they owed greater allegiance to the laws of God than to those of men.[16] The editor of the *Quincy Whig* editorialized that the old issues were not settled — the Mormons under their civil, military, and religious leaders "cannot live in the same community with those who abide our present laws."[17] A citizen from Hancock County said in the *Quincy Herald* that, if the Illinoisans could not approve the murder, they should at least excuse it. Why be so concerned that extralegal process was utilized against the Smiths when law had been long dead in the county?[18] On July 27 a Carthaginian touched on a critical point in the *Missouri Republican,* saying that after the coming August election the Mormons would have controlled the selection of juries in the county, thus insulating their leader and themselves from criminal prosecution and insuring preferential treatment in civil controversies with their non-Mormon neighbors. Mob action, he said, must be viewed in light of this and should not be judged by ordinary standards of right and wrong.[19]

On July 25 Ford again replied to the anti-Mormons, insisting that they must cease to agitate on the Mormon question. He affirmed that although they had been right in demanding the prophet's arrest for the destruction of the *Expositor,* they were now clearly in the wrong and none would sustain them. Ford concluded by urging the anti-Mormons to reconsider their militant policies.[20]

Ford's arguments might have won support for upholding the law among many of the old citizens had it not been an election year. But in the summer of 1844 there were local and national elections impending, and many considered sustaining the law as secondary to winning a party victory at the polls. Thus the editor of the *Quincy Whig* attacked Ford's letter of July 25, charging that his purpose was to win the Mormon vote for the Democratic party.[21] The *Quincy Herald,* a spokesman for the Democrats, promptly denied the allegation, asking how, in the face of continued threats of attack upon Nauvoo, the governor could have acted otherwise.[22] Thomas Sharp answered Ford directly on July 31, saying that it was too late for the anti-Mormons to alter their course. The decision to execute the Mormon leaders had been made in June and was beyond reconsideration. Whether further military moves would be necessary would depend on subsequent events.[23]

On the same day the editor of the *Quincy Whig* made an open bid for Mormon support for his party by reminding the Saints that Governor Ford had failed to protect the prophet at Carthage.[24] Agreeing with this viewpoint, the Mormons initially determined not to vote in the August election.[25] From August 3 through August 8 they were preoccupied with choosing the prophet's successor.[26] However, on August 2, three days before the election, a group of Mormons gathered at the meeting grounds west of the temple and sought to rally the Saints in an effort to gain control of crucial county offices. The chief arguing point was that "the mob party were determined to elect officers who would screen the murderers of Joseph and exterminate the Mormons." The citizens of Nauvoo resolved at this time to support candidates "in favor of preserving order and enforcing the laws." They agreed to support for sheriff General Minor Deming, a neutral militia officer who had deplored the resort to violence; for coroner, Daniel H. Wells, a non-Mormon who would migrate to Utah with them in 1846; for county commissioner, George Coulson, a Mormon who had served an earlier term in that office; and as state representatives J. B. Backenstos, a non-Mormon friend of Joseph Smith, and A. W. Babbitt, a Mormon politico.[27]

In the Hancock County election the Mormons enjoyed a clean sweep, electing all the candidates on their "Old Citizens Law and Order Ticket," and getting a majority vote "well above that of their opponents in every case."[28] It is not clear whether the Mormons initially intended to vote for any of the candidates for state office; if Ford's history is correct, they did not. But just prior to the election Colonel E. D. Taylor, a prominent downstate Democrat, came to Nauvoo and urged the Saints to vote for Joseph P. Hoge, the Democratic candidate for representative in the sixth congressional district, arguing that a vote for Hoge was not a vote for Governor Ford but for the party, and that the party would react favorably should Hoge win his seat.[29] Hoge carried Hancock County by 76 percent and won the election.[30]

There is no proof that Hoge's triumph bolstered the governor's determination to proceed against the murderers, but there is evidence that the Mormon victory in Hancock did, since there were now local authorities who would cooperate with the state officials.[31] The anti-Mormons were well aware of the significance of the recent election returns and voiced their anger and apprehension. Frank Worrell, one of the Carthage Greys on guard at the jail when the Smiths were shot, wrote to Thomas Gregg, the Whig editor of the *Upper Mississippian:* "We are badly beaten in this county — The returns from most of the precincts have arrived in town — Hoge has a majority of between fourteen and fifteen hundred votes over Sweet, Nauvoo alone gave him a majority of over twelve hundred votes. In that place Sweet received about fifty votes." Worrell, thinking of the consequences, reminded Gregg that during the campaign the Democratic candidate for sheriff, Deming, said at Nauvoo that if elected he would bring all those concerned in the death of the Smiths to justice. Worrell exclaimed, "I hope Deming will attempt to arrest some of the mob, if he does — we will then have some more Sport

— & no mistake. I have no time to write much & if I had I could not do it — for I am *Mad Mad* — yes Mad as the Devil."[32]

Although violence against Deming was a distinct possibility, it was not feasible against Governor Ford. Other means were necessary. The anti-Mormons contacted the Whig editor of the *Alton Telegraph,* George T. M. Davis, who was then writing a short treatise that justified the murder as an unfortunate expedient. They persuaded Davis to warn Ford in early August that little could be gained by prosecution. Davis told the governor that to pursue the trial would renew excitement and hostilities, and possibly implicate the governor himself. He told Ford that if he were to proceed with the prosecution, the anti-Mormons intended to embarrass him by having two witnesses testify that they had told Ford prior to the murder that summary execution of the Smiths was imminent. Davis said Thomas Sharp would testify that he spoke to Ford on the matter, and that Ford replied that they must not kill the Mormon leaders while he was there.[33]

But the anti-Mormons focused most of their attention on the newly elected local officials. Thomas Sharp told Sheriff Deming in the *Warsaw Signal* that if he tried to use the state militia to arrest the murderers, he would find few to support him.[34] Commenting on this in a letter to his parents the following day, Deming acknowledged that he had attracted the "venom of party spirit" by "being at the head of the party in the county that contends for the *rights* of the Mormons against robbery and extermination." He added: "There were some 2 or 300 engaged in the murder of the Smiths . . . [who] with their friends and the alliance of the Whig party in the county . . . make a strong party that by threats, violence & desperation aim at supremacy above law and justice."[35]

In the *Warsaw Signal* on September 4 Sharp sought to rally opposition to the new sheriff and to the plans for prosecution of the suspected murderers by publishing a letter written by Deming to the governor in July which affirmed "it is *necessary* for the honor of the state, and the vindication of your *character* that the truth in the matter should be fully known." Sharp termed the letter a "Grand Discovery" and said that it proved the real intentions of the newly elected sheriff.[36]

Fearful of what action officials might take, the anti-Mormons at

Carthage and Warsaw issued a circular on September 7 calling for a "Grand Military Encampment" to be held at Warsaw from September 27 through October 2, for the purpose of "keeping up a proper military spirit among the several companies."[37] Governor Ford maintained that the encampment, designated a "wolf-hunt" by the anti-Mormons, was in reality a call to arms to harass the Mormons.[38] But more particularly the encampment seems to have been a means of intimidating Deming and other officials, especially the county commissioners who were in the process of choosing a grand jury.[39] It is significant that four of the ten militia leaders who called for the encampment were indicted for the murders,[40] and that another, Robert Smith, although not subsequently indicted, was heavily implicated since he had commanded the Carthage Greys guarding the jail.

Despite these moves by the anti-Mormons, Governor Ford proceeded with his efforts to bring the murderers to trial, aware (like the anti-Mormons) that public opinion would have considerable influence on his success or failure. He wrote to the Mormon leader, W. W. Phelps, on September 8 that he was ready to enforce the law should the accused persons offer resistance to legal process, but he urged the Mormons to initiate their complaint outside Nauvoo. He said he would test the loyalty of the militia but that much would depend upon the attitude of the Whigs among them. If they should believe the charge of "corrupt bargain" between him and the Mormons during the August election, they might refuse to assist and even raise opposition.[41]

The anti-Mormons in Hancock must have felt confident that their campaign in the press was effective in some ways, for when a deputy sheriff sought to arrest Thomas Sharp and take him to Nauvoo on September 25, Sharp told him he would not submit unless his friends "said go."[42] Sharp apparently believed he had sufficient community support to resist with impunity any writ issued in Nauvoo.

A direct military confrontation with Governor Ford might be another matter, however, and the anti-Mormons shunned this test of strength. When Sharp learned that Ford had called for 2,500 volunteers on September 15 to prevent a military encampment of merely 500 men, he ridiculed the idea that the military exercise was anti-Mormon in nature and that circulars had been distributed in

Iowa and Missouri.[43] The Whig editor of the *Alton Telegraph* observed, "It does seem as though fate had decreed that Illinois should be the butt of ridicule for the whole nation."[44]

But whatever the intentions of the anti-Mormons with respect to the encampment, it was called off. Before Ford arrived in Hancock with 450 men — all he could muster despite his placing John J. Hardin, a prominent Whig, at the head of the military force — those alleged to have been in the mob took flight to Missouri, believing, according to Thomas Sharp, "that the Governor was the real hunter, and that some arrests were planned."[45]

There is some evidence to suggest that Sharp's suspicions were correct, and that Ford's primary purpose was to arrest the murderers of the Smiths, despite charges by the Whigs that this was an afterthought.[46] Ford said afterward that "as much as anything else, the expedition under General Hardin had been ordered with a view to arrest the murderers."[47] Ford's letter to W. W. Phelps on September 8, cited above, demonstrates that the governor had determined well before the wolf-hunt episode to take action against the murderers, and that he intended to use the state militia for this purpose.[48] Perhaps he was reluctant to call the militia to arms solely to make the arrests, believing that his chances for support would be small. The wolf-hunt may have given him the additional reason he needed to convince his troops that he was justified in an expedition to Hancock County.

In responding to the intervention of Governor Ford, the anti-Mormons shrewdly belittled the governor rather than resisting him with armed force.[49] They mocked the sending of so many militia to prevent a wolf-hunt and criticized the large expenditures for a futile campaign.[50] Whig newspapers across the state and those in Missouri took up the theme,[51] causing Ford and the Democrats much chagrin.[52] But if the purpose of the ridicule was to discredit Ford enough to render him powerless to make the arrests, the attempt was not successful. While it may have had some effect on the troops that Ford brought with him,[53] it did not diminish his determination to proceed against the murderers. Rather, it made their arrest more urgent as a way of justifying the expedition.

On September 22, five days before Ford's arrival, Murray McConnell, a prominent attorney from Jacksonville who had been appointed Ford's special agent to gather evidence for the trial, reached Nauvoo and began taking testimony to be used by the prosecution.[54] The most important was the affidavit of John Taylor, who had barely escaped death at the jail; he gave his oath before Justice of the Peace Aaron Johnson that he "had good reasons to believe and does believe that Levy Williams Thomas C. Sharp — have been and were guilty of committing said criminal act."[55] Upon the basis of this affidavit a warrant was issued for the arrest of these two men. Other writs issued at this time have not survived, but according to contemporary newspaper accounts and other sources, writs were issued for the arrest of William Law, Robert D. Foster, and Charles A. Foster, Mormon dissenters, and for "the whole guard that was placed over the Smiths."[56] A writ was also issued for Joseph H. Jackson, a renegade Mormon who had confessed his part in the murder plan in a letter to Emma Smith.[57]

When Governor Ford arrived in Nauvoo on September 27 and learned that an attempt to arrest Sharp and Levi Williams had failed, he issued a proclamation offering a reward of two hundred dollars each for the arrest of Sharp, Williams, and Joseph H. Jackson. Notice of the reward was published in the *Sangamo Journal* and in the *Lee County Democrat*.[58] Ford also sent an order to General Hardin authorizing him to take command of the Nauvoo Legion, should they be needed to effect the arrests.[59]

Ford now called upon the Mormon leaders to furnish boats to convey him and his men to Warsaw under cover of night. The boats were furnished, but when Bishop George Miller went to the governor's camp that night to deliver them, he was told they were no longer needed. Twice during the night Miller and his party were fired upon.[60] Ford said that many of the militia were "fast-infected" with anti-Mormon prejudices and could not be relied upon to accomplish the arrests.[61]

On September 29 the troops marched to the vicinity of Warsaw and "camped in the suburbs,"[62] but Sharp and Williams had already slipped across the river to Alexandria, Missouri.[63] Angry and frustrated, Ford determined to lead a small force into Missouri to bring the fugitives back. He persuaded three Whigs (Colonels Baker, Merriman, and Weatherford) to accompany him on his expedition, and he secretly procured a boat to cross the river at night and seize the accused, who were encamped with a number of their friends at Churchville.[64] That day, September 30, the anti-Mormon press reported with satisfaction how Ford had only been able to muster about 340 men and how some from McDonough and other counties would not support him in a fight. The *St. Louis New Era* said that Ford "had made himself contemptible, is the laughing stock of everyone."[65]

Perhaps it was this ridicule that prompted the ambitious Colonel Baker, who had a reputation for being "greedy for popular favor," to make a secret visit to Missouri and to bargain with the fugitives. Baker decided during his stay that any hope of arresting the fugitives by coercive measures was futile. Consequently, he attempted to effect a compromise under which the fugitives would receive certain procedural guarantees if they would surrender. When Baker returned from his clandestine visit, he refused to join the expedition planned by Ford and told his friends to do likewise.[66]

Ford now had no choice but to accept the terms negotiated by Baker. He met with those representing the fugitives and signed an agreement drawn up by Sharp and Williams whereby they would surrender themselves to Illinois authorities. The agreement provided that the two men should be brought before Judge Thomas at Quincy rather than being taken to Nauvoo, that Ford was to inform the prosecutor that if bound over to the grand jury they were to have reasonable bail, that if indicted their case would be continued to the next term of the court, and that the state was not to resist a change of venue on the grounds that it was not made in time.[67]

On October 1 Sharp and Williams came back across the river and surrendered themselves at the governor's camp.[68] Thomas Gregg, the historian of Hancock County, said the sheriff read his writ to the prisoners and then turned them over to Colonel Baker and the Quincy troops, who escorted them to Quincy without placing them under custody.[69] The officer's return, executed on the arrest writ, tells a slightly different story. Sheriff Deming stated that he served the writ by "apprehending" Williams and Sharp on October 1, 1844, and delivered them into the custody of John H. Holton, his special deputy. There follows an unsigned certification that Justice Aaron Johnson was absent from the state of Illinois, an apparent expression of official doubts that a writ issued by Johnson could otherwise be returnable in Quincy before Judge Thomas. The last return on the document shows that Holton delivered Williams and Sharp before Judge Thomas in Quincy on October 2, 1844.[70]

In Quincy the arrangement encountered a new obstacle. Judge Jesse B. Thomas of the Illinois Supreme Court, who was the circuit justice for Adams and Hancock Counties, said that he did not intend to be bound by the defendants' arrangement with the governor about bail, but would exercise his own judgment in the matter. In response to E. D. Baker's alarmed inquiry, Judge Thomas wrote a letter to Baker reminding him that under the Illinois Constitution persons charged with a capital offense are not bailable where the proof against the accused is "evident" or the "presumption great." Although the judge said that he would not disregard the prosecutor's admission that there was no such "evident proof" or "great presumption," he emphatically stated his intention to resolve the question "according to the testimony of the witnesses." If, on the basis of that testimony, he reached a different conclusion from the prosecutor, Judge Thomas warned, "I conceive that I could not properly discharge the prisoners on bail."[71]

Judge Thomas's independence presented Sharp and Williams with a difficult situation. If the judge should conclude at their preliminary examination that there was "probable cause" to bind them over to the grand jury and that the proof was evident or the presumption was great, they would go to jail until the grand jury acted in the third week of October. If the grand jury indicted them, they would be in jail until their trial was held, either in October or during the following term of court in May. They wished to avoid this possibility above all, since they feared that if they were incarcerated the Mormons might utilize the same kind of opportunity to dispose of them as the mob had used to eliminate the Smiths.

The situation called for the assistance of clever counsel, and the record shows that Colonel E. D. Baker and O. H. Browning, who represented Williams and Sharp in this matter, were equal to the challenge. With the cooperation of the prosecution an arrangement was made under which the prisoners apparently waived their right to preliminary examination. They solved the question of their custody by voluntarily executing a bond to secure their appearance before the circuit court on the first day of the succeeding term "to answer a charge of murder as is said to have been committed on the 27th day of June 1844 in said county and abide the judgment of the court and not depart without leave." This unusual procedure satisfied both the prosecution and the defense. Judge Thomas, who by this means was not called upon to make any judgment about the sufficiency of the evidence ("probable cause") for holding the defendants to the grand jury or for denying them the privilege of being released on bail, went along with the arrangement to the extent that he specified the relatively small bail of $2,000. The judge took the recognizance of the nine citizens who pledged their "goods and chattels, lands and tenements" as an acknowledgment of this indebtedness to the state of Illinois to secure performance of the above-quoted conditions of the defendants' bond.[72]

The stipulation effecting this agreement shows the uniqueness of the arrangement and the care with which it was drafted.

> The undersigned, counsel respectively for the people of the State of Illinois and Levi Williams and Thos. C. Sharp admit and agree that in appearing and entering into recognizance to appear to answer to any charges preferred against them, they do not make or intend to make any admission of probable cause to bind them over; but that it is done to save time and delay in consequence of the absence of witnesses, and for this reason only; and the said Williams and Sharp, in entering into said recognizance, do so under a protestation of their entire innocence of the offense with which they have been charged.[73]

By this means Sharp and Williams were set free under a nominal bail, at perfect liberty to protest their innocence because there had been no judicial determination of probable cause to hold them to the grand jury. This, as Thomas Gregg sneeringly remarked, left the "whole matter as it was previous to the governor's expedition."[74]

Anti-Mormon newspapers made the most of the terms of surrender. They designated the parties' document a "treaty" between the governor and the fugitives and heaped scorn upon Thomas Ford. The *St. Louis New Era* of October 10, 1844, called the governor "foolish" and "ridiculous" for entering into a "treaty" with the fugitives. "If ever there was a man who deserved a straight-jacket, I think it is Governor Ford."

In his history Ford defends himself against critics who held him responsible for compromising with the murderers. "The truth is,

I had but little of the moral power to command in this expedition. Officers, men, and all under me, were so infected with the anti-Mormon prejudices that I was made to feel severely the want of moral power to control them."[75] But such protests came too late to alter the public image of the debacle. After Judge Thomas refused to be bound by the governor's "treaty" and the defendants won their liberty on small bail under protest of innocence, the "farcical character of the whole proceeding" was all too apparent. According to Thomas Gregg, when the prominent Democrat Stephen A. Douglas entered a "crowd which was making merry at the Governor's ridiculous position," he could only say, 'Gentlemen, this matter has passed beyond ridicule; it is time for sympathy.' "[76]

In fact, however, the governor had done as well as he could in upholding the appearance of law in Hancock County. He later informed the Illinois House of Representatives that the prosecutions would "vindicate the violated honor and broken pledge of the state."[77] Whether the trial itself would be conducted in an impartial and effective manner or whether the governor actually expected this remained to be seen. There were hundreds of anti-Mormons within the county and without who were determined that no jury would find their friends guilty of murder. They believed what Thomas Sharp told the deputy sheriff who had tried to arrest him on September 22: "If my influence helped to produce the state of feeling that resulted in his [Joseph Smith's] death, why I am in common with some hundred of others, guilty, not of murder, but of extra judicial execution."[78] Sharp hoped that by appealing to the concepts of higher law and mutual guilt he might win the sympathy of the uncommitted in the state and gain exoneration for himself and the others who were to go on trial. This was a strategy the anti-Mormons would employ in various ways in the months ahead as the state sought to collect its witnesses, assemble a grand jury, and bring the accused to trial before a jury in Hancock County.

1. Letter of James Gregg to Thomas Gregg, June 28, 1844, Mormon Manuscript Collection, Chicago Historical Society.

2. Marsh, "Mormons in Hancock County," 54-55.

3. *Nauvoo Neighbor,* June 30, 1844.

4. *Ibid.* The governor's original proclamation, dated June 29, 1844, is in the Illinois Historical Survey, University of Illinois Library, Urbana.

5. *Ibid.*

6. Ford's letter of June 30, 1844, is found in the Illinois Historical Survey but is reproduced in Smith, *History of the Church,* VII, 146.

7. Smith, *History of the Church,* VII, 151.

8. *Ibid.,* VI, 625.

9. The editor of the *Sangamo Journal* reproduced an editorial from the *Illinois Register* on September 26, indicating that one reason for delay was the abortive effort to secure regular army troops to be stationed in Hancock County.

10. Ford explained the heavy dependence of the governor upon local authorities in matters of civil disorder in his *History of Illinois,* 366-67.

11. *Quincy Herald,* July 5, 1844.

12. *Quincy Whig,* July 10, 1844. Ford's reply also appears in Smith, *History of the Church,* VII, 160-62.

13. See *Quincy Whig,* July 10, 1844, for the details of a handbill printed by the Warsaw Committee of Safety, and *Warsaw Signal,* July 17 and 19, 1844, for the resolutions of the anti-Mormons at Warsaw on July 14.

14. *Warsaw Signal,* July 10, 1844.

15. *Missouri Republican,* July 22, 1844, and *Warsaw Signal,* July 10, 1844. Sharp said that the "summary execution" of the Smiths brought "the severest censure of nearly the whole newspaper press." Cf. comments of "Adams" in the *Quincy Herald,* August 2, 1844, where mob action is criticized.

16. *Quincy Whig,* July 24, 1844.

17. *Ibid.*

18. See "Let Him That Is without Sin Cast the First Stone," *Alton Telegraph,* July 13, 1844.

19. *Missouri Republican,* July 31, 1844.

20. Reproduced in the *Warsaw Signal,* July 31, 1844; *Quincy Herald,* August 2, 1844.

21. See "Mormon Votes Wanted," *Quincy Whig,* July 31, 1844.

22. *Quincy Herald,* August 2, 1844.

23. *Warsaw Signal,* July 31, 1844.

24. *Quincy Whig,* July 31 and August 7, 1844.

25. Ford, *History of Illinois,* 363.

26. Smith, *History of the Church,* VII, 225-26, 231-42.

27. *Ibid.,* 223. As early as July 17, J. B. Backenstos had warned the Mormons that the anti-Mormons at Carthage were intent on winning the election and choosing their own grand and petit jurors. But the Mormons waited until August to react. See Backenstos's letter in "Journal History," July 17, 1844.

28. Franklin Worrell to Thomas Gregg, August 8, 1844, Thomas Sharp Papers, Yale University. See also Smith, *History of the Church,* VII, 226-27. The election returns can be found in the *Illinois Secretary of State Election Returns* 61 (1844), 67-69, Illinois State Archives, Springfield. These returns show how decisive Mormon bloc voting could be.

State Representatives	Jacob B. Backenstos	1809
	Almon W. Babbitt	1773
	Onias C. Skinner	1080
	Joel Catlin	886
County Commissioner	George Coulson	1830
	Franklin J. Bartlett	832
Sheriff	Minor Deming	1911
	Edson Whitney	871
Coroner	Daniel H. Wells	1838
	David R. Green	867

29. See *Quincy Whig,* August 14, 1844; cf. Ford, *History of Illinois,* 363.

30. Theodore Calvin Peace, *Illinois Election Returns,* Vol. 18 of *Collections of the Illinois State Historical Library* (Springfield, 1923), 147.

31. Cf. Ford, *History of Illinois,* 366.

32. Franklin A. Worrell to Thomas Gregg, August 8, 1844, Yale University.

33. The *Illinois State Register* published Davis's letter on November 8, 1844, after Davis demanded it in a public letter in the *Alton Telegraph* on October 26. Davis denied that he wrote his letter at the instigation of the anti-Mormons of Hancock but seemed unwilling to admit what is obvious from his written editorials and his pamphlet on the martyrdom: that he was greatly influenced by them and had in substance adopted their point of view on the martyrdom. See, for example, his "Let Him That Is without Sin Cast the First Stone," *Alton Telegraph,* July 13, 1844.

34. *Warsaw Signal,* August 21, 1844.

35. Minor Deming to his parents, August 22, 1844, Minor Deming Papers, Illinois Historical Survey.

36. *Warsaw Signal,* September 4, 1844.

37. *Ibid.,* September 25, 1844, reproduces the anti-Mormon version of the circular.

38. Ford, *History of Illinois,* 364-65.

39. See *Illinois State Register,* October 11, 1844, and the next chapter herein, following footnote 5.

40. The four leaders later indicted were Davis, Grover, Levi Williams, and Aldrich.

41. "Journal History," September 8, 1844.

42. *Warsaw Signal,* September 25, 1844.

43. *Ibid.*

44. *Alton Telegraph,* October 5, 1844.

45. *Warsaw Signal,* October 9, 1844.

46. *Sangamo Journal,* October 24, 1844; Gregg, *History of Hancock County,* 752. See "Joseph Smith's Journal Kept by Willard Richards," September 27, 1844, Church Archives, where Richards records that Ford told him and John Taylor that "he had come to execute the law — & was ready to proceed against the murderers of Smiths so fast as the people got out writs."

47. Ford, *History of Illinois,* 367; cf. admission of the *Sangamo Journal* editor (September 26, 1844) that Ford's intimates confessed at that time that the arrests were Ford's main objective.

48. "Journal History," September 8, 1844.

49. *Sangamo Journal,* September 26, 1844, urged the anti-Mormons in Hancock not to resist the governor lest the state have justification for its large expenditures. Obviously the downstate Whigs were largely interested in the political advantage to be gained from Ford's expedition.

50. *Warsaw Signal,* September 25, October 9 and 16, 1844.

51. *Sangamo Journal,* October 10, 1844; *Quincy Whig,* October 16, 1844; *Missouri Republican,* September 28 and October 4, 1844; *St. Louis New Era,* September 30 and October 10, 1844.

52. *Illinois State Register* published testimony as to the anti-Mormon intentions of the wolf hunt as late as October 18, 1844. The *Quincy Whig* editor said on October 23 that "the conduct of Governor Ford, in his crusade against the wolf hunters of Hancock, ought to give us 10,000 votes."

53. Ford, *History of Illinois,* 365.

54. Smith, *History of the Church,* VII, 274; *Nauvoo Neighbor,* October 2, 1844. *Illinois State Register* designated McConnell "as able counsel as the state, or the Western country affords" (October 18, 1844).

55. Oath in support of "Writ for Murder," dated September 21, 1844, in case file, *People* v. *Levi Williams,* Hancock County Courthouse, Carthage, Ill.

56. *Quincy Herald,* October 4, 1844; *Nauvoo Neighbor,* October 9, 1844.

57. John Gillet to Smith Tuttle, July 15, 1844, Illinois State Historical Library, Springfield.

58. *Sangamo Journal,* October 3, 1844; *Lee County Democrat,* October 12, 1844.

59. Smith, *History of the Church,* VII, 276.

60. *Ibid.,* 278.

61. Ford, *History of Illinois,* 365.

62. Gregg, *History of Hancock County,* 327.

63. Ford, *History of Illinois,* 365.

64. Gregg, *History of Hancock County,* 366.

65. *St. Louis New Era,* September 30, 1844; *Missouri Republican,* September 30, 1844.

66. Ford, *History of Illinois,* 366; Arnold, "Recollections," 57-58.

67. Ford, *History of Illinois,* 366; Gregg, *History of Hancock County,* 327. The original document, dated September 30, 1844, and signed by Governor Ford, is located in the Mormon Collection, Chicago Historical Society. See *Missouri Republican,* October 4, 1844, for another account of the arrangement by a correspondent from Warsaw.

68. Ford, *History of Illinois,* 366.

69. Gregg, *History of Hancock County,* 755.

70. Officer's return on "Writ for Murder," case file in *People v. Levi Williams.*

71. Jesse B. Thomas to E. D. Baker, October 2, 1844, Illinois State Historical Library, Springfield. Published in *Warsaw Signal,* October 9, 1844.

72. "Recognizance Bond of Levi Williams & Thomas C. Sharp," case file in *People* v. *Levi Williams.* Also see Gregg, *History of Hancock County,* 755. Those who signed the bond, in addition to Williams and Sharp, were: Robert F. Smith, M. Aldrich, John Harris, Jeremiah Smith, John D. Mellen, Harmon T. Wilson, H. Stephens, Charles C. Stevens, and James Freeman. Several of these men were members of the militia who had called for the wolf hunt in the fall.

73. The agreement, dated October 2, 1844, is in the Thomas C. Sharp Papers, Yale University.

74. Gregg, *History of Hancock County,* 327.

75. Ford, *History of Illinois,* 366.

76. Gregg, *History of Hancock County,* 755.

77. *Report of the Select Committee Relative to the Sinking Fund,* Illinois Legislature, House of Representatives, 1st sess., March 1, 1847, p. 78.

78. *Warsaw Signal,* September 25, 1844.

∾ 4 ∾

Elections and Indictments

The struggle to obtain the arrest, indictment, and conviction of the murderers of Joseph and Hyrum Smith was inseparable from the struggle for control of Hancock County. Control of the county commission was the key. This elected body chose the grand jurors who would determine whether the accused parties were indicted (formally charged), and selected the petit jurors who would hear the evidence and determine their guilt or innocence at trial.

After the August election, the Mormons held the dominant position in county government. George Coulson, a Mormon resident of La Harpe in northeast Hancock County, captured the only county commission seat held by an anti-Mormon. The other two commissioners, now serving the second and third years of their three-year terms, were Andrew H. Perkins, a devout Mormon from Ramus, and John T. Barnett, a Mormon sympathizer.[1] The elected sheriff and coroner were also friendly to the Mormons. These offices were important, because when a juror selected by the county commission was unable to serve, the court would order the sheriff to select a replacement; if the sheriff were disabled, his duties would be performed by the coroner.[2]

The victorious candidates took office in the first week of September, 1844. One of the first responsibilities of the newly constituted county commission was to select the grand and petit jurors for the October term of the circuit court. For purposes of the Mormon controversy, the grand jury was the more important of the two in this term, because it would decide whether there was sufficient evidence to indict and bring to trial persons accused of the murders of Joseph and Hyrum Smith. In addition, the grand jury would decide whether to indict the sixteen prominent Mormons, including church leaders, militia officers, and city council members, who had been accused of riot in the destruction of the printing press of the *Nauvoo Expositor*.[3]

The law required the county commissioners to select "as nearly as may be a proportionate number [of jurors] from each township in their respective counties. . . ."[4] Citizens of Nauvoo, the township with over half the county population, were almost entirely Mormon, and there were significant Mormon populations in several other townships, such as La Harpe, Sonora, and Fountain Green. The selection effort would therefore be expected to produce some Mormons on the jury panels. At least eighteen of the seventy-one grand and petit jurors who had been chosen for service in the preceding May term were Mormons.[5]

Only a deliberate effort to exclude Mormon jurors could result in a grand jury without a single member of a group comprising more than half of the population of the county. Yet that was the result sought by George Thatcher, the anti-Mormon clerk of the county commissioners' court. Thatcher had already fulfilled his bitter official duty of certifying the election results. Now he was required to serve the newly constituted and Mormon-dominated county commission. Himself an elected official, Thatcher was not subject to removal by the commission.[6] The ranking anti-Mormon in the county, he was determined to carry the standard of his group and to oppose the Mormons at every point.

Lacking any vote in the selection of the jurors, Thatcher could only exert his influence in other ways. It seems more than coincidental that, only two days after the county commissioners finished their deliberations, the anti-Mormons circulated their printed invitation for the "Grand Military Encampment" to be held in Hancock County just before the grand jury was to meet. Thatcher, who was one of the signers of the invitation, was obviously aware of the plans for this encampment when he met with the Mormon-dominated county commissioners' court. He probably reminded the commissioners of the very real possibility of civil war in Hancock County and at least hinted that, if they chose a Mormon-dominated grand jury, the planned gathering of anti-Mormon military might intervene in the court proceedings and plunge the county into armed conflict.

Whatever the nature of their effort, the opponents of Mormon jurors could claim total success. The twenty-three grand jurors designated by the county commissioners at their session on September 5, 1844, included *not a single Mormon.*[7]

Instead of being a timid or frightened response to anti-Mormon threats, the exclusion of all Mormons from the grand jury may have been a shrewd effort to cultivate and retain the support and confidence of the important uncommitted citizens of the county and state. This was the motive Mormon representative Almon W. Babbitt cited a few months later; in a speech to the Illinois general assembly he declared that special care was taken in the empaneling of jurors "that not one Mormon shall be put upon them to do away with the groundless apprehensions and foul calumnies that might otherwise be heaped upon them."[8]

While Mormons were missing from the October grand jury, so were prominent anti-Mormons. With but few possible exceptions, the grand jury seems to have been deliberately composed of non-Mormons who were either uncommitted or sympathetic to the Mormon cause. For example, Abram Golden, an early settler of Sonora Township, was a non-Mormon officer in the Nauvoo Legion. Benjamin Warrington of Nauvoo was a non-Mormon member of the Nauvoo city council who had opposed the suppression of the *Nauvoo Expositor.* Thomas H. Owen was a Baptist minister who had served three terms in the general assembly and had been friendly toward Mormon interests in that capacity. Abram Lincoln was a non-Mormon justice of the peace in Fountain Green Township, a cousin of Abraham Lincoln of Springfield. There is no record of his being involved in the anti-Mormon activities of the county; he apparently lived at peace with the Mormon community of Ramus (later Macedonia) in his township. George Walker, an early settler in Walker Township, was a prominent citizen in the county, currently serving as a justice of the peace. The others selected for the grand jury were of similar character.[9]

The circuit court's October term began in Carthage on Monday, October 21, 1844. For a week prior to trial the sheriff and his officers had been serving writs (subpoenas) summoning the principal contestants in the county to come before the court to transact their business as parties or witnesses. Murray McConnell, the prosecution's investigator, had requested subpoenas for thirty-seven witnesses to appear before the grand jury to give evidence against the murderers of Joseph and Hyrum Smith. His list included such names as Emma Smith (the widow of Joseph) and John Taylor, who had been wounded at the jail. Subpoenas were also issued for Warsaw militia officers Jacob C. Davis and Mark Aldrich, who were said to have been implicated in the crime.[10]

Court-watchers were apprehensive. Rumors of possible violence against the court or witnesses by persons opposed to the prosecution were frequent, and they were sufficiently persuasive to prompt Governor Ford on October 9 to order the Nauvoo Legion held in readiness to act under the sheriff's direction to guard the court and protect its participants from mob violence. In his order, the governor repeated his warnings that the situation was "one of great delicacy" and cautioned that the use of the legion in this circumstance might result in civil war in the county.[11]

In this highly charged atmosphere, a man of less courage and determination than Judge Jesse B. Thomas might have found it prudent to be detained in an adjoining county. But this sturdy jurist was not to be turned aside from his duty. Apparently unperturbed by the excitement of armed spectators, he took the bench in the Carthage courthouse on Monday morning in routine fashion and called for the grand jurors who had been summoned the preceding Saturday. All but one of the twenty-three were present, but a handful were unable to serve. Samuel Marshall, a Carthage politician and former clerk of the county commissioners' court, refused to serve and was fined the statutory fee of five dollars. Three other jurors were excused for cause, at least two of them because they had been summoned as witnesses in the case. The remaining nineteen grand jurors were sworn to serve.[12] Under state law any sixteen or more constituted the grand jury; the votes of twelve were necessary to find a true bill or indictment.[13] In his instructions, Judge Thomas advised the grand jury that he had heard reports that the anti-Mormons would prevent the court from meeting, but, the judge stated, he "had never credited them; and was happy to find that he was not mistaken in his opinion." Consistent with his own behavior in that stressful circumstance, the judge charged the jury to "do their duty in the cases likely to come before them, and leave the consequences."[14]

49

In the meantime, the Mormon troops of the Nauvoo Legion were on the march for Carthage. Considering their recent experience with official promises of safety in Carthage, Mormon litigants and witnesses who had business with the circuit court "deemed it inadvisable to venture upon the pledge and promises of others." Consequently, the Mormons came to Carthage in a detachment of about a hundred and fifty men and thirty wagons under the leadership of Major General Charles C. Rich. They went into camp at Crooked Creek, outside Carthage. The official Mormon history notes that "by camping they avoided the necessity of paying hotel bills to enemies and the risk of being murdered in their beds."[15]

About four o'clock on Monday afternoon, the first day of court, word reached Carthage that a portion of the Mormon legion was camped about four miles out of town. A rumor spread rapidly that the Mormons were accompanied by a large group of Indians, having recently met with thirty warriors and having as many as two thousand braves ready to fight in their behalf. Hearing this alarming report, some Carthage residents prepared to fight. Others welcomed this convenient pretext to close down the deliberations of the circuit court. On Monday evening a group of anti-Mormons held a meeting in the courthouse, affirming that two hundred Mormons and three hundred Indians were camped nearby for the purpose of attacking the town. After reviewing the facts and rumors known to the group, the meeting resolved to request Judge Thomas "to adjourn the court, so soon as it may be ascertained to the satisfaction of the court that there is an armed body of Mormons, or Indians, in the vicinity of Carthage."[16] The meeting further resolved that if the court did not adjourn, they would immediately organize an armed force around the courthouse. The ostensible purpose of this force would be to protect the anti-Mormons, but there was a clear implication that it would also be used to prevent court from continuing. Refusing to be intimidated, Judge Thomas responded that any persons who came near the courthouse with arms would be arrested. Faced with this determined response, the anti-Mormons apparently abandoned their effort, and the business of the court went forward. The atmosphere relaxed when it appeared that the Indians were about twenty Potawatamis who were passing through the area on their way to

Iowa to hunt muskrat, and that their presence in the area was a coincidence and had nothing to do with the Mormon group.

On Tuesday, October 22, the grand jury retired to the jury room with the prosecutor, William Elliot, and began to hear evidence on the cases before them. By Wednesday the jury had indicted eleven Mormons for riot in the destruction of the *Expositor,* and the Mormons not indicted had been released from their bonds. Upon the advice of the judge and the states attorney, the Mormon force then returned to Nauvoo "to allay the excitement."[17]

The charges for the murders of Joseph and Hyrum Smith proved more difficult. Seventeen persons testified before the grand jury in this matter, and it was Saturday before the signed indictments were brought to the judge.[18] A Hancock County historian has stated that the grand jury was presented with the names of about sixty persons for indictment. They voted first on the entire sixty, but the evidence was so inconclusive that the number of grand jurors who voted to indict was less than the required twelve. The grand jury then struck off the ten names with the least evidence and voted once more, but again failed to secure the minimum votes. They continued in this manner until the list of potential defendants contained only the nine persons with the strongest evidence against them. In this last instance the requisite twelve votes were finally obtained, and the nine defendants were accordingly indicted or formally charged with the murders of Joseph and Hyrum Smith.[19]

There were separate indictments for the two murders. Each charged the same nine defendants: John Wills,[20] William Voras,[21] William N. Grover, Jacob C. Davis, Mark Aldrich, Thomas C. Sharp, Levi Williams, and two men named Gallaher and Allen, whose first names were not given.[22]

The indictment for the murder of Joseph Smith, on which these defendants were to go to trial seven months later, had two parts or counts, differing slightly in the formal description of the manner in which the defendants had participated in the murder. Using the redundant legalisms common in the nineteenth century, both counts charged that the nine named defendants, "not having the fear of God before their eyes, but being moved and reduced by the instigation of the Devil . . . unlawfully, feloniously, wilfully and of their malice aforethought did kill and murder" Joseph Smith. The second count charged that the gun that discharged "the leaden bullet" that struck Joseph Smith a mortal wound "on the right breast," from which "he instantly died," was "then and there had and held" in the hands of all nine of the defendants. The first count only refers to the gun being in the hands of defendant John Wills, but then uses the same language as the other count in charging all nine defendants with causing the bullet to be shot out of the gun and thus being guilty of the murder.[23]

Any defendant who could be shown to have shot the fatal bullet could be convicted of murder under this indictment — but so could any defendant who merely joined in the mob or deliberately participated in the illegal arrangement. Under the common-law rule in force in Illinois at this time, a person who participated in an illegal arrangement was criminally responsible for all the consequences of that arrangement, even though unintended by him and even though committed out of his presence by persons whose identity could not be established. There are many cases where this theory of conspiracy has been used to convict and hang persons for murders actually committed by their co-conspirators, identified or unidentified, the four persons hanged for Abraham Lincoln's murder being one prominent example.[24] This indictment was apparently drawn to permit proof of the guilt of any or all of these nine defendants on that theory, regardless of who fired the fatal shot and regardless of whether any of them were even present at the jail.

Very little is known about four of the men who were indicted. Allen, Wills, Voras, and Gallaher were never arrested and never appeared for trial. John Hay, who lived in the county as a boy, indicated that Allen was "six feet two in his moccasins."[25] Wills, Voras, and Gallaher were probably named in the indictment because their wounds, which testimony showed were received at the jail, were irrefutable evidence that they had participated in the mob. They undoubtedly recognized their vulnerability and fled the county. A contemporary witness reported these three as saying that they were the first men at the jail, that one of them shot through the door killing Hyrum, that Joseph wounded all three with his pistol, and that Gallaher shot Joseph as he ran to the window.[26] According to Hay, Wills, whom the Mormon prophet had shot in the arm, was an Irishman who had joined the mob from "his congenital love of a brawl." Gallaher was a young man from Mississippi who was shot in the face.[27] Hay described Voras (Voorhees) as a "half-grown hobbledehoy from Bear Creek" whom Joseph shot in the shoulder. The citizens of Green Plains were said to have given Gallaher and Voras new suits of clothes for their parts in the killing.[28]

There is a great deal of information about the other five indicted defendants. All were prominent men with property, reputations, and political ambitions. All left indelible marks in their county's history, both before and after the trial. No doubt it was this prominence that caused them to stay and defend themselves rather than flee like the others.

Defendant Mark Aldrich, age 42, was the oldest of the five by a margin of ten or fifteen years. He was a land speculator and town promoter, one of the four original developers of Warsaw, whose 1834 plat bears his name. Born in New York, Aldrich came in 1832 to Fort Edwards at the site of what would become Warsaw, and a year later erected the second house built outside the fort. He was the first postmaster of Warsaw, serving from 1834 to 1838. In 1836 and again in 1838 he represented Hancock County in the state legislature, being elected as a Whig. In 1836 he was again involved in a land speculation, becoming co-owner of a quarter-section of land that was added to the Warsaw plat.[29]

Aldrich's land development schemes had brought him into direct confrontation with Joseph Smith, with consequences that explain much of his animosity toward Smith and the Mormons. According to the prophet's journal, Aldrich, along with Daniel S. Witter, a Warsaw miller, and Calvin A. Warren, an attorney from Quincy, encouraged the Mormon leaders for about two years to make a Mormon settlement on a section of land they owned on the Mississippi one mile south of Warsaw. Finally, in the summer of 1841, the three men made an agreement with the Mormon presidency, giving the Mormon people the privilege of settling on that section, which had been surveyed and laid out in lots as a new town called Warren. Brigham Young, Heber C. Kimball, and Willard Richards were in charge of making arrangements with the proprietors for building up the place and preparing for the reception of Mormon settlers.[30]

The following November (1841), the Mormon presidency counselled a party of 204 converts from England, led by Joseph Fielding, to settle in Warren. In mid-December Fielding informed the presidency that Witter and Aldrich had raised the price of flour by a dollar a barrel, sold the Mormons mill sweepings at $2.24 per hundred, forbade them collecting old wood on the school section, and raised the rents. The Mormon leaders promptly decided that the immigrants should remove to Nauvoo. Two weeks later Aldrich, Warren, and Witter conferred with Joseph Smith at Nauvoo. His journal reported them as saying that they understood the reasons for the early exodus and "they all agreed that if I did not succeed in the next attempt to establish and build up Warren, that they would fully excuse me from all censure and would feel satisfied that I had done all that could reasonably be required of any man in a like case." Calvin Warren pleaded on this occasion that his "temporal salvation depended on the success of the enterprise." Smith replied that he did not think that the area could be developed in view of the current strong antipathy toward the Mormons existing at Warsaw. The Mormon leader bluntly informed Warren that "the first thing toward building up Warsaw was to break it down, to break down them that are there."[31] To Aldrich and his fellow speculators this statement may have sounded like a declaration of war.

That Aldrich was badly hurt by the Mormon withdrawal is evident from the fact that he and Calvin Warren both took out bankruptcy within three months after their meeting with Smith. Yet these were wily businessmen and potentially dangerous enemies, as is evident from their clever scheme to take advantage of the new national bankruptcy law.[32] Aldrich filed for bankruptcy on March 22, 1842, and Warren (whose law firm, Ralston, Warren & Wheat, represented both men in the bankruptcy proceedings) filed three weeks later. Aldrich's schedule of assets showed twenty-three parcels of land and numerous notes. His debts consisted of twenty-five judgments totaling about $15,000 and an additional $10,000 due to thirty-four other creditors on notes and open accounts. In the course of the bankruptcy proceedings Aldrich's land was sold to his attorney, Calvin A. Warren, and also to attorney Thomas Morrison of Carthage for a total of $163.25. Perhaps because they were subject to large mortgages or unpaid land contract balances, some parcels of this land sold for as little as twelve-and-a-half cents, twenty-five cents, or a dollar. The bills and notes owned by Aldrich were sold to Robert Foster, a Mormon dissenter, to Calvin A. Warren, or to Aldrich himself for about one cent on the dollar of their $3,000 total face value. As a result of these proceedings, Aldrich's debts of $25,000 were totally discharged, and he or his close friends, perhaps acting as straw men in his behalf, came back into possession of virtually all of his property.[33] Such abuses of the first bankruptcy act, common throughout the country, led to its repeal a little over a year after its passage.

At the time of the murder Aldrich was married to Margaret Wilkinson, who had been reared in cultured Baltimore surroundings by her grandfather, a distinguished Revolutionary War general. The couple had three children, ages 1 to 7. Aldrich held a commission as a major in the Illinois militia. He commanded the "Warsaw Independent Battalion," which consisted of at least two companies, the Warsaw Cadets and the Warsaw Rifle Company. These, in turn, were commanded by his two co-defendants, Jacob C. Davis and William N. Grover. During June, 1844, Aldrich's battalion had been attached to the 59th Regiment, which was commanded by another defendant, Levi Williams.[34]

The second defendant, Jacob Cunningham Davis, was an Illinois state senator at the time he was indicted. Born in Virginia, he had received some legal education, but it is not known where. He listed himself as a lawyer in the 1850 census, but there is no record of his practicing law, and he does not appear on the Illinois Roll of Attorneys through 1845. The Warsaw Rifle Company, which he commanded as a captain of militia in 1844, consisted of four officers and sixty-five men. Davis was an unmarried resident of Warsaw.[35]

Only thirty-one years of age, Jacob C. Davis had already embarked upon a promising political career. A Democrat, he had been appointed circuit court clerk by Judge Stephen A. Douglas in 1842; after one year Judge Jesse B. Thomas, who succeeded Douglas in the fifth judicial circuit, appointed Jacob Backenstos, a friend of the Mormons, to succeed him. In 1842 Davis was elected to his first four-year term in the Illinois State Senate. His vote total — 1530 to 620 for his opponent, anti-Mormon Whig William H. Roosevelt — shows that Davis carried the Mormon vote in the county. As late as February, 1844, Davis stood with the moderates in Warsaw in opposing anti-Mormon calls for violence. The anti-Mormons, in turn, ridiculed him as having political ambitions. That spring Davis tried for the nomination for Congress, saying he could get the Mormon vote, but the nomination went to the incumbent, Joseph P. Hoge.[36] Davis's inability to succeed with Mormon support may have turned him against the Mormon prophet.

Defendant William N. Grover, 26, was the youngest of the five principal defendants and was also a captain in the militia. His Warsaw Cadets consisted of four officers and forty-two men. He lived and practiced law in Warsaw, where he had been elected a justice of the peace in 1843. Grover was married but childless.[37] What, if any, grievances he had toward the Mormons and their prophet remain obscure, other than the Warsaw militia's general jealousy of the military establishment at Nauvoo.

Thomas Coke Sharp was probably the best known of the five defendants because of his editorship of the anti-Mormon *Warsaw Signal*. At the time he was indicted, Sharp was only thirty-one years of age, but Mormons and Mormon sympathizers who had been lashed by his venomous prose in the *Signal* had long since scored him with the nickname "Old Tom Sharp." There is no doubt that Sharp was the most hated and feared anti-Mormon in the county. His was the leading voice of the anti-Mormons, and excerpts from his constant barrage of editorial criticism of Mormons and their leaders were widely quoted throughout the state.[38]

Sharp was born in New Jersey, the son of a noted Methodist preacher. He was educated at Dickinson College; in August, 1837, he began eighteen months of study in the law school of Judge Reed of Carlisle, Pennsylvania. He graduated and was admitted to the Cumberland County Bar in April, 1840, but a few months later he left for the west. He opened a law office briefly in Quincy but soon moved his practice to Warsaw. Unfortunately for his legal ambitions, Sharp was hard of hearing, which seriously interfered with his functioning in the courtroom. After about a year he became discouraged and abandoned his practice, although he continued to serve as a justice of the peace, a position to which he was elected in 1841.[39]

Thomas C. Sharp arrived in Hancock County in September, 1840, a year and a half after the Mormons began to settle at Nauvoo. But his belated arrival apparently did not preclude him from promptly becoming the champion and spokesman of the old citizens of the county in their struggles against the Mormons. In November, 1840, just two months after his arrival, Sharp and a partner acquired a newly established Warsaw newspaper, the *Western World.* In the spring of 1841 they changed the name to *Warsaw Signal,* and in November, about the time he abandoned the practice of law, Sharp took over his partner's interest and became the sole publisher. Within a few months Sharp attempted to rally an anti-Mormon movement to offset the political activities of the Latter-day Saints. His editorial opposition to Judge Stephen A. Douglas's appointment of Mormon John C. Bennett as master in chancery in the circuit court brought non-Mormon fears and jealousies into political focus and resulted in the formation of an anti-Mormon political slate for the election of 1842. According to an unidentified informant to the *Illinois State Register,* Sharp may have been a spokesman for the speculators who lost on the proposed Mormon settlement at Warren, but there is no evidence that Sharp lost money himself.[40]

By the end of 1841 Sharp's editorial activities had made him so notorious in the Mormon community that Smith's journal noted that Sharp "devoted his entire time to slandering, to lying against and misrepresenting the Latter-day Saints."[41] Sharp is also credited with coining the term "Jack Mormon" to describe non-Mormons who were friendly to their Mormon neighbors.[42] Notwithstanding his success as a political leader and propagandist, Sharp had his financial problems. By the summer of 1842 he became convinced that his paper could never pay the accumulated debt, and he turned it back into the hands of its original owner. Shortly after he gave up the *Signal* in 1842, Sharp married the young widow of John R. Wilcox, one of the original proprietors of Warsaw, and took up farming for eighteen months. During this time he also participated in anti-Mormon activities, such as the September 6, 1843, meeting where the Warsaw Committee passed resolutions to organize opposition to the Mormons and support Missouri efforts to extradite Joseph Smith.[43]

In February, 1844, Sharp revived the *Warsaw Signal* and reassumed the vocal leadership of the anti-Mormon forces of the county. This was a time of great anti-Mormon excitement, and the opportunities for an editor of Sharp's skill and persuasiveness were considerable. Typical of his efforts, and perhaps best known because it was written at a critical time that gave it unusual notoriety, was his call to arms for an attack on Nauvoo after the suppression of the *Nauvoo Expositor.*

> We have only to state, that this is sufficient! War and extermination is inevitable! CITIZENS ARISE, ONE AND ALL!!! Can you *stand* by, and suffer such INFERNAL DEVILS! to ROB men of their property and RIGHTS, without avenging them. We have no time for comment, every man will make his own. LET IT BE MADE WITH POWDER AND BALL!!![44]

The following day a mass meeting at Warsaw resolved that the time had come for the Mormons to be driven from the surrounding settlements into Nauvoo. If the Mormons did not deliver up the prophet on request, "a war of extermination should be waged to the entire destruction, if necessary for our protection, of his adherents."[45] With the conclusion of the Mormon War and the expulsion of the Mormons in the fall of 1846, Sharp could no longer exploit the issue that kept his newspaper in the forefront of public concern in the county and he once again gave up his editorship of the *Signal.*[46]

Levi Williams, the fifth of the prominent defendants, was a colonel in the Illinois militia, a farmer, cooper, and sometime Baptist minister. He was thirty-four at the time of the indictment, married, with five children. He and his wife had moved from New York in the early 1830's, settling in Green Plains, a few miles southeast of Warsaw. He served his county on two occasions as a commissioner to establish roads. He was commissioned a captain in the 59th Regiment of the Illinois militia in 1835, and in 1840 was commissioned colonel and commanding officer of that regiment, a position he still held in 1844.[47]

If Thomas C. Sharp was the leading spokesman of the anti-Mormon cause, then Levi Williams was probably the leading actor. His activities made him well known to the Mormons. In December, 1843, Williams rode at the head of a mob that forcibly kidnapped a

Mormon named Daniel Avery and his son at gunpoint near Warsaw, threatened them with knives, bound them in chains, and took them into Missouri, where they were briefly imprisoned on horse-stealing charges and then released.[48] The following month a Mormon named William Jones, who had stayed all night at Wilson's Tavern in Carthage, was arrested without process by Williams and his followers and kept in custody until noon without rations. On June 19, 1844, at the height of the excitement preceding Joseph Smith's imprisonment in Carthage, Williams appointed a committee of twelve to tar and feather a militia officer who had refused the unauthorized request of a Carthage constable who wanted him and his company to join a posse to go to Nauvoo and arrest Smith. During that same time Williams took the lead in demanding that militiamen either agree to fight against Joseph Smith or surrender their arms, and in trying to intimidate them into doing so. Levi Williams was involved in mob actions against Mormons in September, 1844, and in anti-Mormon meetings on other occasions.[49] According to Bill Hickman, a renegade Mormon, Williams's anti-Mormon attitudes were based upon political considerations. Williams told Hickman after the murder that while what they had done could not be justified, the Mormons "ruled the county, elected whom they pleased, and the old settlers had no chance; that it was the only way they could get rid of them."[50]

1. Coulson had served one term on the county commission, from 1838 to 1841. (Scofield, *History of Hancock County*, 1045; *Election Returns*, 61:69.) He was later to serve as captain of a company of Mormons in the western move. (Smith, *History of the Church*, VII, 482.) The anti-Mormon incumbent was Robert Miller. (Gregg, *Prophet of Palmyra*, 176-77; Gregg, *History of Hancock County*, 449.)

Perkins had already served as a Mormon missionary and as a delegate to explain the Mormon position to his fellow citizens in eastern Hancock County. He was later ordained a bishop's counselor and a branch president, and appointed captain of a company in the move west. (Gregg, *History of Hancock County*, 820; Smith, *History of the Church*, VI, 340, 483; VII, 306, 375, 482.) Coulsen and Perkins were elected to the first county commission in the valley of the Great Salt Lake. (Hubert Howe Bancroft, *History of Utah* [San Francisco: History Company, 1889], 287.)

Non-Mormon Barnett was an elected member of the Nauvoo City Council, an officer in the Nauvoo Legion, and a spokesman for the Mormon interests. He had been nominated and supported for his county offices by the citizens of Nauvoo. (*Quincy Argus*, June 5, 1842, as quoted in Cecil A. Snider, "Development of Attitudes in Sectarian Conflict: A Study of Mormonism in Illinois in Contemporary Newspaper Sources" [M.A. thesis, Iowa State University, 1933], 32; Smith, *History of the Church,* IV, 287, 295; VI, 483.)

2. *Revised Statutes of Illinois* (1845), 310, 517.

3. The group accused of riot included John Taylor, General Jonathan Dunham of the Nauvoo Legion, W. W. Phelps, and Porter Rockwell. Smith, *History of the Church,* VI, 453. See Oaks, "The Suppression of the *Nauvoo Expositor,*" 862-68.

4. *Revised Statutes of Illinois* (1845), 309.

5. Gregg, *Prophet of Palmyra,* 156; see the Appendix herein for an analysis and classification of the religious preferences of jurors in various terms of court.

6. *Election Returns* 56:63 (August, 1843). Jacob Backenstos names Thatcher as one of those active in the massacre of Joseph Smith. Smith, *History of the Church,* VII, 144.

7. Historical Records Survey, *Hancock County Board Minutes* 4 (September 5, 1844), 160, Illinois State Archives, Springfield; list of grand jurors for October 21, 1844, Hancock County Courthouse, Carthage, Ill. See the Appendix herein for an analysis and classification of the religious preferences of jurors. The *Nauvoo Neighbor* (November 6, 1844) declared that the grand jury was "composed exclusively of men who were not Mormons." The military encampment was discussed in Ch. 3, above.

8. *Nauvoo Neighbor,* January 29, 1845.

9. Scofield, *History of Hancock County,* 1102; Executive Department, *Executive Record* 3 (1837-43), 276, Illinois State Archives, Springfield; Gregg, *History of Hancock County,* 313, 328, 473, 819; *Election Returns,* 50:28; 56:64. Owen wrote a sympathetic and helpful letter to the leaders of the Church immediately following the murder. Smith, *History of the Church,* VII, 192-93; Sandburg, *Lincoln: The Prairie Years,* 47. The other grand jurors were: James Reynolds, Thomas J. Graham, Edward A. Bedell, William M. Owens, Ebenezer Rand, Thomas Brawner, Ralph Gorrell, Brandt Agnert, Martin Yetter, William Smith (of La Harpe), Thomas Gilmore, Reuben H. Loomis, Samuel Scott, James Ward, Samuel Marshall, Samuel Ramsey, David Thompson, and John J. Hickok. List of grand jurors for October 21, 1844, Hancock County Courthouse; Gregg, *History of Hancock County,* 328.

10. Subpoenas in case file, *People* v. *Levi Williams,* Hancock County Courthouse, Carthage, Ill.

11. Gregg, *History of Hancock County,* 328; *Alton Telegraph,* February 22, 1845. Hosea Stout recorded in his journal that the mob at Carthage had sworn to kill any who testified before the grand jury. "Journal History," October 24, 1845; Smith, *History of the Church,* VII, 309.

12. Scofield, *History of Hancock County,* 1414; Gregg, *History of Hancock County,* 328; *Revised Statutes of Illinois* (1845), 310. The man who did not appear was Brandt Agnert. Those excused from serving were George Walker, E. A. Bedell, and Abram Golden. *Circuit Court Record* 162 (October 21, 1844).

13. *Revised Statutes of Illinois* (1845), 309.

14. *Alton Telegraph,* February 22, 1845; Gregg, *History of Hancock County,* 328.

15. Smith, *History of the Church,* VII, 311. On Charles C. Rich, see Leonard J. Arrington, *Charles C. Rich,* vol. 1 of *Studies in Mormon History,* ed. James B. Allen (Provo: Brigham Young University Press, 1974).

16. *Illinois State Register,* November 1, 1844, p. 2; Smith, *History of the Church,* VII, 312, quoting from undated *Nauvoo Neighbor; Missouri Republican,* October 25, 1844, p. 2. Also see *Alton Telegraph,* February 22, 1845.

17. Smith, *History of the Church,* VII, 313. Also see Gregg, *History of Hancock County,* 328-29. These indictments were not resolved until October, 1845,

when a trial resulted in acquittal. Smith, *History of the Church*, VII, 484, and Ch. 11 herein.

18. *Circuit Court Records*, 207. The following witnesses are listed on the "Indictment for the Murder of Joseph Smith," case file, *People* v. *Levi Williams:* "Joseph Staunton, Jonas Hobert, Walter Bagby, William M. Daniels, John Peyton, Benjamin Brackenbury, William Garret, Hon. Thomas Ford, Walter Bagby, Marvin M. Hamilton, [illegible; deleted; probably Artois Hamilton], Thomas Dixon, George Walker, Plat Fairchild, John Taylor, Eli H. Walker, William Houk and Henry Mathias [or Matthews]." Most of these persons later testified at the trial. Yet, concerning testimony before the grand jury, there is reason to doubt the entire accuracy of the list. Contemporary accounts carry no mention of Governor Ford's being in the area or testifying, a fact that surely would not have gone without notice. Likewise, Mormon historians make no mention of John Taylor's giving testimony, and there is even a contemporary statement from another witness, William Daniels, that he was the only Mormon to give testimony before the grand jury. *Nauvoo Neighbor*, November 6, 1844, p. 3. Perhaps Ford and Taylor were listed as witnesses because the grand jury made some use of documents signed by them.

The prosecution made an effort to subpoena an eighteenth person, Willard Richards, to prove that Joseph and Hyrum Smith were dead. But on learning that Richards was sick in Nauvoo, the judge refused to issue a writ of attachment, observing that this formality could be proved without bringing a sick man out of his bed.

19. Gregg, *Prophet of Palmyra*, 301-2. The *Warsaw Signal*, October 30, 1844, maintains that no indictment could be obtained from Tuesday through Friday, but that on Saturday the Mormons "smuggled" in two additional witnesses who provided the basis for indictment.

20. A Mormon source gives this as "John Patrick Wells." Smith, *History of the Church*, VII, 162.

21. So in indictment. Other sources often show it as "Voorhees."

22. There were three Gallahers in the Warsaw militia units: Charles, Patrick, and William. "Muster Roll of the Commissioned and Non-Commissioned Officers, Musicians and Privates belonging to the 59th Regiment 4th Brigade and 5th Division, Illinois Militia, under the command of Levi Williams," Chicago Historical Society. Hereafter cited as "Muster Roll." John Hay, "The Mormon Prophet's Tragedy," *Atlantic Monthly* 24 (December, 1869), 675, gives Gallaher's first name as William. There was a Nathan N. Allen in Captain Grover's company of Warsaw Cadets, but no other Allen is listed in the militia from Warsaw. "Muster Roll."

23. "Indictment for the Murder of Joseph Smith," case file, *People* v. *Levi Williams.*

24. *Brennan* v. *People*, 15 *Illinois Reports* 511 (1854) (individual conspirator's responsibility for murder by mob, discussed in Ch. 8); *Spies* v. *People*, 122 *Illinois Reports* 1, 12 *Northeastern Reports* 865, 17 *ibid.* 898 (1887) (a report of the trial proceedings against these defendants, the "Chicago Anarchists," is contained in *American State Trials*, XII, ed. John Davison Lawson [St. Louis: F. H. Thomas Law Book Co., 1919], 8). For a legal discussion of the trial of Lincoln's murderers, see Lawson, *American State Trials*, VIII, 32.

25. Hay, "The Mormon Prophet's Tragedy," 675.

26. Statement of Jeremiah Willey, August 13, 1844, Brigham Young correspondence, Church Archives.

27. Hay, "The Mormon Prophet's Tragedy," 669, 675. Another source says Wills was a former Mormon elder who had left the Church. Davis, *An Authentic Account*, 24.

28. Statement of Jeremiah Willey, August 13, 1844.

29. U.S. Bureau of Census, Hancock County, Ill., 1850, p. 325-A, located and indexed in Illinois State Archives, Springfield (hereafter cited as Hancock County Census, 1850); Scofield, *History of Hancock County*, 720, 1105, 1108; Gregg, *History of Hancock County*, 448, 637, 654; John Moses, *Illinois Historical & Statistical*, II (2nd rev. ed., Chicago: Fergus Printing Co., 1895), 1163; *Illinois Laws of 1836/37*, 155.

30. Smith, *History of the Church*, IV, 405, 471; VI, 470-71.

31. *Ibid.*, IV, 486, 471-72.

32. *United States Statutes at Large* 5 (1841), 440.

33. "General Bankruptcy Records, District of Illinois," IV, 258, 259-63, 280, 283, 284-86, 471, 493, Federal Records Center, Chicago.

34. Sources cited in note 29 above. Military organization shown in "Muster Roll."

35. "Roll of Attorneys of the Supreme Court of the State of Illinois," *Illinois Reports* 3-4 (2 and 3 Scammon and 1 Gilman) (1841, 1843, 1844, 1846); "Muster Roll."

36. Gregg, *History of Hancock County*, 240, 449, 749; Smith, *History of the Church*, IV, 471; *Warsaw Signal*, February 14, 1844; Simeon Francis to John J. Hardin, April 22, 1844, Hardin Collection, Chicago Historical Society. William D. Abernethy, a Whig, said he hoped Davis could obtain the nomination for Congress since he felt the Whigs in the county could beat a "thorough Jack Mormon" with a "strait out antimormon." William D. Abernethy to John Hardin, March 19, 1844, Hardin Collection, Chicago Historical Society.

37. *Hancock County Census, 1850*, p. 381-B; *Election Returns*, 56:64.

38. *Hancock County Census, 1850*, p. 315-B. Anti-Mormons claimed that Hyrum Smith announced in June, 1844, that if anyone were to go to Warsaw in broad daylight and break the press in the *Signal* office with a sledge hammer, he would "bear him out in it if it costs me a farm." Gregg, *History of Hancock County*, 319; Ford, *History of Illinois*, 319. Hyrum Smith denied this. Smith, *History of the Church*, VI, 495.

39. Most of the information about Sharp is taken from the detailed biography in Gregg, *History of Hancock County*, 748-57.

40. *Ibid.*, 283, 749-50. See the letter to the *Register* quoted in *Nauvoo Neighbor*, November 13, 1844. Cf. Joseph Smith's comments in Smith, *History of the Church*, IV, 487.

41. Smith, *History of the Church*, IV, 489-586.

42. *Illinois State Register*, November 1, 1844, reproduced in *Nauvoo Neighbor*, November 13, 1844. This article says Sharp earlier coined the term "Jack Mason" to describe persons unwilling to join the anti-Masonic movement in western New York, where he was a newspaper editor. This statement is at least partly and perhaps wholly inaccurate, as is evident from the above biographical information. *Missouri Republican*, July 31, 1844, p. 2, refers to Jack Mormons as "a class of men who adhere to the Mormons for the sake of *votes* and *lucre* — a class more to be despised and feared than the Mormons themselves."

43. Gregg, *History of Hancock County*, 749-50; Smith, *History of the Church*, VI, 8.

44. *Warsaw Signal*, June 12, 1844.

45. Smith, *History of the Church*, VI, 463-64. Sharp also appeared with several other anti-Mormon attorneys of Hancock County as counsel for the state in the preliminary examination of Joseph Smith for the charge of treason. This occurred in the courthouse in Carthage on June 26, the day before he was murdered. *Ibid.*, 596; VII, 98.

46. Gregg, *History of Hancock County*, 756.

47. Brigham H. Roberts, *Comprehensive History of the Church of Jesus Christ of Latter-day Saints* (Provo: Brigham Young University Press, 1965), II, 322; Smith, *History of the Church,* VII, 143; *Hancock County Census, 1850,* 280, 293; Scofield, *History of Hancock County,* 656, 670; *Executive Record,* 3:187 (1837-40).

48. Smith, *History of the Church,* VI, 145-48, 123. The Avery case occasioned great excitement in Nauvoo (*ibid.,* VI, 100-148). A Nauvoo justice of the peace issued a writ to arrest Williams for kidnapping. Upon receiving reports that a mob was congregating at Williams's house and soliciting additional armed assistance from Missouri, a hundred Nauvoo Legion members were detached to assist the constable in executing it. The force went to within two miles of Williams's house, but on being informed that a body of armed men had assembled there, they "judged it prudent" to return to Nauvoo for weapons and help (*ibid.,* 120). At this point cooler heads prevailed and conflict was averted. Affidavits covering the whole matter were collected and forwarded to Governor Ford, with the comment that "it was deemed most advisable to let Colonel Levi Williams and his mob flourish until indictments could be made at the Circuit Court of Hancock County" (*ibid.,* 153).

49. Smith, *History of the Church,* VI, 8, 175, 464, 471, 504, 509-13; VII, 270.

50. Bill Hickman, *Brigham's Destroying Angel* (New York: George A. Crofutt, 1872), 39.

∞ 5 ∞

To Secure Pre-Trial Advantage

Once the indictments were secured, the state officials, Mormons, and anti-Mormons engaged in a series of moves and counter-moves to secure pre-trial advantage, each group with its own special interests to promote and each with a general distrust of the other. In these maneuvers the state's primary objective was to proceed with the trial and thus vindicate the honor of the state. The anti-Mormons' objective was to harass and intimidate the state's witnesses, while courting public favor so as to lessen the likelihood of conviction.[1] The Mormons sought to protect their members and principal leaders from further legal involvement and possible assassination while finishing their temple and making ready for an exodus to the West.

As soon as the indictments were returned, the defendants demanded an immediate trial. Appearing for the state, Murray McConnell objected, declaring that the prosecution was not ready. Its witnesses had left without recognizance to appear, and William Elliot, the states attorney, had departed. The defendants agreed that their cases could be postponed until the following term of court, in May, 1845, but insisted that the clerk issue no *capias* (arrest warrant) in the interim if they gave their pledge that they would appear at the stipulated time.[2] Short of being forced to trial without prosecutor and witnesses, the state apparently had no choice but to agree.

To offset a state law that required a clerk of court to issue the sheriff a *capias* for apprehension of indicted persons,[3] McConnell signed a communication ordering the clerk not to issue a *capias* until so directed by the prosecuting attorney or the court.[4] Despite that protection, on November 20 a *capias* was issued for the arrest of all nine of the defendants. It appears that Judge Thomas, who had already shown some independence of mind earlier in the case, directed the clerk to issue the *capias* notwithstanding the arrangements made between the prosecution and the defense.[5] But it seems peculiar that, so far as the record shows, the only defendant actually arrested under the *capias* was Jacob C. Davis, whom Sheriff Minor Deming took into custody on December 26 in Springfield during a session of the state legislature — nearly a month after the *capias* was issued.[6] Davis's arrest under such circumstances could not have come without careful planning. Deming may have hoped that by seizing Davis in Springfield he would escape the interference of Davis's many friends in Hancock County.[7]

The fact that Davis alone was arrested, and that it was done while he was participating in a session of the state legislature, gives reason to suspect that political considerations were involved. According to a correspondent of the *Missouri Republican,* the administration was fearful that Davis would spearhead a movement to investigate Governor Ford's anti–wolf hunt campaign. The correspondent charged that "the whole effect seems to have been to get hold of him and prevent his being in the Senate where he could expose the whole *burlesque,* whenever that body attempted an investigation of the late Mormon difficulties, and the expenses of the state arising from them."[8] Another possible reason for the executive's apparent antipathy toward Davis was that the senator from Hancock was actively seeking the repeal of the Nauvoo Charter.[9] In his address to the legislature in December Governor Ford indicated that he favored revision of the Mormon charter, but that he was against repeal.[10] Whatever the reason, Deming arrested Davis despite some personal threats to his life. Deming wrote that the anti-Mormons have so "long threatened me that I have become familiar with the talk of lynchings and death."[11]

Davis's arrest infuriated the Illinois Senate. The senators appointed a committee of three to investigate the cause of arrest and issued a process to compel Deming to appear before them for examination.[12] After hearing Deming, the committee affirmed that "base motives" were involved. The entire Senate voted to order Davis's release, threatening punitive action if the Hancock sheriff did not comply. After consulting with Ford and prosecutor Murray McConnell, Deming released his prisoner. Ford maintained that the Senate's order was arbitrary and unheard of, but a correspondent to the

Illinois State Register justified the Senate with precedents from Blackstone regarding legislative privilege.[13]

At the same time the arrest of Davis was initiated, the prosecuting attorney directed the clerk to issue attachments for nine witnesses to appear as state's witnesses at the trial, including Benjamin Brackenbury, George Walker, and John Taylor.[14] Under this process the witnesses were to be arrested and not released until bail or recognizance was given as security. Available sources indicate that the sheriff did not arrest any of these until early May, when some were arrested and released on fifty-dollar bail. The document also requested subpoenas for Thomas Ford and William Daniels, and they were served in December.

In the meantime, the defendants were apparently trying to strengthen their position by new allegiances within the influential Masonic order. Mark Aldrich was a member of Warsaw Lodge No. 21, founded in January, 1843.[15] With an immediacy and urgency that cannot have been coincidental, Jacob Davis, Thomas Sharp, and Levi Williams were all initiated into the small Warsaw lodge in October and December, 1844. Before spring all three had been passed to the second degree, and Davis and Williams had been raised to Master Masons. How much advantage the defendants expected to derive from this association is unclear, though it is a fact that many of the most influential men in the county and state at this time were Masons. The list includes Justice Richard M. Young of the Illinois Supreme Court, who was to be the judge at the trial; James H. Ralston, former states attorney; Judge Stephen A. Douglas; former circuit judge O. C. Skinner, who was to be among the defense counsel at the trial; George W. Thatcher, the anti-Mormon clerk of the county commissioners court; and various members of the Warsaw militia such as Charles Hay, Henry Stephens, and several of the Chittenden family.[16]

Whatever uncertainties may exist in the benefits the defendants expected to derive from their Masonic affiliation, there is no doubt that the state officers in the Masonic order identified an impropriety in this maneuver and took decisive disciplinary action. In its annual meeting in 1845 the Grand Lodge of Illinois appointed a select committee to investigate reports that the Warsaw lodge had violated

Masonic regulations by conferring degrees upon persons who were under indictment. In response to this investigation, officials of the Warsaw lodge admitted that the degrees had been conferred on Davis, Williams, and Sharp, but pleaded that the men in question were "worthy members of society, and respected by their fellow citizens. . . ." Their standing in the community "had not been at all impaired by the indictment, but, on the contrary, they were regarded with greater consideration than before, from the fact that they had been particularly selected as the victims of Mormon vengeance." The Grand Lodge was apparently unimpressed with this defense. A year after this report was submitted, the Warsaw lodge surrendered its charter, ostensibly because "the members of Warsaw Lodge No. 21 have no suitable room to work in. . . ."[17] This voluntary relinquishment of a charter because of a supposed housing shortage in Warsaw was undoubtedly a face-saving disposition in lieu of involuntary suspension for violation of the regulations of the order.

At Nauvoo the Mormons were also active. On February 11 they arrested John C. Elliott for murder and brought him before three Nauvoo justices of the peace for preliminary hearing.[18] They apparently hoped to add Elliott to the list of those already indicted for the murder. Elliott was a former deputy sheriff and constable at Warsaw[19] who had joined with Levi Williams in the kidnapping of Daniel Avery in December, 1843.[20] The May, 1844, grand jury had indicted Williams and Elliott for that crime,[21] but their trial had not yet been held. The principal evidence against Elliott in the charge of murder was Daniel Avery's testimony that he heard Elliott threaten the prophet's life during the kidnapping, and the testimony of Benjamin Brackenbury that Elliott was in the company of men who went toward the Carthage jail on the afternoon of June 27 and was among those who confessed afterward that they had killed Joseph Smith. Finding probable cause to believe that Elliott was guilty of murder, the Nauvoo justices of the peace committed him to the Carthage jail to await the action of the May, 1845, grand jury.[22] Elliott later escaped and was never brought to trial.[23]

On March 3 the Mormon majority on the county commissioners' court, perhaps after consultation with Brigham Young, abandoned the policy followed the previous October of not choosing Mormons for jury duty. Mormons comprised almost half of those chosen for the grand and petit juries for the May term.[24]

The significance of these choices could not have been lost on the anti-Mormons of the county. They retaliated by getting a justice of the peace in Augusta (in the southeast part of the county) to issue a writ for the arrest of Benjamin Brackenbury for the crime of perjury before the grand jury in October, 1844. A witness for the state in the forthcoming murder trial, Brackenbury was accused by a member of the grand jury, who said that he had testified falsely that Levi Williams was present on horseback at the Carthage jail during the murder.[25] On March 10 Brackenbury was arrested in Nauvoo, but a party of approximately 125 armed Mormons took him from the custody of the sheriff.[26] Brigham Young and the Mormon leaders were convinced that Brackenbury would be killed if he were taken to Carthage.

The anti-Mormons promptly sent a messenger to the governor reporting that the Mormons had resisted county officers and urging him to order a *posse comitatus* to take Brackenbury. Fearing this would lead to confrontation between the state and the Mormons, Brigham Young sent Brackenbury to Augusta under a guard of six armed men for a hearing before the justice of the peace who issued the writ.[27] The prosecution was not prepared and asked for postponement. Brackenbury offered to admit to the charge for purposes of examination, and to give bond to appear at the May term of the court (the same procedure followed by Sharp and Williams in their September preliminary hearing). But the justice of the peace refused, scheduled the hearing for March 19, and remanded Brackenbury to Sheriff Deming for confinement in Nauvoo until that date. That same week, thoroughly disgusted with lawyer's fees and legal maneuverings, Brigham Young declared that he would spend no more money "feeing" lawyers, and that he "would rather have a six shooter than all the lawyers in Illinois."[28]

The Mormons still feared that witness Brackenbury might be killed on his way back to Augusta. On March 19 Sheriff Deming notified the justice of the peace that he could not have the accused before him in Augusta because he had just been served with a writ of *habeas corpus* to have Brackenbury before the judge of the fifth judicial circuit in Quincy.[29] The case file in the Hancock County courthouse shows only one writ being issued by the fifth circuit judge, however, and it is dated March 22. Deming may have had no more than Brackenbury's petition for a writ when he refused to take his prisoner to Augusta. Deming's delay may have been encouraged by Brigham Young, who conferred with church leaders and a lawyer on March 21 and decided that Brackenbury should sue for a writ of *habeas corpus* returnable before Judge Young at Quincy.[30] Brackenbury was taken to Quincy the following day, where he alleged that Judge Dunn, the Augusta justice of the peace, had imprisoned him on a malicious charge. Brackenbury's petition for the writ stated "that he verily believes that his person will not be safe from violence in appearing again before judge Dunn that he is a material witness in a criminal proceding now pending in Hancock Circuit Court and [that] . . . it is the intention of his prosecutors either to take his life . . . or intemedate [*sic*] your petitioner so that he will not appear at said court in Hancock County."[31] Circuit Judge Richard M. Young, who by this time must have known that he was due to preside at the forthcoming trial of the accused murderers of the Smiths, was apparently persuaded of the reality of the threat to Brackenbury's safety. He signed an order that allowed Brackenbury to enter into a recognizance to appear at the May term of court under bond of $1,000,[32] thus giving him liberty to return to Nauvoo to await action by the grand jury on his own case and the trial of the accused assassins.

There is evidence that Governor Ford was also apprehensive on the eve of the trial, fearing that the anti-Mormons might do harm to the state's witnesses and prevent them from appearing at Carthage for the May term. Ford wrote to Sheriff Deming on May 13 that he had received information that "certain persons in Hancock county were preparing a force, with the view to prevent the witnesses on the part of the state in the murder cases . . . from attending court." Ford told Deming that if necessary he could call out the Nauvoo Legion. Ford said he did not think the situation warranted another expeditionary force — that if the danger of armed intervention seemed imminent, the cases might be continued to another term.[33]

Ford's changing attitude on the use of the Mormon militia bears some scrutiny, for he apparently considered the risk of a Mormon–

anti-Mormon military clash less dangerous to the image of the state and the Democratic party than he did the embarrassment of another "wolf hunt" campaign with its attendant frustrations. Ford's unwillingness to repeat his direct involvement in the Hancock controversies was typical of an attitude prevailing among most state officials and party members at this time. Ford acknowledged in a letter to the sinking fund committee of the legislature in 1847 that "Everyone desired to keep as much out of these difficulties as possible, who had anything in future to expect from public opinion." Proof that Ford's characterization of the situation is accurate comes from the fact that the state had to use four prosecutors in the course of gathering the evidence and trying this case, and that none with political ambitions remained with it very long. William Elliot, a prominent political figure, was states attorney but would take no part in the murder trial itself. Ford indicated that Elliot had deliberately stayed away from the preliminary hearing before Judge Thomas in Quincy and implied that the same attitude kept him from attending the trial.[34]

To carry on the prosecution Ford employed Josiah Lamborn, formerly attorney general of the state, who was highly regarded among the legal profession in Illinois for his forensic talents and persuasive powers. Relying on the preparatory work of his predecessors, Lamborn had the sheriff and his deputies serve dozens of subpoenas on potential prosecution witnesses.[35] The returns on these processes show that many witnesses could not be found. One witness who evaded the deputies was John Taylor, the Mormon apostle and editor of the *Times and Seasons,* who had been wounded at the jail on June 27. It is clear that Taylor and other Mormon leaders went to unusual lengths to avoid being served with a summons to testify. In a public address given on April 13, 1845, Taylor had affirmed emphatically that "if they made an attempt to serve writs on him it would cost them their lives." Taylor said that if the state wished to magnify the law and make it honorable, they would bring the murderers of Joseph and Hyrum Smith to justice. He denounced state officials who had allowed the brothers to be "treacherously butchered while in the custody of officers pledged for their safety" and concluded that "he would not submit any more to such outrages on our lives and liberties, for under present circumstances the law is only powerful to hold men still while the lawless massacre them."[36] Ten days later in an editorial in the *Nauvoo Neighbor* Taylor said, "Until the blood of Joseph and Hyrum Smith have been atoned for by hanging, shooting, or slaying in some manner, every person engaged in that cowardly assassination, no Latter-day Saint should give himself up to the law."[37] Taylor voiced a strong feeling of many Mormons: that state officials were not trustworthy when it came to protecting them, and that cooperation with the state in prosecuting the cases against the men accused of the murders should be minimal.

In truth, many Mormon leaders had little confidence in the ability of the state to prosecute the murderers successfully. Apostle George Albert Smith wrote in January, 1845, that "we have not the least idea of any of the guilty will be punished by the laws of Illinois." They feared, as John Taylor expressed it, that if their leaders went to Carthage to participate in the trial, it would only endanger their lives while accomplishing nothing toward punishing the murderers. For ultimate justice they looked to themselves and to the Lord. George A. Smith said, "God will execute his vengeance no doubt in due time."[38]

The Mormons had already begun preparations for a mass exodus from Illinois,[39] believing that both state and federal governments had failed to grant them justice and to right the wrongs done in Missouri and Illinois. Their primary reason for remaining in the state was to complete the temple and receive certain religious rituals prior to departure. This necessitated good public relations in the interim. Early in March the General Council resolved that those "hunted with writs" should go on missions, so the anti-Mormons could not succeed in their strategy of securing "vexatious writs in order to provoke resistance to the form of legal authority and thereby produce a collision between us and the state." Brigham Young said he hoped "if possible [to] evade the blow until we can finish the Temple and the Nauvoo House."[40]

When the editor of the Democratic *State Register* criticized John Taylor sharply for advocating "resistance to the law" in his April editorial in the *Neighbor*,[41] and when rumors circulated in Hancock of intended Mormon threats against the court, the Council of Fifty met on May 6 to consider the situation and work out a counteracting policy. William Clayton recorded in his journal that the anti-Mormons were affirming that, if the court did not convict the murderers, the Mormons intended to destroy the courthouse and the citizens of the county. Such tactics, Clayton wrote, were intended "to bring us into collision with the State, so as [to] bring about our expulsion or extermination forthwith."[42]

The Council decided that none of the Mormon men should leave Nauvoo during court week, except those with business at Carthage. They also decided that Willard Richards and Orson Hyde should write an article to appear in the *Neighbor* the next day to define what Brigham Young termed a "medium course" in relationship to the trial and the anti-Mormon strategies, which would avoid "extremes that might raise an excitement in the county."[43] In part the medium course consisted of the Council's repudiation of John Taylor's protest in April against honoring of legal process by the Mormon people. Richards and Hyde wrote "in behalf of the church" that "we have no knowledge of the '*Neighbor*' until we read it, as do others, and therefore cannot be responsible for it . . . and we further declare to all men, that as a people we are still determined to abide our pledge, and await the action of the executive and judiciary, and tarry at home, and attend to our own business as usual during the sitting of the court . . . and we wish, decidedly wish, that those whose business it is to keep the peace during court, should do it, and let us as a people alone, for we do not wish to be brought in collision with our neighbors, and we are determined to abide the law."[44]

1. Brigham Young wrote to Phineas H. Young on January 21, 1845: "Our enemies without in the surrounding counties are endeavoring to do all they can to frustrate the execution of the laws of this state upon the murderers of our Prophet . . . by publishing false reports against the Saints as a community, and by raising an excitement in the adjoining counties. . . ." Letter in Brigham Young Letter File, Church Archives.

2. Gregg, *History of Hancock County,* 329. For further details on the "compromise" negotiated by counsel, see the account of N. Bushnell in the *Warsaw Signal,* December 18, 1844.

3. *Revised Statutes of Illinois* (1845), 183.

4. "Order for Capias," October 26, 1844, in case file, *People* v. *Levi Williams.*

5. "Capias on Indictment," November 20, 1844, and M. McConnell letter to Clerk of Circuit Court, November 20, 1844, both in case file, *People* v. *Levi Williams.*

6. *Ibid.;* see also sheriff's return on "Capias on Indictment."

7. This was suggested in *Missouri Republican,* December 30, 1844. According

to a correspondent, an abortive attempt was made to arrest Davis while he was en route to Springfield. See *Missouri Republican,* December 4, 1844.

8. *Ibid.,* December 4, 1844.

9. Almon Babbitt to Elias Smith, January 7, 1845, in which Babbitt says that Jacob Davis read the *Nauvoo Neighbor* to the Committee on Banks and Charters. Cf. Smith, *History of the Church,* VII, 363. See also Babbitt to Brigham Young, December 19, 1844, Almon W. Babbitt Papers, Church Archives. E. M. Webb claimed in the *Kalamazoo Gazette* that the Senate would not give Davis up to Deming for fear they would not have enough votes to repeal the charter. Webb's letter was republished in *Times and Seasons* 6 (May 1, 1845), 894.

10. Reproduced in *Warsaw Signal,* January 15, 1845.

11. Minor Deming to his parents, December 22, 1844, Illinois Historical Survey, Urbana.

12. *Illinois State Legislature, Senate Arrest of Hon. Jacob C. Davis,* S.R. 14th Assem., 1st sess., December 26, 1844, pp. 157-58.

13. *Missouri Republican,* December 30, 1844; *Illinois State Register,* January 3, 1845.

14. "Attachment," issued December 14, 1844, in case file, *People* v. *Levi Williams.*

15. John C. Reynolds, *History of the M. W. Grand Lodge of Illinois* (Springfield: by H. G. Reynolds, Jr., 1869), 210, 331. For a general discussion of previous Mormon contacts with the Masons, see Kenneth W. Godfrey, "Joseph Smith and the Masons," *Journal of the Illinois Historical Society* 64 (Spring, 1971), 79-90.

16. *Ibid.,* 140, 203, 229, 253, 305-6, 315, 351.

17. *Ibid.,* 305-6, 351-52, 395.

18. Smith, *History of the Church,* VII, 373.

19. *Nauvoo Neighbor,* February 19, 1845.

20. Smith, *History of the Church,* VI, 145-47.

21. *Circuit Court Record,* 119. The charges were later dismissed. *Ibid.,* 198, 377.

22. Case file in *People* v. *John C. Elliott,* Hancock County Courthouse, Carthage, Ill. The testimony and arguments of counsel were published in *Nauvoo Neighbor,* February 19, 1845.

23. *Warsaw Signal,* February 19, 1845.

24. *Hancock County Board Minutes,* 4:226, 255, 260-62. See Appendix herein for analysis and classification of religious preferences of jurors. Since Andrew H. Perkins, one of the commissioners, was in close touch with Brigham Young at this time on the business of the county commissioner's court, it seems likely that he would also have consulted Young on the matter of the use of Mormons on the juries, but no letter on this subject has been preserved. See Perkins's letter to Young on Mormon voting and voting precincts, dated May 11, 1845, Brigham Young Correspondence, Church Archives. See also Smith, *History of the Church,* VII, 388, for further evidence of communications between Perkins and Young.

25. Writ dated March 8, 1845, in case file in *People* v. *Benjamin Brackenbury,* Hancock County Courthouse, Carthage, Ill.

26. *Davenport Gazette,* April 3, 1845.

27. Smith, *History of the Church,* VII, 380-81, 384.

28. *Ibid.,* 383-84, 386. Petition for Habeas Corpus and Sheriff's Return, in case file in *People* v. *Benjamin Brackenbury.*

29. Sheriff's return on writ in case file in *People* v. *Benjamin Brackenbury.*

30. Smith, *History of the Church,* VII, 387.

31. "Petition for Habeas Corpus," in case file in *People* v. *Benjamin Bracken-bury*. On habeas corpus, see, generally, Dallin H. Oaks, "Habeas Corpus in the States — 1776-1865," *University of Chicago Law Review* 32 (Winter, 1965), 243-88.

32. Order signed by Judge Richard M. Young, March 22, 1845, in case file in *People* v. *Benjamin Brackenbury*.

33. Smith, *History of the Church*, VII, 409.

34. *Illinois State Legislature, House, Report of the Select Committee, Relative to the Sinking Fund*, H.R. 15th Assem., 1st sess., March 1, 1847, 346.

35. Subpoenas and Attachments in case file, *People* v. *Levi Williams*.

36. Smith, *History of the Church*, VII, 396.

37. "Our Rights," *Nauvoo Neighbor*, April 23, 1845.

38. George A. Smith to Wilford Woodruff, January 25, 1845, Church Archives.

39. "Journal History," March 1 and March 19, 1845.

40. Smith, *History of the Church*, VII, 380. See also *ibid.*, 417-18.

41. *Illinois State Register*, May 2, 1845.

42. "Journal of William Clayton," May 6, 1845, Church Archives.

43. *Ibid.;* "Journal History," May 6, 1845.

44. *Nauvoo Neighbor*, May 7, 1845, also published in Smith, *History of the Church*, VII, 406.

✤ 6 ✤

The Courtroom and the Contestants

The people of Carthage arose early on Monday morning, May 19, 1845. On foot, on horseback, and by wagon hundreds of eager spectators gathered to Carthage from the fifteen-mile radius of Hancock County and from adjoining counties for the beginning of court term. Most came fully armed because, in the words of a St. Louis newspaperman, "great fears were entertained that a collision would take place between the Mormons and the anti-Mormons."[1] The possibilities of armed conflict must have enlivened the breakfast conversations in the tavern room of the Hamilton House, in the crowded dwellings of the town, and around the campfires that dotted the outskirts. Most would agree that if conflict came, it would be touched off by some militant action by the Mormons or by something that happened at the trial. The prospects turned on the intentions of the Mormons and the outcome of the trial.

Those who predicted war could point to the fact that the Mormon-dominated county commission had chosen Mormons to serve on the juries for this term of court. This seemed to show that they were determined to bring about the conviction of the men indicted for the murder of their leaders, and conviction would surely result in bloodshed. The law required death for all convicted of murder, and Carthage was filled with violent men who vowed they would never see their friends hang. Persons who still thought that the county could avoid war could be encouraged by the fact that the Mormon leaders had instructed their people to stay away from Carthage unless they had specific business with the court. The peacemakers would watch anxiously to see how many Mormons appeared in Carthage and how carefully they avoided giving offense.[2]

The courtroom filled to capacity as soon as it was opened. The two hundred persons who climbed the stairs to the second floor were a cross-section of the residents of Hancock County, except that the fifty Mormons in attendance represented only about half of their proportionate share of the county's population. About one-third of the men who crowded into the courtroom had been summoned as jurors — twenty-three for the grand jury, and forty-eight others to serve on the two panels of petit jurors.[3] Also present were lawyers, witnesses, indicted defendants, and others whose cases would be called at the beginning of court.

The courtroom was fifty feet from side to side and forty feet from front to rear. The judge's bench was located on the north; on the south side were three doors. The stairway led up to the center door at the rear of the courtroom. The two jury rooms, one apparently for the grand jury and the other for the petit jury, were located on either side of the stairway and were accessible through twin doors on the left rear and right rear of the courtroom. Spectators settled into the benches on the east, west, and south sides of the room. The lawyers took their places on chairs inside the knee-high railing or bar that separated them from the spectators' section. The floor inside the bar was covered with matting.[4]

After all were in place, Judge Young entered the courtroom from one of the jury rooms, stepped through the railing, and made his way to the judge's bench at the front. Though not the regularly assigned circuit judge, Richard M. Young was known to all. A former senator from Illinois, he was probably the best known and most experienced of the justices of the Illinois Supreme Court. Erect and well proportioned, his 6'2" height made him a commanding figure in any crowd. One of his contemporaries called him "the finest-looking man in the state."[5] He was a splendid horseman and a man who did not flinch at personal physical hardship. Twelve years before, when he was named the first judge for the circuit including Chicago, he had ridden there on horseback, a round trip of more than three hundred miles, just to hold court for three days. Judge Young had other talents that made him popular on the circuit. He was an outstanding fiddler who used his fine old violin, which he purchased as a law student in Kentucky, to contribute to the gaiety of social life during court week. He was also considered to be an unsurpassed conversationalist, "having an exceedingly entertaining style of expression and a limitless store of anecdotes and apt illustrations always at his command."[6] His Quincy home was famous for its festive social gatherings. At forty-seven, Judge Young was now older than most of the lawyers who appeared before him. Though affable, with the stately politeness and courtly manners of his southern birth, he was always dignified, never tolerating undue familiarity. Judge Young's courts were models of decorum and order.[7]

As the crowd rose to acknowledge his appearance and then quieted for the beginning of business, Judge Young must have experienced at least a moment of satisfaction. Hancock County had a fine courtroom — a far cry from the unfinished tavern in which he and Thomas Ford, then states attorney, had held the first circuit court in Chicago in 1833, or from the log cabins, crude platforms, and plank seats in other locations where he had held court during his many years on the circuit.[8] Here the judge had an appropriate bench in a dignified, well-lighted, second-floor location, and the spectators had comfortable seating on wooden benches.

The first order of business was to organize and charge the grand jury. As the grand jurors stood to take the required oath to perform their business with integrity, alert spectators could confirm the rumor that the county commissioners had abandoned their October, 1844, policy of not choosing Mormon grand jurors. Nine of the twenty-three persons who stood before the judge as prospective grand jurors were Mormons, and some were Mormon leaders.[9] An example was Daniel Spencer, an alderman of the city of Nauvoo. There were anti-Mormons among the grand jurors also, including Robert Miller, who had recently finished a term as a county commissioner. He and other grand jurors had served in the Warsaw militia on the day the Smiths were killed.[10] This grand jury was a volatile mix of both factions.

Judge Young appointed Daniel Spencer foreman of the grand jury, an action which probably provoked a growl of protest from some in attendance. The judge next explained that William B. Elliot, the elected states attorney for the fifth circuit, was not present at this term of court, so it would be necessary for him to appoint a states attorney pro tem to perform the duties of that office by presenting the prosecution's evidence to the grand jury and representing the state in various criminal prosecutions.[11] Judge Young stated that he was appointing James H. Ralston. "Judge" Ralston was well known as a prominent Democratic politician who had served on the Illinois Supreme Court, as fifth circuit justice, and in the legislature. He had a history of very friendly relations with the Mormons.[12] After the judge completed these organizational arrangements, the acting states attorney led the grand jurors to one of the jury rooms to begin the performance of their duties.

The next order of business was for Judge Young to complete the venires or panels of petit jurors. Consistent with the usual practice, the county commissioners had summoned two panels of twenty-four each, one to function during each of the two weeks of court. When the panel was complete, the clerk of court would write the names of each of the potential jurors on tickets placed in a box and draw forth names at random whenever it was necessary to empanel a twelve-man petit jury to hear a case.[13] The Mormon or anti-Mormon sympathies of these potential petit jurors were critical, since twelve of these men would make a life or death decision for defendants Aldrich, Davis, Grover, Sharp, and Williams. Just as important, the anti-Mormons' resort to violence to offset Mormon control of the county government was also on trial in this case. A verdict of guilty would impart an unmistakable message that the community was rejecting illegal violence and seeking a peaceful accommodation with the Mormon majority.

The clerk called the potential petit jurors' names, one by one. When a man was absent, the judge would issue a writ of attachment, sending a deputy sheriff out to arrest him and compel him to attend court and perform his duty. Some persons sought to be excused, and occasionally one refused and was fined the statutory five dollars. Vacancies were filled by the sheriff's choosing replacements from the bystanders. In practice, this meant choosing a responsible individual who was present in the courtroom, or perhaps lounging on the square outside. Before the two jury panels were complete on this Monday morning, ten bystanders had been chosen in this manner, some Mormon and some non-Mormon.[14]

As the potential jurors were identified one by one, defendants and spectators could verify that the county commissioners had made a determined effort to assure that Mormons would be represented on the jury at the trial. The final count showed that the two panels of twenty-four included ten Mormons for the first week and eleven for the second. Many were prominent leaders like Major General Charles C. Rich of the Nauvoo Legion, a member of the city council in Nauvoo, and Jonathan H. Hales, a Mormon bishop from Nauvoo who was a lieutenant colonel in the Legion. But the panels also included prominent anti-Mormons, like Calvin Cole and Samuel Brown. Both of these prospective jurors were lieutenants in Warsaw militia companies on the day that Joseph was killed, each one serving under one of the indicted defendants, Captains Davis or Grover.[15] Like the grand jury, the group of potential petit jurors represented the extremes of Mormons and anti-Mormons in Hancock County. The court concluded its organization business at noon and adjourned for lunch.

The first case called when court convened at two o'clock that afternoon was *People* v. *Levi Williams,* the case of the five indicted assassins of Joseph Smith.[16] Defendants Levi Williams, Thomas C. Sharp, Mark Aldrich, Jacob C. Davis, and William N. Grover all stood to acknowledge their presence. None of the other four indicted defendants, John Wills, William Voras, William Gallaher, or Allen, made any appearance at the trial. A newspaper reported a rumor that three of them had left the state.[17]

Judge Young announced that this case would be prosecuted by Josiah Lamborn, special counsel appointed by the governor. Every eye was upon Lamborn's tall figure as he stood to acknowledge his readiness to proceed. Though crippled from birth by a defective foot, Lamborn's personal appearance was dramatic and appealing. After a decade of political and legal competition with the greatest men at the Illinois bar, including two years as attorney general of Illinois and almost fifty cases before the Illinois Supreme Court, Lamborn was one of the most colorful, successful, and feared criminal lawyers of his day. The defendants were represented by four lawyers: O. H. Browning, Archibald Williams, and Calvin A. Warren of Quincy; and Colonel William A. Richardson of Rushville in Schuyler County.[18]

Defense counsel immediately asked the judge to fix a recognizance bond to secure the appearance of their clients from day to day during the term, rather than taking them into custody. Because a free defendant could intimidate witnesses or choose to flee if the weight of evidence tipped against him, such a request was unusual in a capital case. Nevertheless, the prosecutor agreed with the request, the judge fixed their bonds at $1,000 each, and the defendants signed a recognizance for one another in that amount. That formality having been concluded, the judge set the trial for Wednesday morning, May 21, at seven o'clock, and instructed the sheriff to notify the witnesses to appear at that time.[19]

After Judge Young concluded with the murder case for that day, there must have been a considerable exodus from the courtroom as defendants and spectators hastened to share the latest information with their friends waiting outside. The new well just outside the courthouse was always surrounded by a crowd of loungers on a warm day during court week, and those who wanted to quench their thirst by something more fiery than the water in the well bucket had no difficulty finding a bottle or a jug in the crowd.[20] The spectators during this first day of court week included newspapermen from the St. Louis *Missouri Republican* and the *Sangamo Journal*. The correspondent of the latter, perhaps persuaded by the small attendance of Mormons in court that morning or by word that the Mormon leaders were not cooperating in the gathering of evidence for the prosecution, sent a report that minimized the possible effect of Mormon participation in the trial.

> The impression appears to be, that the Mormons will not attempt a very rigerous [sic] prosecution, although they have witnesses who are ready to swear to the actual participation of some of the defendants in the death of the Smiths; yet, being convinced of the entire incredibility of their testimony in a court of justice, will rather let things take their own course, and after the trial of the prisoners endeavor to create sympathy in their behalf, from the fact that the testimony failed to establish the guilt of the prisoners.[21]

As defendants and their counsel left to prepare for the trial on Wednesday, the circuit court proceeded with the normal business of court week. A civil damage action by apostate Mormons Francis and Chauncy Higbee, William and Wilson Law, and Robert and Charles Foster against Mormons Edward Hunter, Orson Spencer, John Green, and Stephen Markham, probably for damages in the destruction of the *Nauvoo Expositor* press, was dismissed for want of prosecution, with defendants granted costs against the plaintiffs. The grand jury returned indictments against three persons for larceny. Some indictments found by earlier grand juries were dismissed on technicalities with the consent of the states attorney. John Brannan, whom the grand jury had indicted for larceny just a few hours before, pleaded guilty and was sentenced to a year and a day in the penitentiary, a proceeding that must have made some kind of record for swift dispensing of justice even by brusque frontier standards.[22] And, with impartiality that seems too convenient to be coincidence, the grand jury refused to indict either John Elliott, who had been charged with complicity in the murder of Joseph Smith, or Mormon witness Benjamin Brackenbury, who had been charged with perjury before the grand jury that had returned the murder indictments.[23]

The lawyers for the defendants must have met on Monday or Tuesday to confer on their strategy for the trial; they could not have met on Sunday, because Orville H. Browning would not have left his home in Quincy until he had completed an entire Sabbath of worship. Browning was a devoutly religious man, a supporter of temperance movements, who did not think it right even to take passage on a river steamer on Sunday.[24] The three lawyers from Quincy, on the Mississippi River about forty miles southwest of Carthage, probably came by river boat to Warsaw and then by buggy or horseback over the sixteen miles of prairie from Warsaw to Carthage. Colonel Richardson probably covered the forty miles from his home in Rushville, southeast of Carthage, on horseback.

Browning was the natural leader of the group. The bold and self-assured manner of this thirty-nine-year-old lawyer would not permit him to occupy a trivial or obscure role in any undertaking. Like many members of the bar in western Illinois, Browning was born in Kentucky, where he served in the legislature before coming to Illinois. In Illinois he was already a veteran of one four-year term in the state senate and two years' service in the lower house. In a time when public speaking was a signal qualification for anyone in public life, Browning was considered "perhaps the ablest speaker in the state."[25] His forensic powers, along with his obvious brilliance, his extensive political contacts, and his close affiliation with the powerful *Quincy Whig* in his home city, had made him a leading spokesman for the Whig party.[26]

Ironically, of all the participants in the Carthage trial it was

Browning, the chief counsel for the defense, who had been most closely identified with the Mormons and their murdered leader. Browning had been the principal counsel for Joseph Smith when the Mormon prophet was arrested for extradition to Missouri on old charges and sought his liberty by a writ of habeas corpus before Judge Stephen A. Douglas, then holding circuit court in Monmouth. Joseph Smith credited Browning with taking his case despite threats that anyone who was "engaged on the side of the defense . . . need never look to the citizens of that county for any political favors." He wrote that Browning stood up "in the defense of the persecuted in a manner worthy of high-minded and honorable gentlemen."[27] The editor of the Mormon *Times and Seasons* described Browning's two-hour speech in favor of releasing the prophet on that occasion as "one of the most eloquent speeches ever uttered by mortal man in favor of justice and liberty." He said that Browning "soared above the petty quibbles which the opposite counsel urged" and "boldly, nobly, and independently stood up for the rights of those who had waded through seas of oppression and floods of injustice and had sought a shelter in the State of Illinois."[28] Joseph Smith's journal stated that when Browning traced the persecuted women and children from Missouri to Illinois by their bloody foot-marks in the snow, his words were "so affecting that the spectators were often dissolved in tears. Judge Douglas himself and most of the officers also wept."[29] Browning won his case, and Joseph Smith went free. Three years later, on June 27, 1844, that memory prompted Joseph Smith to dispatch a letter from Carthage jail asking Browning to hurry to his side to represent him at the forthcoming examination on the charge of treason.[30] Nothing came of that request because the prophet was murdered just a few hours after this letter was sent. Now, a little less than a year later, Browning was chief counsel for the men indicted for that murder.

Colonel William A. Richardson was a contrast to the polished Browning in virtually every important characteristic, except their common interest in politics and their common birth and early education in Kentucky. A thirty-four-year-old Jacksonian Democrat, Richardson was a protege of Stephen A. Douglas. His ascending political star was to bring him repeated elections to Congress, and service in the Senate as well.[31] In most of his election campaigns Richardson's opponent was Whig O. H. Browning, who was no match for this popular Democrat at the polls. In contrast to Browning's religious attitudes, careful grooming, and cultivated manners, Richardson's manner was "unguardedly rough, almost crude at times." He "laughed, drank, swore, and fought with relish." He was "uninterested in acquiring a wide knowledge that would develop him into an educated man," but he was "a spirited and loyal party worker," much favored by the masses.[32] At the time of the trial Richardson had already served a term in the state senate and two terms in the house of representatives. In the house session that concluded in March, 1845, he had been elected speaker by a large majority. In that position "Dick" Richardson was one of the most potent Democrats in the state. The relationship he would occupy with Browning in the trial of this case was similar to the relationship he enjoyed with his mentor, Stephen A. Douglas. Richardson's biographer observed that his subject "was not endowed with the faculty for proposing significant ideas," but he was a "faithful, diligent worker, one who would execute the plans that had originated in the mind of another."[33]

The other two advocates for the defense were Democrat Calvin A. Warren and Whig Archibald Williams. New York–born Warren, a law partner of J. H. Ralston and Almeron Wheat, was thirty-eight at the time of the trial. Before taking up residence in Quincy, Warren had practiced law in Warsaw for several years; his continuing business interests in that area gave him the closest contacts with the residents of Hancock County of any of the circuit-riding members of the defense team. Until 1843 he had frequently served as a lawyer for Joseph Smith. In 1841 Warren and defendant Mark Aldrich had attempted to use Mormon immigrants to populate their real estate development of "Warren," with consequences already explained. He blamed the Mormons for his business failure, and soon gave his support and voice to the increasingly strident anti-Mormon activities in western Illinois.[34]

Archibald Williams, at forty-four, was the eldest and most experienced of the defense counsel, but his role in the trial was a minor one. Kentucky born and educated, Williams had come to Illinois in 1829, settling in Quincy. An ardent Whig, Williams was a successful candidate for political office even when his party was in a minority.

The key to his personal popularity was similar to Richardson's, a direct homespun manner and easy identification with the people of the frontier, without pretensions to culture or superior knowledge. A biographer has written that Williams was regarded as "the homeliest man in the legislature," with the possible exception of his close friend, Abraham Lincoln.[35] Both these men were tall and angular, similar not only in homeliness but also in humor. Carl Sandburg says that Williams's clothes were so careless that a hotel clerk who observed him loafing in a chair asked him if he was a guest of the hotel. Williams replied with a snarl, "Hell, no! I am one of its victims, paying $5.00 a day!"[36] Williams was not an orator, but a master of direct, plain, and earnest reasoning.[37]

This distinguished team of lawyers was aided by two others, young Onias C. Skinner of Quincy and Thomas Morrison of Carthage.[38]

Though they outnumbered the prosecutor six to one, the defense counsel could not afford to be overconfident about their contest. Josiah Lamborn was a formidable adversary. Usher F. Linder, one of Lamborn's contemporaries in the Illinois bar, has left this description:

> He was a very remarkable man. Intellectually, I know of no man of his day who was his superior. He was considered by all of the lawyers who knew him as a man of the tersest logic. He could see the point in a case as clear as any lawyer I ever knew, and could elucidate it as ably, never using a word too much or one too few. He was exceedingly happy in his conceptions, and always traveled the shortest route to reach his conclusions. He was a terror to his legal opponents, especially those diffusive, wordy lawyers, who had more words than arguments.[39]

Born in Pennsylvania and just thirty-six years old at the time of the trial, Lamborn was educated at Transylvania University in Kentucky. He came to Jacksonville, in Morgan County of western Illinois in the early 1830's. He soon became active and prominent in politics, championing the anti-Jacksonian faction of the Democratic party against Stephen A. Douglas.[40] In 1834, the first year he was admitted to law practice in Illinois, he suffered a setback that almost ruined his career. Disbarment proceedings were initiated against Lamborn by an angry client who charged that the young lawyer had sold out to the opposition in pending litigation, once by agreeing to throw a case, and in other instances by offering to give confidential information to his adversaries. After investigation the Illinois Supreme Court found Lamborn's conduct in some instances "highly censurable" or "not free from censure," but took no disciplinary action because, the court said, there was insufficient proof of any "corrupt motive." Lamborn was admonished, however, to "guard his reputation with a jealous watchfulness . . . that the indiscretions which have been committed may not be repeated."[41]

Despite this embarrassing setback, Lamborn gained increasing recognition at the Illinois bar. He took an important step in his career when he and John J. Hardin conducted the successful prosecution of some rowdies who had attempted to break up a camp meeting of the celebrated frontier revivalist, Peter Cartwright. Afterward, Cartwright wrote that although Lamborn was "somewhat dissipated at times, he was a talented gentleman of the bar, and a friend of religious order."[42] During the presidential campaign of 1840 Lamborn and Stephen A. Douglas took an active part in debating the champions of the Whig party, including Hardin and E. D. Baker, as they followed the circuit court from county to county. Lamborn's political career took a new turn in December of that year when he was elected attorney general of the state, an office he occupied until January, 1843. While attorney general, Lamborn appeared for the state in forty-six cases before the supreme court. In the same capacity he represented the State of Illinois in its second attempt to arrest Joseph Smith and return him to Missouri on the extradition warrant, which the Mormon prophet successfully resisted before Judge Pope in the federal court in Springfield.[43]

A contemporary called Lamborn "one of the most able, untiring yet merciless prosecutors that ever lived."[44] But despite his undoubted ability, his advancement was impeded by recurrent rumors of corruption, even while he was attorney general. At the conclusion of his term he failed to win his party's support for reelection. With his career in decline, he began to drink excessively.

Though flawed in character and diminished in politics, Lamborn was still a powerful advocate, and he could well have been the best lawyer available to the harassed governor, who had already experienced several defections by others who had originally accepted assignments in connection with the prosecution. Governor Ford may have sought Lamborn not only for his ability but also because he sensed that Lamborn had some personal ambition to gratify by agreeing to assume the difficult and unpopular task of prosecuting the indicted murderers of Joseph Smith. Lamborn might seek to use this case as a vehicle to win the esteem of the large Mormon electorate and ride a tide of popular resentment against the murderers, thus regaining some political prominence. Or perhaps Lamborn had some other favor he sought to earn from the Mormons or from the governor.[45]

Whatever circumstances may have brought Whig Browning and Democrat Lamborn to oppose one another in this trial of the indicted murderers of Joseph Smith, the contrast was richly ironic. To vindicate its broken pledge and regain its tarnished honor, the state chose as its champion an increasingly intemperate and flawed genius whose own character and loyalty were subject to doubt. In opposition, to defend the indicted murderers, was the personal attorney of the murdered man, a teetotaler so devoutly religious that he faithfully attended church even on circuit, would not travel on Sunday, and was once so shocked by the sight of his neighbors playing cards on the Sabbath that he concluded that he should "have them indicted."[46]

As the defense attorneys met with their clients to confer about trial strategy, each of them knew that Joseph and Hyrum Smith had been killed by the men of the Warsaw militia. This was common knowledge in the circuit.[47] Four of the defendants, Colonel Williams, Major Aldrich, and Captains Davis and Grover, were officers in this militia. The fifth, Thomas C. Sharp, was the acknowledged spokesman for the most rabid anti-Mormon element in Warsaw. His *Warsaw Signal* had called for the killings before they took place and had justified them afterwards. How would the defendants deal with this situation?

The defendants could not go on the witness stand themselves, since the criminal law of that time did not permit a person accused of crime to testify in his own behalf.[48] They would have to make their defense out of the mouths of other witnesses. Could someone establish an alibi that the defendants were at their homes in Warsaw during the killings in Carthage? That would not do, since it was well known that all five of the individuals were in Carthage at or about the time of the murder. In fact, they had come there with or at about the same time as the men who had just been discharged from their militia duties. In truth, the defendants had no affirmative defense. Their primary defense tactic would be to attack the truthfulness of the prosecution's witnesses and to contend that the evidence was insufficient to convict.

Rarely have defendants been provided with material more suitable for attacking the truthfulness of a witness (impeachment) than was presented to them by William M. Daniels, the prosecution's key witness before the grand jury. Two weeks before the trial he published a twenty-four-page booklet containing "the names and proceedings of the principal murderers of Joseph and Hyrum Smith."[49] Defense counsel obviously lost no time in obtaining a copy of this publication, which sold for twenty-five cents. Now, on the eve of the trial, they could savor its contents and enjoy the opportunity it gave them to prepare a careful, advance cross-examination of the testimony of the key witness for the prosecution. They would exploit this opportunity to the fullest.

Daniels's booklet describes how he had overheard some Warsaw militiamen plotting to assist the Carthage Greys in murdering Joseph and Hyrum Smith while the governor was in Nauvoo. Persuading them of his sympathy with their cause, Daniels joined them in their march for Carthage. About noon the troops were met at an intermediate point by Sharp and others, who bore dispatches from the governor disbanding the troops. Sharp then made "an inflammatory speech to the companies, characteristic of his corrupt heart."[50] Daniels quotes the speech at great length. In substance, he has Sharp telling the disbanded troops that the law "is insufficient" for their problem and that they must take matters into their own hands to end "the mad career of the Prophet."[51] They should murder the Smiths in Carthage and have the news reach Nauvoo while the governor was still there. The enraged Mormons will then fall upon and murder Tom Ford and "we shall then be rid of the d———d little Governor and the Mormons too."[52]

Captain Grover was the first to step forward, followed by eighty-four others. Daniels followed to "see what they would do." Colonel Williams rode back and forth several times to the Carthage Greys. When they were within four miles of Carthage, one of the Greys brought a note assuring them that this was an excellent time to murder the Smiths, and that the guns of the jail guards would be loaded with blank cartridges. Daniels says he left the mob at this point and went directly to the jail, but he was unable to inform the prisoners of the plot because of the complicity of the guards. Soon the mob appeared and surrounded the jail. They had blacked themselves with wet gunpowder "which gave them the horrible appearance of demons." Colonel Williams, mounted on a horse, shouted to the mob, "Rush in! — there is no danger boys — all is right!"[53]

The Daniels booklet then relates the familiar account of what took place as the mob ran up the stairway and fired through the wooden door into the prisoners' chamber. He adds one unfamiliar detail: that the pistol Joseph fired at the mob "wounded three of them — two mortally."[54] Joseph then sprang to the window, but, seeing an array of bayonets below, he caught the window casing and hung there by his hands and feet with his head to the north and his feet to the south for "three or four minutes" before he fell to the ground. While he was hanging in that position, Colonel Williams shouted: "Shoot him! God d———n him! Shoot the d———d rascal!"[55] However, according to Daniels, no one fired at him. Presently he fell to the ground, landing on his back and right shoulder.

The next portion of Daniels's pamphlet provided the defense with some of their choicest opportunities for impeachment:

> He rolled instantly on his face. From this position he was taken by a young man, who sprung to him from the other side of the fence, who held a pewter fife in his hand, — was bare-foot and bare-headed, having on no coat — with his pants rolled above his knees, and shirtsleeves above his elbows. He set President Smith agains [*sic*] the South side of the well-curb, that was situated a few feet from the jail. While doing this, the savage muttered aloud, "This is Old Jo; I know him. I know you, Old Jo. Damn you; you are the man that had my daddy shot." The object he had in talking in this way, I supposed to be this: He wished to have President Smith and the people in general, believe he was the son of Gov. Boggs, which would lead to the opinion that it was the Missourians who had come over and committed the murder. This was the report that they soon caused to be circulated through the country; but this was too palpable an absurdity to be credited.[56]

After commenting briefly about what was going on inside the jail, Daniels continues with the following:

> When President Smith had been set against the curb, and began to

recover, Col. Williams ordered four men to shoot him. Accordingly, four men took an eastern direction, about eight feet from the curb, Col. Williams standing partly at their rear, and made ready to execute the order. While they were making preparations, and the muskets were raised to their faces, President Smith's eyes rested upon them with a calm and quiet resignation. He betrayed no agitated feelings and the expression upon his countenance semed to betoken his inly prayer to be, "O, Father, forgive them, for they know not what they do."

The fire was simultaneous. A slight cringe of the body was all the indication of pain that he betrayed when the balls struck him. He fell upon his face.[57]

Daniels continued his account with this embellishment:

The ruffian, of whom I have spoken, who set him against the well-curb, now secured a bowie knife for the purpose of severing his head from his body. He raised the knife and was in the attitude of striking, when a light, so sudden and powerful, burst from the heavens upon the bloody scene, (passing its vivid chain between Joseph and his murderers,) that they were struck with terrified awe and filled with consternation. This light, in its appearance and potency, baffles all powers of description. The arm of the ruffian, that held the knife, fell powerless; the muskets of the four, who fired, fell to the ground, and they all stood like marble statues, not having the power to move a single limb of their bodies.

By this time most of the men had fled in great disorder. I never saw so frightened a set of men before. Col. Williams saw the light and was also badly frightened; but he did not entirely lose the use of his limbs or speech. Seeing the condition of these men, he hallooed to some who had just commenced a retreat, for God's sake to come and carry off these men. They came back and carried them by main strength towards the baggage waggons [sic]. They seemed as helpless as if they were dead.[58]

The remaining pages of Daniels's booklet recount how he saw Joseph Smith in a vision and received his blessing. After reporting his observations to the Mormons in Nauvoo and to the governor, he moved his wife and children to Quincy for safety from the mob. While he was living in Quincy two unnamed men told him they would pay him $2,500 if he would leave the county and not appear against the murderers. Daniels said he refused. He concluded his pamphlet by stating that he had joined the Mormon Church and by reaffirming that he had seen "the heavens exert a power" to prevent the ruffian from severing the head of General Smith from his body.[59]

Though apparently comforting to the rank and file of Mormons still mourning their fallen leader, Daniels's account of the wondrous light was never accepted in official Church accounts and has been rejected by responsible Mormon historians.[60]

The Daniels booklet gave the defense an unequaled opportunity for impeachment of this chief prosecution witness. The incredible portions could be used to ridicule him, and if he deviated from any portion of the published version he could be attacked for lying. Contacts in Quincy and in Hancock County had already lined up several witnesses who would challenge the truthfulness of various statements in the pamphlet. Witnesses were also prepared to contradict the testimony and impeach the credibility of several other witnesses who had furnished the most damaging testimony before the grand jury.

Although defense counsel had a strong basis for impeachment, they could not base their sole reliance on this kind of "answering" defense. It was too risky, since the prosecution might produce one or more surprise witnesses whom the defense had not anticipated and were not prepared to answer. Consequently, the lawyers had to consider additional lines of defense.

One obvious objective was to secure a favorable jury. Concern therefore centered on the identity of the panel of twenty-four men from whom the twelve-member jury would be chosen. A third to half of this group were Mormons. Did this make inevitable the inclusion of Mormons on the twelve-man petit jury that would hear evidence in the case?

In the process of selecting the jury, both defense and prosecution could eliminate potential jurors without giving any reason by a peremptory challenge. Every person tried for a crime punishable by death was entitled by law to the peremptory challenge of twenty jurors; the state was entitled to half as many peremptory challenges as the defense.[61] In this joint trial of five defendants, the defense could therefore use a maximum of a hundred peremptory challenges and the state could use fifty. But to what effect? If the prosecution challenged all of the anti-Mormons on the panel and the defense challenged all of the Mormons until all of their challenges were exhausted, the jury would then be composed of the remaining panel members, who would probably be a cross-section of the relatively uncommitted citizens in the county.

Could the defendants afford to be tried before a relatively disinterested jury of their peers? If they wanted a disinterested jury,
they could obtain one as a matter of legal right by requesting a
change of venue (transfer) for trial in another county.[62] In his
September 30, 1844, agreement with Sharp and Williams, Governor
Ford had already committed the prosecution not to resist such a
transfer.[63] But the defendants apparently did not want a trial before
an impartial jury. In this respect their position was like that of the
modern Chicago politician who retained a large law firm to defend
him against vote-stealing charges. When his lawyers assured him
they would get him "a fair trial," he fired them and sought other
legal assistance, observing that "those odds are not good enough."
The defendants clearly wanted a trial in Hancock County, but they
wanted a trial before a jury selected from their friends and sup-
porters. The defendants needed a way to challenge the panel of
potential jurors selected by the county commissioners and to substitute twenty-four men of their own choice. Was there any legal basis
upon which counsel for the defense could persuade the judge to
discharge the entire panel and substitute another?

Questions addressed to legal theory were most uncommon in the
law practice of the frontier. Lawyers generally had little opportunity
or disposition for legal research, or even for advance preparation of
their cases. Law libraries were tiny or nonexistent in frontier Illinois;
there were only a few libraries of more than fifty volumes in the
entire state. The *Revised Statutes,* the *Illinois Form Book,* and a
few elementary treatises like *Chitty, Starkie, Coke on Littleton,* or
a set of *Blackstone* were all that was available in most county seats.
Otherwise, the only law books lawyers had on circuit were the few
volumes they chose to include in their saddlebags or buggy. Cases
generally went to trial without preliminary study, and principles of
law remembered from reading Coke or Blackstone or from observing
the practice of the circuit judge were applied on the spot to solve the
legal questions that arose. What he lacked in scholarly study, the
frontier lawyer made up in shrewdness, eloquence, and common-
sense application of principle.[64]

But common sense and frontier rhetoric were not adequate to
the challenge of upsetting the whole statutory mechanism for selecting a jury panel. Such an undertaking was probably beyond the

experience of any of the lawyers in attendance at the court in Carthage. This was a challenge to the most creative legal mind and the most diligent research. Only one of the defense counsel had that kind of mind and any disposition for that kind of research; although the author of the defense's key strategic move is unknown, credit undoubtedly belongs to O. H. Browning. Though unprecedented, the suggestion he made to his fellow lawyers was logical and persuasive and had some support in the most respected common-law authority on the frontier, *Blackstone's Commentaries on the Law of England*. The decision to follow Browning's suggestion assured his preeminence and controlling authority in the conduct of the case. The lawyers and their clients set about preparing the papers to present when the trial began on Wednesday.

1. *St. Louis New Era,* May 29, 1845.

2. *Nauvoo Neighbor,* May 6, 1845, quoted in Smith, *History of the Church,* VII, 406; *Revised Statutes of Illinois* (1845), 155 (specifies death penalty).

3. *Sangamo Journal,* May 29, 1845. The sheriff's certificate of service of subpoenas for the jurors for the May term, 1845, is on file in the Hancock County Courthouse.

4. Scofield, *History of Hancock County,* 694.

5. Moses, *Illinois Historical,* I, 408.

6. J. F. Snyder, "Forgotten Statesman of Illinois, Richard M. Young," *Transactions of the Illinois State Historical Society* (1906), 323.

7. The biographical information on Judge Young is taken from Snyder, "Forgotten Statesman," 302, 312, 323-24; Caton, *Early Bench and Bar,* 38, 53, 222; Thomas Hoyne, "The Lawyer as a Pioneer," *Chicago Bar Association Lectures,* Fergus Historical Series, no. 22 (Chicago, 1880), 76-77; Moses, *Illinois Historical,* I, 408.

During 1839 and 1840 Senator Young had performed some routine political chores for the Mormons, such as assisting them in having the post office at Commerce changed to their desired name of Nauvoo, and aiding Joseph Smith in his unsuccessful effort to have the Nauvoo postmaster ousted and to have himself appointed in his place. Smith, *History of the Church,* III, 348-49; IV, 111-12, 121-22; V, 184, 266, 274.

8. Arnold, "Recollections," 11; Hoyne, "Lawyer as Pioneer," 76-77.

9. Jury lists for May term, 1845, on file in the Hancock County Courthouse, verified by reference to the same names in *Hancock County Board Minutes* 4:255 (March 3, 1845). The religious preference of jurors is tabulated in the Appendix herein.

10. Smith, *History of the Church,* VII, 370; *Executive Record,* 4:200 (1843-47), Gregg, *History of Hancock County,* 449; "Muster Roll."

11. *Circuit Court Record,* 231, 243. The December, 1844, session of the legislature had reelected William Elliot as the states attorney for the fifth judicial circuit (certificate signed by Clerk of General Assembly and Secretary of Senate, December 16, 1844, Executive File, Illinois State Archives, Springfield).

12. Ralston had been the lawyer for Joseph Smith in some of the proceedings

growing out of Missouri's attempt to extradite him to face charges in that state. In the 1840 election the Mormon voters of Nauvoo paid him a unique compliment; although the Mormons generally voted the Whig ballot, in that election about two hundred of them marked out the name of the Whig presidential elector, Abraham Lincoln, and wrote in the name of James Ralston in its place. On the evening when the Smiths were murdered, Ralston had called on the wounded John Taylor in Carthage and expressed his sympathy. Biographical information on Ralston is found in Scofield, *History of Hancock County,* 747; Moses, *Illinois Historical,* II, 1147, 1181; Smith, *History of the Church,* IV, 367; V, 89, 103; VII, 111; Gregg, *History of Hancock County,* 449.

13. *Revised Statutes of Illinois* (1845), 310.

14. *Circuit Court Record, 232.*

15. The names of the petit jurors are taken from the jury lists for the May term, 1845, on file in the Hancock County Courthouse, verified by reference to the same names in *Hancock County Board Minutes,* 4:260-62 (March 3, 1845). The religious preference of jurors is tabulated in the Appendix herein. Membership of the Warsaw militia was established from the "Muster Roll."

16. Watt Manuscript, 1. (See Bibliographical Note for information on this source.)

17. *Missouri Republican,* May 27, 1845; there was an unverified report that two of the men had died of their wounds. Smith, *History of the Church,* VII, 103.

18. Smith, *History of the Church,* VII, 421; Watt Manuscript, 1.

19. *Circuit Court Record,* 235 (May 19, 1845); *Sangamo Journal,* May 29, 1845; Watt Manuscript, 1.

20. Scofield, *History of Hancock County,* 693-94.

21. *Sangamo Journal,* May 29, 1845.

22. *Circuit Court Record,* 237, 245, 250, 251.

23. *Missouri Republican* (May 31, 1845) reported that the grand jury had agreed to find bills in a number of perjury cases involving Mormon witnesses, but when the prosecuting attorney prepared the bills, they refused to endorse them. Consistent with that suggestion, the case file in *People* v. *Benjamin Brackenbury* contains a fully drawn indictment against Brackenbury for perjury. It bears the signature of J. H. Ralston, states attorney pro tem, but below his signature is the notation "not a true bill," followed by the signature of Daniel Spencer, foreman of the grand jury. The indictment shows that five witnesses testified in this matter, most of them grand jurors who could describe Brackenbury's testimony the preceding October. The key witness was Jason H. Sherman of Warsaw, a prominent anti-Mormon (Smith, *History of the Church,* VI, 466), whose testimony was evidently necessary to demonstrate that Brackenbury had lied. Apparently Sherman could not persuade the statutory minimum majority of twelve jurors that there was "good and sufficient evidence" to believe that Brackenbury had been guilty of a crime. *Revised Statutes of Illinois* (1845), 309.

24. Baxter, *Browning,* 52, 59-61.

25. Moses, *Illinois Historical,* I, 509.

26. The biographical information on Browning is from Baxter, *Browning;* Robert D. Holt, "The Political Career of William A. Richardson," *Journal of the Illinois State Historical Society* 26 (1833-34), 222, 232, 233; Moses, *Illinois Historical,* I, 509.

27. Smith, *History of the Church,* IV, 367.

28. *Ibid.,* 369. In pointing out the impossibility of Joseph Smith's obtaining justice in Missouri, Browning painted a vivid picture of the Mormons' ejection

from Missouri and their arrival in his own city of Quincy. The editor's account shows Browning's oratory in full flower: "Great God! have I not seen it? Yes, my eyes have beheld the blood-stained traces of innocent women and children, in the drear winter, who had traveled hundreds of miles barefoot, through frost and snow, to seek a refuge from their savage pursuers. 'Twas a scene of horror sufficient to enlist sympathy from an adamantine heart. And shall this unfortunate man, whom their fury has seen proper to select for sacrifice, be driven into such a savage land and none dare enlist in the cause of Justice? If there was no other voice under heaven ever to be heard in this cause, gladly would I stand alone, and proudly spend my latest breath in defense of an oppressed American citizen." *Ibid.*, 370.

29. *Ibid.*, 369.

30. *Ibid.*, VI, 613.

31. The biographical information on Richardson is taken from Baxter, *Browning*, 69-70; Holt, "The Political Career of William A. Richardson," 222-67; Gregg, *History of Hancock County*, 240, 414-15; Moses, *Illinois Historical*, II, 1132, 1190.

32. These descriptions are quoted from Baxter, *Browning*, 70; and Holt, "The Political Career of William A. Richardson," 232.

33. Holt, "The Political Career of William A. Richardson," 263.

34. Bateman, *Historical Encyclopedia of Illinois*, 577. In his youth Warren had worked for a time as a typographer in Vermont with Horace Greeley, later the founder of the *New York Tribune*. Later he lived in Ohio and Kentucky; he completed his law studies at Transylvania University in 1834, after which he came to Illinois. Joseph Smith's journals for 1842 and 1843 contain repeated references to legal consultations with "Squire Warren." The Warren real estate venture is described in Smith, *History of the Church*, IV, 486-87, and in Flanders, *Nauvoo*, 138. Warren's bankruptcy case is recorded in "General Bankruptcy Records, District of Illinois," III, 471, Federal Records Center, Chicago. He was discharged in bankruptcy on October 4, 1842. His creditors received a total of $283.56, about 10 percent of the amount of their claims. He subsequently repurchased all nine parcels of his real estate for $23.12 ("General Bankruptcy Records," 493, 500-501). Such was the operation of the first bankruptcy law.

35. Holt, "The Political Career of William A. Richardson," 233-34.

36. Sandburg, *Abraham Lincoln: The Prairie Years and the War Years*, 51-52.

37. Biographical information on Archibald Williams is taken from Gregg, *History of Hancock County*, 414; Moses, *Illinois Historical*, I, 408, 455; II, 1188; Scofield, *History of Hancock County*, 590.

38. Skinner was born in Oneida County, New York, twenty-six years before the trial. He studied law in Ohio, coming to Illinois and beginning his practice in Warsaw in 1841. Like Warren, Skinner had considerable contacts with the Mormons and had done some legal work for their leader. In June, 1844, just before the murder, he took a leading role in the anti-Mormon Warsaw meeting that resolved upon the extermination of the Mormons, and was appointed to carry the meeting's resolution to the governor. Two weeks later he was special counsel to prosecute Smith in his preliminary hearing on the charge of treason. Bateman, *Historical Encyclopedia of Illinois*, 482; Smith, *History of the Church*, V, 317, 415; VI, 53, 462-66, 596-97.

Another source lists Morrison as one of the defense counsel. He may have been associated to give the defense team a Carthage representative acquainted with many persons in the county who could assist in the selection of the jury. Morrison was a Whig politician who had come from Tennessee a few years before the trial; he was elected as a justice of the peace in 1843, but never obtained a large legal practice. A notorious anti-Mormon, Morrison had issued the writ on which Joseph Smith had been arrested and brought to Carthage on the charge of riot. Smith, *History of the Church,* VI, 454, 460, 466, 553, 567, 596; VII, 66-67; Gregg, *History of Hancock County,* 418; *Election Returns,* 64:418 (1843).

39. Usher F. Linder, *Reminiscences of the Early Bench and Bar of Illinois,* 2nd ed. (Chicago: Chicago Legal News Company, 1879), 258.

40. The biographical information on Lamborn comes from Cornelius J. Doyle, "Josiah Lamborn, Attorney General of Illinois, 1840-43," *Journal of the Illinois State Historical Society* 20 (1927), 185-200; Linder, *Reminiscences,* 258; Moses, *Illinois Historical,* I, 426; II, 551; Scofield, *History of Hancock County,* 327; Baxter, *Browning,* 33.

41. *People* v. *Lamborn,* 2 *Illinois Reports* 123, 124-25, 126 (1834); Doyle, "Josiah Lamborn," 193-94.

42. Doyle, "Josiah Lamborn," 192.

43. Smith, *History of the Church,* V, 220-45.

44. Moses, *Illinois Historical,* II, 697.

45. A letter Josiah Lamborn sent to Brigham Young from Springfield on January 28, 1845, seems clearly intended to have endeared Lamborn to the Mormons. At a time when public outcry and official hostility were bringing repeal of the valued Nauvoo Charter, Lamborn praised the Mormons and assured them that they had "many true friends" in Springfield, including "most of the intelligent gentlemen of the Legislature," who felt that the Mormons "were an injured and an outraged people." He attributes the repeal of the Nauvoo Charter to "the body of the Whig party, together with such demagogues of the other party as could be cajoled and bamboozled by the Whigs." He criticized Senator Jacob C. Davis, who "has done much to poison the minds of the members" against anything in the Mormons' favor, and expressed outrage at the way "he walks at large in defiance of law, an indicted murderer." His letter counseled Mormons to be "quiet, submissive to the law and circumspect in your conduct." In this way, he predicts, "there will be a mighty reaction in the public sentiment, which will ultimately overthrow all of your enemies." Smith, *History of the Church,* VII, 370-71.

46. Baxter, *Browning,* 59-60.

47. George R. Gaylor, "Governor Ford and the Death of Joseph and Hyrum Smith," *Journal of the Illinois State Historical Society* 50 (1957), 405.

48. This was the general common-law rule. John Henry Wigmore, *A Treatise on the Anglo-American System of Evidence in Trials at Common Law,* 3rd ed. (Boston: Little, Brown, 1940), II, §§575, 579; Simon Greenleaf, *A Treatise on the Law of Evidence,* 7th ed. (Boston: Little, Brown, 1854-58), I, §26-27. This rule was not changed by statute in any American state until over twenty years later. "Testimony of Persons Accused of Crime," *American Law Review* 1 (1866), 443; Scofield, *History of Hancock County,* 762.

49. *Nauvoo Neighbor,* May 7 and May 14, 1845.

50. William M. Daniels, *Correct Account of the Murder of Generals Joseph and Hyrum Smith, at Carthage on the 27th Day of June, 1844* (Nauvoo: By John Taylor, 1845), 8. There are copies of this rare book in the Church Archives and in the Wilford C. Wood Museum in Bountiful, Utah. Its contents were republished in Lyman Omer Littlefield, *The Martyrs: Joseph & Hyrum Smith* (Salt Lake City: Juvenile Instructor Office, 1882), 71-86.

51. *Ibid.*

52. *Ibid.* (quoted as in original).

53. *Ibid.,* 8-10.

54. *Ibid.*, 11.

55. *Ibid.*, 13 (quoted as in original).

56. *Ibid.*, 13.

57. *Ibid.*, 14.

58. *Ibid.*, 15.

59. *Ibid.*, 19.

60. There is no reference to any light or miraculous circumstances in the events of the martyrdom in the official account in Section 135 of the Church's *Doctrine and Covenants*. B. H. Roberts, the Mormon historian, has this comment on the Daniels account, which he elsewhere refers to as "a sensational pamphlet" (Smith, *History of the Church*, VII, 163): "The story of Daniels is incredible, not because it involves incidents that would be set down as 'miraculous,' but because the story is all out of harmony with what in the nature of things would happen under the circumstances and the incidents he details are too numerous, too complicated, too deliberate, and would have occupied too much time to be crowded into the space within which necessarily they must have happened, if they happened at all." (Roberts, *Comprehensive History*, II, 325, n. 14). Nevertheless, the Daniels account has had a persistent currency in unofficial publications identified with the Mormon Church. The pamphlet was originally listed as a Church publication (Smith, *History of the Church*, VII, 558-59). Daniels's account of the light, together with numerous other hearsay or secondhand accounts apparently relying on it, are set forth in N. B. Lundwall, ed., *The Fate of the Persecutors of the Prophet Joseph Smith* (Salt Lake City: Bookcraft, 1952), 226-33.

61. *Revised Statutes of Illinois* (1845), 185.

62. *Ibid.*, 528.

63. Agreement signed by Governor Thomas Ford at Camp Edwards, Ill., September 30, 1844, Mormon Collection, Chicago Historical Society.

64. Baxter, *Browning*, 9; Arnold, "Recollections," 12; Conkling, "Recollections of the Bench and Bar of Central Illinois," *Chicago Bar Association Lectures*, Fergus Historical Series, no. 22 (Chicago, 1880), 38.

ᘰ 7 ᗘ

A Jury of
"Intelligence, Probity and Worth"

When the clerk called the case of *People* v. *Levi Williams* on Wednesday morning, May 21, Colonel William A. Richardson stepped forward and made the key motion of the trial.[1] He asked the court to discharge the panel of potential jurors chosen by the county commissioners, disqualify the county commissioners and sheriff from their statutory duties in selection of jury panels, and appoint successors to assemble a new panel of jurymen. In support of this audacious proposal he handed the clerk two affidavits signed by the five defendants.

M. Aldrich

Levi Williams

Wm. N. Grover

Jacob C. Davis

J. Cunningham Davis

In the first affidavit the defendants swore that the three county commissioners were prejudiced against them and consequently selected the potential petit jurors with partiality so as to prejudice their trial.[2] In the second affidavit the defendants swore that sheriff Minor Deming and his deputies were "very much prejudiced" against the defendants and were "so influenced by partiality" and such "bias of opinion and feelings in favor of said prosecution" that, if permitted to officiate, they would discharge their duties "in such partial,

97

unfair, oppressive and unjust manner, as greatly and improperly to prejudice the rights and lives" of the defendants.[3]

What alternatives were open to the court if the defendants' charges of prejudice were found justified? Illinois law provided that if a sufficient number of jurors chosen by the county commissioners did not appear, or if "by reason of challenges, or for any other cause" there were insufficient qualified persons to make up the panel, the judge could order the sheriff to designate additional "men of the county."[4] If the court met before the county commissioners had selected a panel of potential jurors, or if for any reason the whole panel failed to attend court, the judge could have the sheriff "summon [qualified persons] from the bystanders" to supply the deficiency.[5] If both the commissioners and the sheriff were unable to function, the law provided that the judge could direct the coroner to perform the sheriff's duties in the selection of the jury, at least in civil cases.[6] The elected coroner in Hancock County at this time was Daniel H. Wells, the prominent Nauvoo justice of the peace, but for some unknown reason he had failed to qualify and refused to serve as coroner.[7] Consequently, the prior coroner, George W. Stigall of Carthage (also jailer at the Carthage jail), continued in office. The defendants' carefully prepared affidavit took notice of the coroner as the final alternative for official selection of the jury, but alleged that Stigall was then absent from the State of Illinois. The defendants concluded their affidavit by swearing that they feared and believed that they could not obtain a fair trial "unless an Elisor be appointed on attendance at the present term of this court."[8]

Here, then, was the proposal: disqualify the county commissioners; quash (set aside) the panel of jurors they had chosen; disqualify the sheriff; bypass the coroner; and appoint substitutes (called elisors) to select an entirely new panel of petit jurors.

The principal or sole authority for this proposal was *Blackstone's Commentaries,* which declared that where the sheriff and the coroner are persons of whose partiality there is "tolerable ground of suspicion" the whole panel of jurors can be challenged and the selection of substitutes "shall be directed to two clerks of the Court, or two persons of the County, named by the Court and sworn and these two [who] are called Elisors or Electors shall indifferently name the jury."[9]

Though the defendants' sudden and unprecedented maneuver probably caught him by surprise, Lamborn made a spirited and effective response. The defense's proposal was "a novelty," he declared, since "the affidavits of the defendants predicated no charge against the present panel of jurors, either individually or collectively."[10] Illinois statutes made no provision for quashing an entire panel of jurors, Lamborn pointed out, and the laws were utterly silent on the subject of entirely displacing the county commissioners or sheriff from their statutory functions. The statute referred to by Colonel Richardson applied to civil, not criminal cases.[11] If charges of prejudice were made against county officers, Lamborn continued, the court ought to hold a hearing and receive evidence before displacing them from their official functions. Elected officers surely should not be displaced upon a mere *ex parte* (unanswered) affidavit, especially one executed by five indicted murderers. Having clearly demonstrated that the defense argument was wrong on principle and unsupported by its purported authority, Lamborn concluded his powerful argument by challenging the defense to produce a precedent "in all the experience of this state or any other, in criminal cases. He defied them to produce a single case."[12]

As a powerful Democratic politician, Colonel Richardson had served his clients well by making the defendants' key motion. But he was not qualified to deal with Lamborn's devastating argument in opposition. That challenge was best handled by the probable author of the motion, O. H. Browning, who rose to respond. Browning admitted that "there had not been a precedent, in the United States for such a proceeding," but he sought to explain this by asserting that "there has never been a case like this in the United States." On reason and authority the defendants had lost the argument, but their advocate held the crowd intent by his oratory. With no more legal authority than his enormous forensic skill, Browning concluded with the emphatic assertion "that in a case like this, the County Commissioners, the Sheriff, and his Deputies can be discharged, and in their place, can be appointed two Elisors for the purpose of choosing another jury."[13]

The arguments were over, and the focus of attention shifted to Judge Young. It behooved him to ponder the implications of his decision. As an experienced politician and a resident of nearby Quincy, Judge Young was all too familiar with the current struggle for control of Hancock County and the charges that the Mormon-dominated county commission would control the criminal justice system by controlling the selection of jurors. As a faithful Democratic party leader and worker, he was also conscious of the political dilemma of his long-time associate, Governor Thomas Ford, who had made a special appointment of this prosecutor and pursued the prosecution of these cases with such public concern for vindicating the violated honor of the state. If he reflected on Ford's abortive military action of the past fall as he looked out upon the well-armed audience in this courtroom, Judge Young may have wondered whether the governor really desired a conviction. Would the price of a conviction be civil war in the county? The judge may also have wondered about the Mormons, conspicuous by their absence and apparent indifference to the prosecution, and pondered whether they wanted a conviction. But most of all Judge Young probably weighed the probable effect of his ruling on the voters of Illinois.

Defendants and their counsel knew that Judge Young was not immune to political pressure; in this respect they considered him clearly preferable to the regular circuit judge, Jesse B. Thomas, whose sturdy independence and lack of political ambition led him to rule solely on the basis of the law as he saw it. The defense must have been overjoyed when they learned that Young and Thomas had exchanged circuit assignments for this term of court.[14] Judge Young was an honest man and an able judge who would not move solely by political expediency, but his view of the merits of a legal argument like party leader Richardson's could well be influenced by political considerations.

As careful students of Illinois politics, Richardson, Browning, and the others knew that Judge Young had not yet relinquished his political ambitions. They had not forgotten how Richard M. Young, serving in the U.S. Senate by election of the Democratic majority of the state legislature in 1836, had bungled his important assignment to obtain a $4 million loan from English financiers to rescue the state from bankruptcy by completing the Illinois and Michigan

canal.[15] Illinois lost over a half-million dollars because of misman-
agement of that assignment. Senator Young was, in the words of his
biographer, "destitute of financial tact and skill."[16] When his six-
year term expired in 1842, he found little support for his bid for
a new term and was induced to withdraw as a senatorial candidate
by promise of a place on the Illinois Supreme Court.

In his service on the bench, both before and after his term in
the Senate, Judge Young commanded the respect and affection of
the bar. He was, nevertheless, reluctant to relinquish the limelight,
and in that spring of 1845 he was known to be considering how he
could win support to succeed his fellow Democrat, Thomas Ford,
in the governor's seat.[17] Thus Judge Young was likely to be taking
a political view of matters submitted for his decision, using care not
to make himself inaccessible to the interests whose support he would
need to further his ambitions. His vulnerability was aptly described
by his biographer, who observed that Judge Young "conducted his
courts with dignity and conscientious rectitude, but neglected no
opportunity to keep himself in the limelight of popular favor."[18]

The record is silent on how long the judge pondered his decision.
We know only that, when he was ready to rule, he began with a
brief review of the law on the subject of quashing a panel or array
of jurors, followed by a statement of his determination "to do strict
justice to both parties, so that there may not be any cause of complaint on either side, that justice has not been administered by this
court."[19] After that introduction he announced his decision: "I believe it is my duty to quash the array, and to appoint persons as
elisors, to select another jury."[20] Apparently sensing some resentment
on the part of the twenty-four who had been regularly chosen and
summoned to the courtroom for service, Judge Young explained
that "there was no charge against them, but the charge was predicated against the officers of the county only." To aid him in the
selection of elisors, "since he was a stranger in the county," Judge
Young invited the prosecution and defense to "agree upon two persons."[21] He thereupon adjourned the case until eight o'clock Thursday morning, and turned his attention to the other pressing civil
and criminal business scheduled for this term of court.

With this unprecedented ruling Judge Young had taken the bare
affidavits of indicted defendants and set aside the action of regularly

101

elected county officials without giving them any opportunity to be heard, thus upsetting the entire legal process of jury selection in Hancock County. The anti-Mormons had professed fear that Mormon control and corruption would use the criminal courts as engines of oppression and the civil courts as instruments of favoritism against their enemies. But under Judge Young's precedent all that an anti-Mormon had to do was sign an affidavit that a Mormon or a Mormon sympathizer was involved in the judicial system — even in elective office — and the court could set aside any official action in which he was involved and appoint a non-Mormon to act in his place.

Careful observers immediately recognized the long-range significance of this decision. Writing from Carthage immediately after the ruling, a shrewd St. Louis newspaperman made this observation:

> This decision is considered a great victory by the defendants, inasmuch as it takes the power out of the hands of the present officers of the county (who are all Mormons, or what is called 'Jacks') of selecting a jury to suit their own purposes, and it will also be used as a precedent by the anti-Mormons hereafter, to quash the Mormon juries that may be summoned, and it will tend considerably to curb the Mormon power of controlling the courts of the county.[22]

A writer in the *Burlington Hawkeye* (Iowa) made a similar prediction: "The decision of Judge Young will hereafter be plead [*sic*] as a precedent whenever a Mormon jury is to sit in judgment in the trials of anti-Mormons and will in great measure lessen the power the Mormons have heretofore possessed in controlling the courts of that county."[23] In addition to its use to prevent the exercise of some of the important ingredients of Mormon political power in Hancock County, this court decision was important for its tacit recognition that the Mormons were no longer respected as a significant political force in the county or state.

Word of Judge Young's decision reached Nauvoo on Wednesday evening with the return of the discharged jurors. Brigham Young and some others were hiding in the home of one of these jurors, Robert Pierce, who probably brought them the news. At nine o'clock that evening a group of leaders assembled at the home of Willard Richards to discuss this development and Josiah Lamborn's urgent request for assistance in hunting up witnesses for the trial. Those present included five members of the Twelve: Brigham Young, Willard Richards, John Taylor, Heber C. Kimball, and George A. Smith.[24]

Any leaders who had previously held hope for the viability of legal authority in resolving some of the Mormons' differences with their adversaries now apparently abandoned that hope.[25] George A. Smith was appointed as spokesman to advise Lamborn that "the Mormons wanted nothing to do with the prosecution."[26] His letter, composed and sent to Lamborn by messenger that night, expressed wonderment at laws that would permit the discharge of the jurors and the disqualification of the sheriff. The author said he could not understand the state's willingness to allow "indicted murderers to roam at large month after month without arrest." He reaffirmed the Mormon leaders' original refusal to assist in procuring witnesses. They had given Murray McConnell all the information in their possession when he visited them in Nauvoo, but had informed him that they "had nothing to do with the affair and wanted nothing to do with it," lest any effort on their part should be misconstrued as "a persecution or a desire to pick a quarrel on our part." The difficulty in the pending trials, George A. Smith's letter told Lamborn, is not between the Mormons and the anti-Mormons or the murderers, but "between the state and the prisoners or offenders." While the Mormons would like the state to "redeem her pledge" by prosecuting the case to final judgment, they would even submit peaceably "if she choose to abandon the prosecution."[27]

In truth, the Mormons had now ceased to place any reliance on Illinois justice and wanted only peace until they could plan and carry out their exodus. The letter concludes: "We shall be ever ready to assist in favoring the ends of right so far as we can do it and not give any occasion of excitement which would be detrimental to public peace." This was the Mormon leaders' last communication with Illinois officers about the trial. The era of Mormon reliance on and cooperation with Illinois criminal justice had ended.

Despite changing Mormon attitudes, the trial continued on its course. When Judge Young took the bench on the morning of Thursday, May 22, he expressed pleasure "that two men had been agreed upon" to act as elisors in the case, particularly since "they were old citizens of Hancock County, and men with whom he had been

acquainted for many years." He was satisfied that William D. Abernethy and Thomas H. Owen, the men he was appointing by agreement, would act "without prejudice or partial feelings on either side,
in the selection of a panel of jurors, to judge the case now before
the court."[28]

Abernethy was a minor Whig politician who had served as county
sheriff from 1840 to 1842. Like most other Whigs, he had been
turned out of office by the Mormons' Democratic vote in the election
of 1842. Thereafter he had been active in anti-Mormon activities
of the county.[29] Owen, the other elisor, was a forty-nine-year-old
North Carolina-born Baptist clergyman, known as a Jack Mormon.
Thomas Owen claimed the distinction of being the first resident of
Carthage, where he settled in 1831. In 1833 he had supervised the
building of the original log cabin courthouse in Carthage. Often
selected for responsible offices by his fellow citizens, Owen had
served in the general assembly from Hancock County in 1834 and
1842. In the latter election he was supported by the Mormon vote
and had loyally and capably represented their interests, notably in
opposing the unsucccessful efforts to repeal the Nauvoo Charter.
Since that time, he had been sympathetic with the Mormon cause
in resisting what he called the "wretched purposes" and "blood-
thirsty dispositions of those demons" who were advocating anti-
Mormon mob action.[30]

After Abernethy and Owen executed an oath to "faithfully and
diligently perform all of the duties appertaining to [their] respective
offices as Elisors,"[31] Judge Young ordered them to "Summons *from
the bystanders* Twenty-four of like good & lawful men citizens of
the said county of Hancock" to serve as petit jurors in this case.[32]
The italicized words, which were inserted above the line in this
handwritten order, were of critical importance. Jurymen chosen
"from the bystanders" would of course be persons in attendance at
court. Mormon leaders had told their followers to stay at home unless they had business with the court; now that the Mormon jurors
had been discharged, they had probably departed, so that the only
bystanders remaining in Carthage, aside from an occasional and
apprehensive Mormon with a civil or criminal case before the court,
would be non-Mormons. And even those non-Mormons were likely
to be the more militant element whom Governor Ford's history iden-

tified as "more than a thousand men [who] had assembled under arms at the court, to keep away the Mormons and their friends...."[33] In short, this order gave the elisors no opportunity to choose a jury representative of a cross-section of citizens in the county.

At two o'clock on Thursday afternoon of the same day they were sworn, the elisors submitted a list of twenty-four men they had summoned for service as petit jurors. One observer recorded that each elisor had chosen twelve.[34] The elisors were to choose three more panels of twenty-four, a total of ninety-six, before the twelve petit jurors were finally selected from the group.

The array of potential jurors summoned by the elisors differed in one important respect from those chosen by the county commissioners. Whereas the forty-eight on the county commissioners' array included twenty-one Mormons, the ninety-six chosen by the elisors included only four who can be identified as Mormons (There is doubt as to the religious persuasion of thirteen; the remaining seventy-nine were definitely non-Mormon.) In other respects the panels from whom the twelve-man petit jury was to be chosen appear to have been made up of a fair cross-section of Hancock citizens in attendance at court.[35]

The examination and selection of individual jurors commenced at a special session on Thursday evening. First, Judge Young called the defendants before the bench for formal arraignment. In conformity with Illinois law, the prosecutor gave them a copy of the indictment, a list of the states witnesses, and a list of the persons the elisors had summoned to be examined for service on the jury. The judge then asked the defendants how they would plead. All five pleaded not guilty.[36]

The process by which prosecution and defense counsel examine and select a twelve-man petit jury from the panel members available for service is considered one of the most important stages of a trial. First, the clerk draws four names from a hat containing all twenty-four in the panel, and these four are sworn to give correct answers to the questions the lawyers ask them. Then the examination begins. If a lawyer can show that a potential juror is prejudiced against his cause, such as by having already judged the matter, the juror can be excused for cause. In addition, each lawyer can use one of his peremptory challenges to excuse a potential juror without giving any reason.

Judge Young laid down the rules to be observed in determining the competency of jurors to serve in this case. A potential juryman should be asked: "Have you made up and delivered an opinion, that the Defendants are guilty or innocent of the charges laid in the indictment?" A juror would not be disqualified for cause if he had formed an opinion but had not expressed it.[37] Moreover, the judge ruled, if a person had formed and expressed an opinion from *reports* as to the guilt or innocence of the defendants, without hearing the statements of any persons who professed to know the *facts* in the case, then even expressions of opinion expressly based on these reports would not render the juror incompetent to serve.[38] These rulings permitted almost any bystander to qualify as a juror, despite having formed and expressed an opinion on the guilt or innocence of the accused. Consequently, the only way counsel could keep an apparently biased panel member off the trial jury was to eliminate him by a peremptory challenge.[39]

As the Thursday evening session wore on into the weary hours, five of the persons on the elisors' first panel of twenty-four were selected to serve on the jury. Of the other nineteen, both prosecution and defense eliminated several by peremptory challenges, and the rest either did not appear in response to the summons or were excused for cause.

As soon as the first twenty-four were used up, the elisors provided a new panel. Only two jurors were selected from this second group. The prosecution excused thirteen by peremptory challenges, and the defense excused three. There were two Mormons in this second panel, William E. McKay and Thomas D. Woolsey. Both were excused by peremptory challenge. But, surprisingly, it was not the defense that challenged them but the prosecution. Lamborn apparently explained his strategy in his closing argument when he claimed credit for the fact that "we did not ask that a Mormon should be put upon the jury."[40]

In the session on Thursday evening the prosecution and defense examined forty-eight prospective jurors and selected only seven to sit on the jury for the trial. As court adjourned, Judge Young ordered that these seven jurors "be kept together, separate and apart from all other persons, and without speech to any in some private, convenient, and comfortable place in said Town of Carthage by the said Elisors." He also ordered the elisors to "cause the said jurors to be furnished with such meat and drink, fire, candle and bedding as may be necessary for their comfort and convenience."[41]

Judge Young turned his attention to other judicial business on Friday, but the selection of the jury resumed on Friday evening. Four more jurors were selected from the elisors' third panel, and with one juror remaining to be chosen, the elisors tendered a fourth panel of twenty-four. In examining this last group the prosecution excused seven jurors and the defense excused one before the final juror was chosen. In total, the prosecution used thirty-three of its challenges in selecting this jury, and the defense used only eleven.[42] This unusual discrepancy is mute testimony to the fact that the persons composing the various panels of jurors were thought by both parties to be much more favorable to the defense than to the prosecution. Once the jury was completed, Judge Young committed the remaining jurors into the custody of the elisors and announced that the trial would commence the following morning, Saturday, May 24, at seven o'clock.[43]

Like the panels from which they were chosen, the twelve jurors who would determine the guilt or innocence of the indicted defendants were representative of a cross-section of the non-Mormon citizens of Hancock County.[44] Two were in their early twenties, two in their fifties, and the rest were thirty to forty years of age. Except for two jurors who were born in Vermont and Connecticut, all members of the jury were born in the South, mostly in Kentucky or Tennessee. Most came to Illinois in the 1830's. One juror was a tanner, and the others were farmers, at least one of whom, James Gittings, was very wealthy by the standards of that day. Another juror, Frederick M. Walton, was later elected a county commissioner.[45] All but one of the jurors were married, with from two to seven children. The seven whose place of residence is known came from five different townships in the county. None of their names was reported in connection with anti-Mormon activities in the county. Historian Thomas Gregg says he knew some of the jurors, and that they were "men of intelligence, probity and worth."[46]

Whatever confidence non-Mormon observers may have reposed in this jury and the manner of its selection, to the Mormon community it was symbolic of the rejection of their aspirations to find justice within the legal system of their county and state. After the elisor decision the Mormon press, including the weekly *Nauvoo Neighbor* and the bi-weekly official *Times and Seasons,* gave their readers no more than a passing reference to the trial. There was no summary of the testimony or other news reporting of the sort carried in the Springfield, St. Louis, and Burlington press. As the Carthage community looked forward to the beginning of the trial on Saturday morning, the Mormons' attention was focused on their own important event on that date.

When Joseph Smith was murdered, the Nauvoo Temple was only one story high. Yet the Mormons had pushed construction so rapidly that the walls were now complete and ready for the capstone, which had to be placed promptly to avoid delay in construction. In normal times this would have called for a large public ceremony and celebration, but Brigham Young and the rest of the Twelve were now in hiding because of court week. Legal activity in the county was always at a high pitch just before and during court week. In this May term there were writs out for many of the Mormon leaders, summoning them to give testimony, such as for the murder trial, or arresting them to answer civil or criminal charges, such as the charges of riot in the destruction of the *Expositor* press.[47] Consequently, just a few days before the beginning of court week the top Mormon leaders retired to semi-seclusion "to keep out of the way of the writs reported to have been issued against us."[48]

At six o'clock on the morning of Saturday, May 24, the Twelve and other church leaders met at the temple site "with great secrecy" to lay the capstone. Despite secrecy, the brass band was there playing "The Capstone March," which William Pitt had composed specially for the occasion, and a crowd of several thousand quickly gathered. At precisely 6:22 A.M. the capstone was pronounced set. Brigham Young then uttered a prayer, which suggests the importance he attached to the temple endowment ceremonies which the Mormons could not conduct until the building was completed, and his consciousness of the risk that they would be driven out of Nauvoo before that time: "The last stone is now laid upon the Temple, and I pray the Almighty in the name of Jesus to defend us in this place and sustain us until the Temple is finished and we have all got our endowments."[49] John Taylor noted in his journal that the audience at the Temple site included "several officers watching for us to take us," but the leaders escaped by leaving abruptly during the closing song.[50] As the temple crowd dispersed in Nauvoo a few minutes before seven o'clock the courthouse crowd was just assembling in Carthage, some fifteen miles across the prairie to the southeast, to attend the trial of the indicted murderers of Joseph Smith.

1. Watt Manuscript, 1-2.

2. "Affidavit for Quashing Jury Panel," May 21, 1845, case file in *People v. Levi Williams.*

3. "Affidavit for Appointment of an Elisor," May 20, 1845, case file in *People v. Levi Williams.*

4. *Revised Statutes of Illinois* (1845), 149, 310.

5. *Ibid.,* 310. Massachusetts also filled its jury panels from the bystanders. William E. Nelson, "The Legal Restraint of Power in Pre-Revolutionary America," *American Journal of Legal History* 18 (1974), 1, 14.

6. *Revised Statutes of Illinois* (1845), 310. The coroner was generally authorized to fill the office of the sheriff in case of a vacancy "by death, resignation, removal, or otherwise." *Ibid.,* 517.

7. *Election Returns,* 61:69 (1844). M. R. Deming Letter to General Ewing, July 17, 1845, Illinois State Historical Library, Springfield.

8. "Affidavit for Appointment of an Elisor," note 3 above.

9. "Minutes of Trial," 35, quoting from *Blackstone's Commentaries,* IV, 354, 359. ("Minutes of Trial" cites this source by its original designation: Book 3, p. 355.)

10. Watt Manuscript, 2. (Edited version in Smith, *History of the Church,* VII, 421.)

11. In this point Lamborn probably relied on the provision authorizing the coroner to replace the sheriff if the latter "is related to either of the parties." *Revised Statutes of Illinois* (1845), 310. He may also have observed that Blackstone was not authority for the suggested relief, since Blackstone's description of the appointment of an elisor only concerned cases where a sheriff or coroner was disqualified because he was "a party in the suit, or . . . related by blood or affinity to either of the parties" (*Blackstone's Commentaries,* IV, 354).

12. Watt Manuscript, 2. (Edited version in Smith, *History of the Church,* VII, 421-22.)

13. *Ibid.,* 3. (Edited version in Smith, *History of the Church,* VII, 422.)

14. It is tempting to speculate why Judge Young apparently traded his circuit assignment with Judge Thomas, but the causes may have had nothing to do with this trial. Such trades were authorized by law and were common in Illinois at this time. *Revised Statutes of Illinois* (1845), 147; Scofield, *History of Hancock County,* 746; Hoyne, "Lawyer as a Pioneer," 77. Judge Young's substitution may have been related to the fact that Judge Thomas was soon to resign from the Illinois Supreme Court (because the emoluments of his office were insufficient). Resignation dated August 8, 1845, Executive File, Illinois State Archives, Springfield.

15. This biographical information on Richard M. Young is principally drawn from Snyder, "Forgotten Statesman," 302-7; Caton, *The Early Bench and Bar,* 41; Ford, *History of Illinois,* 192-94.

16. Snyder, "Forgotten Statesman," 318.

17. Richard Young offered his name as candidate for governor in the Democratic convention the following February (1846). On the first vote the 235 ballots were spread among six candidates; Young was tied for fourth place with 35 votes. He was then induced to withdraw in favor of Augustus C. French, who was later elected to the office. Snyder, "Forgotten Statesman," 321.

18. *Ibid.,* 308. This source gives an illustration of Young's attempt to create favor with his fellow politicians.

19. Watt Manuscript, 3.

20. *Ibid.; Circuit Court Record,* 261 (Wednesday, May 21, 1845).

21. Watt Manuscript, 3.

22. *Missouri Republican,* May 27, 1845, p. 2.

23. *Burlington Hawkeye,* June 5, 1845.

24. Smith, *History of the Church,* VII, 414-15.

25. On the day when the trial commenced, the Mormon press, perhaps with some irony, publicly affirmed their confidence that justice would be done: "We have great confidence in the court and officers. . . . No doubt they will, as heretofore, acquit themselves with honor and increase the dignity and peace of the people" (*Nauvoo Neighbor,* May 21, 1845). There were no further expressions of this sort from Nauvoo after the elisor decision.

26. "Journal of Willard Richards," May 21, 1845, Church Archives.

27. The letter is published in Smith, *History of the Church,* VII, 415-16.

28. Watt Manuscript, 3-4; *Circuit Court Record,* 269 (May 22, 1845).

29. Scofield, *History of Hancock County,* 667-68, 1055; Gregg, *History of Hancock County,* 449; *Election Returns,* 38:84; Smith, *History of the Church,* V, 537-38; VI, 4-8.

30. Smith, *History of the Church,* VII, 193. The biographical information on Owen is from Moses, *Illinois Historical,* II, 1180; Gregg, *History of Hancock County,* 427-28, 449, 687; Scofield, *History of Hancock County,* 690, 1050; Hancock County Census, 1850, p. 278-B.

31. Elisors' oath in case of *People* v. *Levi Williams.*

32. Order dated May 22, 1845, in case of *People* v. *Levi Williams.*

33. Ford, *History of Illinois,* 367.

34. List from case file, *People* v. *Levi Williams;* Watt Manuscript, 4.

35. The 96 names were obtained from the original lists in the case file, *People* v. *Levi Williams.* See the Appendix herein for their classification by religion. Biographical data on the potential jurors was obtained from census reports and county histories. Over three-fourths of the 65 who are identified in the 1850 census were farmers, owning their own land. Almost all were married, between the ages of 25 and 40, with goodly numbers of children. A smattering of other occupations appear: a few laborers and merchants, a tanner, a wealthy nurseryman, a physician, two young men who were listed as lawyers by 1850, a miller, a carpenter, and a grocer. Six of the group had been elected justices of the peace in the county, some for many terms. Several had served in minor offices, such as road commissioner, clerk of elections, township supervisor, and postmaster. Thirty of the 96 are mentioned in the county history as prominent early settlers of their respective areas. Every populous township in the county was well represented, except Nauvoo.

36. *Circuit Court Record* 269 (May 22, 1845).

37. "Minutes of Trial," 33, citing as authority 1 *Burr's Trial,* 418; *Noble* v. *The People, Breeze's Reports,* 29, 30; accord, Watt Manuscript, 4.

38. "Minutes of Trial," 33, citing as authority *Gardner* v. *People, 3 Scammon* 88. This ruling is also consistent with the ruling in Aaron Burr's trial, as described in *Reynolds* v. *United States,* 98 *United States Reports* 145, 147, 155-56 (1878).

39. The succeeding information on peremptory challenges is from the "Minutes of Trial," 2-3, where the various persons challenged by each side are listed by name. Religious classification of the jurors is based on the study summarized in the Appendix herein.

Examples of individuals summoned by the elisors who would have been excused from jury service are Derrick Fuller and Larkin Scott, who had been summoned to testify as witnesses for the defense. John Houckins or Hukins was probably excused because of his anti-Mormon reputation. A county historian credits him with organizing "a company of men of the anti-Mormon stripe known as 'Brick-Batters.'" Scofield, *History of Hancock County,* 1092.

40. "Minutes of Trial," 22.

41. *Circuit Court Record,* 270.

42. Another source indicates that the prosecution used 36 challenges and the defense 12, a slight discrepancy from the "Minutes of Trial" reference. *Trial of the Persons Indicted in the Hancock Circuit Court for the Murder of Joseph Smith* (Warsaw, Ill.: *Warsaw Signal,* 1845), 2, cited hereafter as Sharp, *Trial of the Persons.* This pamphlet, apparently authored by defendant Thomas C. Sharp, is an enlarged and selectively edited version of the "Documents Relating to the Mormon Troubles," discussed in the Bibliographical Note.

43. *Circuit Court Record,* 274.

44. The jurors were as follows:

Jabez A. Beebe	Solomon J. Hill
Gilmore Callison	Joseph M. Jones
Jonathan Foy	Joseph Massey
James Gittings	William Robertson
Jesse Griffitts	William Smith (of Bournes Creek)
Silas Griffitts	Frederick M. Walton

"Minutes of Trial," 2; Gregg, *History of Hancock County,* 329. (We have followed Gregg in the spelling of these names.) Biographical information on these jurors appears in: Hancock County Census, 1850, pp. 273, 278, 301, 333, 351, 376; Gregg, *History of Hancock County,* 448, 510, 546, 607, 819-20; Scofield, *History of Hancock County,* 665-66, 708, 719, 1047, 1053, 1076, 1112, 1135; sources cited in note 45 below.

45. The Census of Hancock County, 1850, pp. 393, 435, states that the real estate of James Gittings of La Harpe Township was worth $10,000. As a young man he had freighted flour from Ohio to New Orleans, making profits he later used to purchase extensive lands in Illinois after his arrival there in 1835. Gregg, *History of Hancock County,* 903.

Frederick M. Walton was probably the best known of the jurors. He and his wife and children came to Illinois from Kentucky in 1835, settling on a farm in Augusta Township. A year after the trial 33-year-old Walton was elected a county commissioner. His biographer describes him as a forthright and honest man. Gregg, *History of Hancock County,* 527, 793; Scofield, *History of Hancock County,* 1390; Hancock County Census, 1850, 306.

46. Gregg, *History of Hancock County,* 330. Gregg's evaluation of the jury is more consistent with the biographical facts than the disparaging descriptions of two other historians. John Hay, who seems to have been most interested in a nice phrase, says that "the Elisors presented ninety-six men, before twelve were found ignorant enough and indifferent enough to act as jurors" (Hay, "The

Mormon Prophet's Tragedy," 669, 678). Governor Ford stated that the jury was made up of "military followers of the court" (Ford, *History of Illinois,* 367).

47. Roberts, *Comprehensive History,* II, 472.

48. Smith, *History of the Church,* VII, 408. Brigham Young's journal for this period refers to the "Brethren of the Twelve" who had "retired to our places of retreat, out of the way of constables and officers who are prowling around the city from Carthage." *Ibid.,* 418 (journal entry of May 24, 1845).

49. Smith, *History of the Church,* VII, 417-18; John Taylor's journal entry of May 24, 1845, quoted in Roberts, *Comprehensive History,* II, 472-73.

50. Roberts, *Comprehensive History,* II, 472-73.

Joseph Smith, from the death mask, by Gary E. Smith.

Illustration from Daniels, *Correct Account.*

Carthage Jail, from the southeast.

Defendant Mark Aldrich.

Defendant Thomas C. Sharp.

Governor Thomas Ford.

Judge Richard M. Young.

Defense counsel Orville H. Browning.

Defense counsel William A. Richardson.

Defense witness John Peyton.

Defense witness George Walker.

Juror James Gittings.

Juror Frederick M. Walton.

Hamilton House in Carthage, 1886.

Hancock County Courthouse, after 1866 alterations.

CHAPTER

8

"Quiet Perjury to Screen a Murder"

The preliminary routine of trial started at seven o'clock on Saturday, May 24, 1845. Complaining of the absence of Jonas Hobert and two other potential witnesses under subpoena, Lamborn had Judge Young direct the deputies to find them, arrest them, and bring them in by force.[1] In other preliminaries, Colonel Richardson withdrew his earlier request for the court to order the arrest of Governor Ford for failure to appear as a witness for the defense. The prosecution had served a subpoena on the governor, but on second thought Lamborn apparently decided not to press the issue, and Richardson made the same decision.[2] In this inauspicious manner the prosecution began.

The spectators, armed and partisan, were impatient with these incidentals and anxious for the action to begin. Among these spectators was the capable correspondent of the *Missouri Republican* of St. Louis, who wrote of the "deep and intense anxiety" that pervaded all classes of persons in attendance at the trial: "Everybody almost attending court comes armed to the teeth, and frequently, muskets and rifles will be seen taken out of wagons with as much deliberation as if they were attending a militia muster instead of attending a court of justice. This is a bad state of things, but extraordinary cases demand extraordinary remedies."[3]

Preliminaries completed, it was eight o'clock before Lamborn finally opened the case for the prosecution. He spoke for thirty minutes. First he read the indictment to the jury; then he described the legal theory of his case. He spoke in broad generalities, making no specific reference to the evidence he would introduce. "You are here called upon to judge a truly extraordinary case," Lamborn told the jury — extraordinary because of the "peculiar celebracy [*sic*] of the person killed, and on account of the peculiar circumstances attending the killing."[4] Referring to the "array of learned counselors" against him, Lamborn reminded the jury that he had to stand alone, without even the assistance of the states attorney. He did his duty not for the applause of the community "but for the applause of my own conscience, and for the applause of heaven." He was here not "to court the favor or smiles of any men or party of men," but to act with "decision and firmness, in spite of the consequences, and vindicate the supremacy and majesty of the law."[5]

Referring briefly to the facts of the case, Lamborn reminded the jury that a citizen of Hancock County had been murdered by a mob while confined in jail under the protection of the law and with the "plighted faith" of the governor and the state. He identified the five defendants as "the men who were the movers, and instigators, of that mob who committed the crime, and shed blood, upon the soil of your town." This reference to the leadership of the mob led to Lamborn's explanation of the legal theory of the prosecution's case:

> It is not necessary to prove that these men entered the jail or shot the gun or any of these instruments by which his death was accomplished in order to convict them, but that the mob got its spirit, impulse, movements, and blood thirstiness from the minds and dispositions of these men, and that they were the instigators of that mob, gave countenance to it and that they did stir up others to commit the murder we shall be able fully and substantially to prove. And it is frequently the case, when crime is committed, for the instigator of the crime to pass away, and let the blood be spilt or the crime perpetrated by underlings, they did direct the arm that did strike the fatal blow to the heart of the unfortunate victim.[6]

Lamborn conceded that the prosecution had an uphill battle for the sympathies of the jury: "There are hundreds here I have no doubt [who] are ready to applaud you, and rejoice with you if you should return a verdict of not guilty against these men." He nevertheless called upon the jurymen to do their duty. "The guilt of this crime," he told them, "hangs over you as a blight and a curse which is destroying your character, and gnawing at the root of your prosperity. It is a bloodstain upon your character, and a foul blot, which cannot be erased but with vengeance, and rigor, to deal out the law, as the law is." There can be no liberty, Lamborn declared at the conclusion of his argument, "no equal rights, no patriotism, in an agricultural county like this, where such things [as mob murder] are permitted to exist." The prosecutor was appealing to the jury's concern with preserving the force of law in their county, but he also appealed to their concern with the religious higher law: "Justice we ask, and justice we expect to get, for whoso sheddeth man's blood, by man shall his blood be shed, here is the law of God, and the law of God, is higher than the law of man."[7]

Considered in light of the complexity and seriousness of his case, Lamborn's opening statement was surprisingly brief. It can hardly have given the jury sufficient overview of what the prosecution expected to prove. Faced with the necessity of linking these defendants to the mob action by a theory of conspiracy, with proof from the mouths of numerous prosecution witnesses, the prosecutor should have given the jury an extended and carefully organized chronological account of the evidence he would introduce. Then, when his evidence was being assembled piecemeal from many different witnesses, the jury would be able to relate it to the overall picture of the prosecution's case. Lamborn's statement was long on rhetoric but short on substance.

Colonel Richardson replied for the defense. Not having to respond to any specifics alleged by the prosecution, he could be brief — and he was. After accusing Lamborn of trying to work upon the feelings and prejudices of the jury, Richardson cleverly used the weakness of the prosecution's opening argument to his own advantage by reminding the jury that the defendants could only be convicted by specific evidence introduced by the prosecution. At that task they will fail, he predicted. Then Richardson invited the jurors to draw an inference of innocence from the "clamorous reports" in the county (a clear appeal to the popular prejudice of the area) and from the fact that the defendants had made no attempt to evade a trial but had promptly presented themselves at the bar of the court for judgment upon the evidence to be produced.[8]

While these opening statements were being delivered, deputies were out looking for the missing witnesses, John Morrison, Henry Stephens, and Jonas Hobert. This could be dangerous work, since some of these Hancock County men were deadly determined not to testify for the prosecution. Just the previous Tuesday one of Sheriff

Deming's deputies had arrested Henry Mathews on an attachment to testify, but Mathews had managed to pull a gun on the deputy and escape.[9]

As they waited for the first witnesses, the courtroom spectators watched the lawyers, especially Browning, the handsome and graceful cavalier. His ruffled shirt, large cuffs, and Prince Albert coat with yellow outside pocket handkerchief set him elegantly apart from every other person in the courtroom. The dandy Browning was a conspicuous contrast to the impassive Lamborn, whose drab apparel covered a huge and crippled frame, sometimes bent over a cane and occasionally leaning for support on the arm or shoulder of a friend.[10]

Lamborn was the underdog and he knew it. The crowd was hostile to his cause, and the jury had been chosen from that crowd. He was a stranger hardly anyone knew, sent by a governor no one liked, prosecuting a case nobody wanted. To top it all off, the theory by which he had to link the defendants to the murder was conspiracy, an agreement or common design to commit an unlawful act. Since direct evidence of agreement is rarely available, a prosecutor who seeks to establish the guilt of a group of defendants by the theory of conspiracy must usually assemble a mosaic of evidence piece by piece in order to show the jury the whole picture of the defendants' design. Only when the common design and the individual's connection have been demonstrated beyond a reasonable doubt can that individual be held responsible for the acts of a co-conspirator. Without conspiracy, only the man who pulled the trigger would be guilty of the murder. But if conspiracy is proven, then all who took part in the plan would be criminally responsible for the consequences of its execution. Thus, in a case decided just nine years after this trial, the Illinois Supreme Court affirmed a conviction and death sentence for nine men who had been among a mob who killed a storekeeper, even though there was no evidence that any of these nine men had actually struck the blow. The court said:

> It is sufficient that they combined with those committing the deed to do an unlawful act, such as to beat or rob [the deceased]; and that he was killed in the attempt to execute the common purpose. If several persons conspire to do an unlawful act, and death happens in the prosecution of

the common object, all are alike guilty of the homicide. The act of one of them done in furtherance of the original design is, in consideration of law, the act of all. And he who advises or encourages another to do an illegal act is responsible for all the natural and probable consequences that may arise from its perpetration.[11]

The prosecution's testimony began at 9:45 A.M., soon after the deputies returned with the arrested Jonas Hobert.[12] The prosecution's first three witnesses had testified before the grand jury. All three were solid Hancock County men who had no desire to sit in the witness chair and face their disapproving fellow-citizens. As each testified, it was obvious that he knew more than he told.

From the unwilling Jonas Hobert, Lamborn drew not much more than the fact that Joseph Smith had been killed at the Carthage jail. When Hobert heard firing and hurried to the nearby jail from his home in Carthage, he found a crowd of about a hundred and fifty men armed with muskets or spring breech rifles. Smith's body lay outside on the east side of the jail, with wounds in the right breast, abdomen, and left shoulder. Apparently seeking to determine how long he had been dead, Lamborn asked the witness, "Was the blood still fresh and warm?" It was.[13] Hobert was at the jail about two minutes before the mob walked away toward the west. He said he knew all the defendants except Grover, and he had not seen any of them at the jail. Apparently probing for a lead to another witness who would be more talkative, Lamborn asked Hobert to name anyone he knew among the men at the jail, but Hobert solemnly denied knowing any of them.[14] Confident that this witness had not harmed the defense, Browning waived cross-examination, and the witness stepped down. Lamborn must have concealed his disappointment, but the defendants probably made no attempt to hide their satisfaction that the witness had implicated no one. This pattern would be repeated frequently during the trial.

Still seeking to establish an important initial advantage for his case, Lamborn relied heavily on his next two witnesses, John Peyton and George Walker. Both enjoyed the reputation of honest and respected citizens.[15] Both had been with the Warsaw militia when they started for Nauvoo. Both recalled how Colonel Williams's regiment had marched up river toward Golden's Point, reaching what was called "the railroad shanties"[16] five or six miles from Warsaw at about noon. There Colonel Williams discharged the militia. Aldrich, Davis, Grover, and Sharp were also present at this time. After the troops were discharged, Aldrich and Williams began to "beat up" for volunteers to go to Carthage. Peyton said that Aldrich "spoke of the grievances of the people, and that the Mormons had the power themselves and they must do something to stop it."[17] Sharp also made a speech. "Did he say anything about Joseph Smith?" Lamborn asked. The record shows that Peyton "waited some considerable time" before he answered cautiously: "I think he said that Joe Smith was now in custody, and the Mormons would elect the officers of the county, and by that means Joe would select his own jury and get free."[18] Sharp told the men that "the Governor had said that whatever was done should be done quickly."[19]

Despite Lamborn's determined efforts, neither Peyton nor Walker would give more specific testimony on the speeches at the shanties. Neither would admit hearing anyone say why they wanted to go to Carthage, or that they intended to kill the Smiths. Lamborn's examination of Peyton on this subject illustrates the stubborn reticence with which the prosecutor had to contend:

Q: Was anything said about killing Joseph Smith?

A: No.

Q: Did he say what should be done with him?

A: No.

Q: Was there anything said about their coming in here, with the troops?

A: Some of the officers, I think Aldrich, said something about it.

Q: Then it was Aldrich that was in favour of going to Carthage?

A: I don't know that it was Aldrich, or some other of them. There was something said in the crowd on going to Carthage I think.

Q: What did the people there, upon the ground, in common with these men, say they were going to Carthage for?

A: I could not tell what their intention was. They did not say.[20]

Both witnesses testified that, after the speeches, over half of the disbanded troops, about a hundred armed men, started in the direction of Carthage, approximately ten miles to the east. The Carthage-bound group included defendants Aldrich, Grover, Sharp, and Williams, but not Davis, who turned back toward home.[21]

When George Walker's testimony reached this point, he gave the prosecution its first tangible evidence of conspiracy. Lamborn asked what Captain Davis had said to explain why he and some of his men were heading home instead of going with the group to Carthage. In a surprisingly forthright response, Walker told the jury that he heard Davis say "he would be damned if he would go to kill a man that was confined in prison."[22] There must have been many a grave glance in the courtroom when Walker spoke those words. That fragment of testimony could be sufficient to establish the purpose of the speeches at the shanties and the objective of the men who were walking toward Carthage on that hot summer afternoon. After an hour's examination of his first three witnesses, Lamborn had the advantage he sought; he could now call his next witness from a position of some strength.

There would certainly have been a stir in the crowded courtroom as the clerk read the name of the prosecution's next witness, Franklin A. Worrell. Here was a witness of extraordinary importance, since this young Carthage merchant, a lieutenant in the Carthage Greys, had been in command of the guard at the jail when Joseph Smith was killed.

A sophisticated observer would note Lamborn's boldness in calling as a prosecution witness a man who might be implicated himself. Worrell's participation in anti-Mormon activities in the county was well known.[23] Some may have known that Worrell had told Dan Jones, a Mormon who visited the Smiths on their last night in the jail: "We have had too much trouble to bring Old Joe here to let him ever escape alive, and unless you want to die with him you had better leave before sundown."[24] The Carthage Greys were widely supposed to have been in collusion with the Warsaw militia in the murders, and there were rumors of a prearrangement by which the guards at the jail had removed the balls from their muskets so as to fire into the attacking mob without doing injury.

What would Lamborn be able to prove by this witness? Those who surrounded the defense table may have regarded Worrell with some concern as he took the stand, but Lamborn must have been the most nervous of all. In fact, his calling of the hostile Worrell was a reckless probe, and he could not have had more than an inkling of the probable content of his crucial testimony.

Worrell was on the witness stand for fifteen minutes. He gave the jury some explicit but harmless details about the events of that bloody afternoon. He said the mob "came from the direction of Nauvoo on the Nauvoo road." About thirty of the mob of one or two hundred men had disguised themselves "by wetting their hands in powder, and then putting their hands on their faces." Worrell described how he was sitting on the doorstep of the jail when the mob approached. "They came up in front of the jail, and when they had got formed there," he told the jury, "they made a rush for the door."[25] He described how the mob pushed him and the other guards out of the way. "There was a great crowd," Worrell explained, "as thick as in this courtroom. Their pieces were going off all the time and [there was] so much noise and smoke that I could not see or hear anything what was said or done."[26]

Here Lamborn should have asked Worrell more details about his personal actions, the names of his fellow guards at the jail, where each was stationed, whether their muskets were loaded or unloaded, and whether any of them had fired into the mob. But the commanding demeanor and apparent popularity of this confident young witness may have disarmed the veteran prosecutor. In any case, without probing these crucial lines of inquiry, he thrust boldly into a question about whether Worrell had seen any of the defendants at the jail. Here was a critical point, and Lamborn should have foreseen the inevitable answer. Although Worrell admitted seeing Aldrich and Williams in Carthage not long after the killing, he solemnly told the jury he "did not see any of the defendants" at the jail.[27] Another question permitted Worrell to add that although he was acquainted with about one-third of the people in the county, he "did not recognize any" of the mob at the jail.[28] Commenting on this testimony later, an eminent fellow citizen of Hancock County, John Hay, observed that "it would be difficult to imagine anything cooler than this quiet perjury to screen a murder."[29]

Lamborn could do nothing further. There was no cross-examination. Worrell's testimony had not incriminated the defendants to the slightest degree, and had in fact worked in their favor by denying their presence at the jail. The testimony of the witnesses from the Warsaw militia at least had implied a murderous intent in the noontime speeches at the shanties, had shown that one militia officer understood that they were proposing to go to Carthage to kill the Smiths, and had placed defendants Aldrich, Grover, Sharp, and Williams with about a hundred other men on the road to Carthage about five hours before the murder.

Lamborn's next strategy was to show the jury that the defendants arrived in Carthage at or before the time of the murder. He would also try to identify them in the execution mob or implicate them in some collusion with the guards at the jail, or with the larger contingent of the Carthage Greys who had been camped on the courthouse square for guard duty.

The next three witnesses were interrogated with these objectives in mind. Baldwin Samuels and George Backman were privates and Eli H. Williams was an orderly sergeant in the two companies of Carthage militia who had been left to guard the jail. One was commanded by R. F. Smith (the Greys), and the other by Wesley Williams (the Riflemen). All three witnesses had been with the troops camped on the courthouse square when the firing commenced at the jail.

Each witness told how the troops assembled as soon as they could and commenced their march toward the jail. On the way they saw Colonel Levi Williams standing on the northwest corner of the courthouse square; he came along with them as they marched to the jail. Two of them also saw Aldrich on the square at about that time. Eli Williams said that when the Greys were about a hundred and fifty yards from the jail, he saw Joseph Smith fall from the window. There was some firing after that. By the time the troops arrived at the jail, the mob was in retreat, some two or three hundred yards away, and the Smiths were dead. The troops made no pursuit. None of these witnesses could identify any members of the mob, but each testified that defendants Aldrich, Sharp, and Williams were in Carthage on or around the courthouse square shortly before the shooting started around five o'clock. Despite Lamborn's prolonged questioning, none of these witnesses would admit to overhearing any conversations of the defendants that afternoon.[30]

At this point in each man's testimony Lamborn might have asked whether he saw any of the defendants in conversation with any of the officers or men of the Carthage Greys, but it appears that the lawyer neglected to search for that missing piece in the mosaic of conspiracy. In an apparent attempt to establish some prearranged signal between the mob and the Carthage Greys, Lamborn did question Eli Williams about whether he had seen anyone on the cupola of the courthouse. The witness admitted that he had seen some men up there, but he "did not see any signals." Apparently sensing that he was on the trail of something, the prosecutor turned his fiercest manner on this young witness and finally secured an admission that he "might have heard a gun" — but the witness insisted that he was unsure whether he saw the men on top of the courthouse "before or after the gun was fired."[31]

This trio of witnesses, who testified just before and just after the noon adjournment, had provided Lamborn with a few necessary facts and some suspicious circumstances, but no important breakthrough. The task of proving conspiracy from the mouths of unfriendly witnesses in a hostile environment was difficult and frustrating. Lamborn was not measuring up to the challenge, and he must have known it. Two witnesses whom he called and questioned briefly during this same period illustrate his difficulty.

John D. Mellen, a thirty-two-year-old Warsaw merchant, began his testimony by swearing that he had been in Westboro, Massachusetts, when the Smiths were killed and had not arrived back in Hancock County until about the first of August.[32] The embarrassed Lamborn had no further questions. If he had known the content of this testimony, he obviously would not have called Mellen to the witness stand. That he did so probably indicates either that he had omitted the routine preparatory work of speaking with his own witnesses before they were called to the stand, or that Mellen refused to speak with the prosecutor, who was careless enough to call him anyway.

Canfield Hamilton, a Warsaw tavernkeeper, provided testimony that he had seen Grover, Davis, Aldrich, and Sharp in Warsaw at about eight or nine o'clock that evening. Apparently seeking to exploit the tavernkeeper's undoubted access to the common understanding and confidences of the residents of his small town, Lamborn questioned him about his conversations with the defendants on this subject. Although the defendants were the five leading citizens of the town, and although the killing of the Smiths in Carthage was the most notorious event of the year, the tavernkeeper solemnly testified that he had not heard "any of these men say a word about the transaction . . . one way or the other since it occurred."[33] This response was incredible on its face, but Lamborn could not challenge it, since lawyers are considered to vouch for the credibility of their own witnesses.

By now Lamborn's frustrations must have been almost routine to the judge, jury, and courtroom crowd. Anyone who has ever experienced a warm, late spring afternoon in downstate Illinois can imagine how minds wandered and eyelids grew heavy. But at this point Lamborn provided the first surprise of the trial, which doubtless shook the torpor. He asked Judge Young for permission to recall Franklin Worrell to the stand.

Defense counsel, who had not cross-examined a single prosecution witness up to this point, had to shake off their own lethargy to confront this first challenge of the day. Orville Browning strode to the bench to take issue with Lamborn, arguing that normal procedures prevented the prosecutor from bringing Worrell back to the witness stand because the defense had not cross-examined the witness after his original testimony. Consequently, the proposed testimony, instead of clarifying unfavorable inferences brought out on cross-examination, could only supplement his original testimony. Witnesses are generally expected to give their whole testimony at one time, and Browning urged Judge Young not to grant an exception in this circumstance. But the prosecutor's plea, delivered with all the intensity and fluency for which Lamborn was renowned, prevailed. Judge Young ruled that Franklin Worrell could be recalled and examined as to any material facts not already covered in his testimony.[34]

The crowd probably responded angrily. This young merchant had made credit sales to hundreds of citizens in the county,[35] and the courthouse crowd might have been afraid that this second effort would incriminate their popular and generous friend. Apparently disturbed by their hostility, Judge Young sought to placate them by explaining that this was a privilege which he would not refuse to the defendants' counsel under like circumstances, and therefore ought not to withhold from the prosecuting attorney.[36] Governor Ford later deplored how Judge Young "was compelled to permit the court-house to be filled and surrounded by armed bands" during the progress of this trial, and how the coercive pressure of the mob, stamping their feet and yelling in the courtroom, forced the judge not only to hear their commentary, "but to lend it a kind of approval."[37] To the dignified and courteous Judge Young, whose courtrooms were always models of decorum,[38] these outbursts must have been especially distressing.

Lamborn had only a few questions when Worrell took the stand, all dealing with one of the vital subjects which he had earlier overlooked: "Do you know if the Carthage Greys, that evening, loaded their guns with blank catridge [sic]?" Before Worrell had time to feel more than a brief moment of alarm, Browning and Richardson both spoke out to the witness saying, "You need not answer that question." Not one to miss a cue, Worrell responded: "I will not answer that question, I know nothing about the Carthage Greys, only the six men that I had to do with."[39] Tenaciously Lamborn pressed forward: "Do [Did?] those six men load their guns with blank cartridge that evening?" "I will not answer it," Worrell replied.[40]

Browning was immediately on his feet to support the witness in his refusal, but the determined Lamborn persisted in his question. Aware of the sensitivity of this inquiry, the members of the jury must have listened with special interest while focussing their attention on the grave-mannered judge who would rule whether the witness was required to answer. Young could not have missed the meaning of the crowd's angry outbursts. According to Governor Ford, Judge Young later explained that he was "in duress" during the entire conduct of the trial and "did not consider his life secure any part of the time."[41]

The judge ruled that the witness was not bound to answer the question about whether the guard's muskets had been loaded with blanks if he could not do so without incriminating himself.[42] While the crowd noised its approval, Worrell savored the cue the judge had given him, and then concluded his testimony by what later came to be known as "taking the Fifth Amendment": he declared that he refused to answer on the grounds that he might incriminate himself.[43] To the jury, theoretically bound by legal rules, that answer was supposed to be neutral on the issue of guilt. But to a practical-minded Hancock County juror, Worrell's refusal to testify on this ground could have seemed a practical admission that Worrell and the guards at the jail were part of the plot and had cooperated with the mob that killed the Smiths.

Despite a few momentary gains, thus far the trial had not gone well for the man who was called "the strongest prosecutor in the state."[44] Men who were willing to testify said they knew nothing, and men who knew something (or were in a position to know something) about the planning or membership of the mob gave evasive testimony or swore they had recognized no one. The afternoon was wearing on, and the Sabbath adjournment was just a few hours away. If Lamborn's case was to have a chance, he should conclude this first day of trial with some seriously incriminating evidence of guilt. Jurors who were accustomed to criminal trials of no more than an hour or two were not likely to take a criminal case seriously if the prosecutor could not show some persuasive evidence of guilt in the first six or eight hours of testimony. The time was ripe for Lamborn to call his key witness, and he motioned for the deputies to bring in William M. Daniels.

The excitement created by Worrell's recent testimony may have heightened as the youthful Mormon worked his way through the crowd to the witness stand. Some had read his sensational booklet, just published in Nauvoo, which contained his eyewitness account of the murders. Everyone knew that this young cooper had been a key witness before the grand jury that had indicted these defendants. Here was a man who had been with the mob and who *was* willing to testify to what he had seen.

The tenor of Lamborn's initial questions reflected his obvious satisfaction with what was to come. "Mr. Daniels," he began, "stand up and tell the jury what you know about these five men."[45] After leading Daniels through the now-familiar account of the militia's march north to the railroad shanties, where Colonel Williams read the orders disbanding them, Lamborn inquired about the speech delivered by Thomas Sharp. Daniels told the jury that Sharp's speech "pointed to the necessity of killing the Smiths to get rid of the Mormons." Sharp had said that he wanted the troops to go on to Carthage, but Daniels did not recall hearing any such proposal from Williams or Aldrich. Soon there was a call for volunteers "to kill the Smiths." Daniels testified that he heard Grover say "he would come alone if nobody else would come."[46] Sharp asked Captain Davis to come with his company. Davis replied that if they would go to Nauvoo he would go with them, but he would go home rather than go to Carthage. "They called him a damned coward," Daniels reported, and said "they would never elect him [Captain] again."[47]

Responding to Lamborn's rapid questions, Daniels told the jury how sixty or a hundred men then started toward Carthage, scattering out along the road. Most were on foot. He did not see either Sharp or Williams on the way to Carthage; Aldrich was there, on horseback, but he left the troops about four miles from Carthage, where most of the group turned off the road to the left into a timbered hollow. Daniels continued on the road into Carthage, along with several other men and the two or three baggage wagons which had accompanied them.[48] He went directly to the jail, but he had no conversation with the guards. "Why not?" Lamborn asked. "Because they knew about it as well as anybody else," Daniels explained, adding that he had understood from the other men that the guards were to have their guns loaded with blank cartridges.[49]

Daniels was standing fifteen or twenty feet in front of the jail when the men arrived a few minutes later. He heard two or three guns fire just before they appeared. They came in a single file along the fence that ran from the jail to the timber;[50] some of their faces were blackened, apparently with wet powder. Did you see any of the defendants at the jail? Lamborn asked, confidently. Daniels nodded in the affirmative. He had seen Grover, carrying a double-barrelled shotgun, running toward the door of the jail just before the killing. Colonel Williams was standing in the middle of the road on the south side of the jail just before the mob arrived. Williams had cried, "Rush in, boys, there is no danger." He also hallooed to them to come around on that side to the window, Daniels related, "and then told them to shoot the damned scoundrel." What about Aldrich, Sharp, or Davis? The witness had not seen any of them with the mob at the jail. Daniels told the jury that he had seen Joseph Smith when he fell from the window, and he thought the

Mormon leader hadn't as yet been shot. Three or four guns were fired after he fell. It was all done in a great deal of confusion. The men had been drinking whiskey in the wagons coming up, and some of them acted as if they were drunk.[51]

At last the jury had some real evidence of guilt. If believed by the jury, Daniels's testimony could convict Grover, Sharp, and Williams as fully responsible participants in the murder of Joseph Smith.

Lamborn concluded Daniels's direct examination with a skillful attempt to draw the sting of the forthcoming cross-examination by having Daniels explain the booklet that bore his name. Lamborn held up a copy and asked Daniels if he was the author. No, Daniels replied, "Lyman Omar Littlefield is the author." (Littlefield was a twenty-six-year-old typesetter for the *Nauvoo Neighbor,* publisher of the booklet.[52]) "I suppose he got it from what I told him," Daniels continued. "I told him the story a good many times."[53]

The most questionable part of the Daniels-Littlefield booklet was the miraculous light that was supposed to have appeared and baffled the mob immediately after the death of Joseph Smith. Knowing that the defense was sure to use this material to ridicule Daniels, Lamborn gave his witness a chance to explain it to the jury under friendly questioning. "I suppose it will astonish you to tell you that I saw a light," Daniels began.

Q: Well explain it to us.

A: It is represented in the book rather different than what it was.

Q: But it is true that you saw a light?

A: Yes.

Q: Might it not have been the reflection of a musket?

A: I don't say what it might have been.

Q: Was the light seen by any that was standing by except yourself?

A: I cannot tell. . . .

Q: Was you alarmed at the time you saw the light?

A: Yes I was considerably excited.[54]

Apparently seeking to attribute the exaggerations to Littlefield,

Daniels told the jury that he had related the circumstances to Little-field "substantially as I have related them here."[55] For the second time he insisted that "the whole composition of that book is Little-field's."[56] In response to Lamborn's final questions, Daniels admitted that he was now a Mormon and lived in Nauvoo, although he was not a Mormon at the time of these events.

Each of Daniels's statements was noted carefully by the lawyers at the defense table — especially Browning, who would conduct the cross-examination. A copy of Daniels's booklet was close at hand, ready for its contemplated use. Browning was a little disappointed to hear Daniels disclaim authorship, but he was not surprised. Lamborn was too clever to let a youthful craftsman with little formal education claim to have written the pedantic prose in this publication.[57] Daniels's disclaimer of authorship would complicate his task, but Browning could still use the booklet for impeachment purposes since Daniels had admitted it had been written from his account. He carefully observed discrepancies between Daniels's trial testimony and the story in the booklet, confident that Daniels would be unable to explain them sufficiently to avoid casting doubt upon his credibility as a witness.

Browning was superbly prepared to commence his cross-examination of this vulnerable witness. He was aware that the youthful Daniels, only twenty-four years of age, had made few friends in Illinois since coming from New York seven or eight years before. Probably none of these friends were in the courtroom to sustain him in this ordeal. Most of the spectators were outwardly hostile, eagerly anticipating Daniels's downfall.

The dignified and gentlemanly Browning was a marked contrast. Putting aside the expansive oratorical style for which he was famous, he shrewdly sought to exploit Daniels's vulnerability by a disarming friendliness. Suave and searching, but never oppressive, Browning's technique sought to reassure Daniels that he was the witness's true friend, perhaps his only friend in the courtroom. Yet his plan of attack on Daniels's credibility was designedly devastating. He would seek to show that Daniels was not worthy of credence because some of his testimony was contrary to common experience, that Daniels had a motive to lie about the events since he was implicated in the crime himself, that Daniels was making money by selling the booklet with his account of the crime, that Daniels had taken money to influence the content of his testimony at trial, and that Daniels had already shown himself to be a liar by telling one thing to one person and just the opposite to another. This last point was to be achieved not by the cross-examination alone, but by encouraging Daniels to testify to facts that would later be contradicted by other witnesses.

First, Browning exploited the apparent inconsistency between Daniels's insistence that he was opposed to the murder and his story that he joined a Warsaw militia unit that he said was committed to the killing. In attempting an explanation, Daniels insisted that he joined the militia because this was the only way he would be permitted to leave Warsaw. He said he had overheard militia officers Aldrich, Davis, Grover, and Williams in conversation on the night before the march; they were agreeing that the Smiths must be murdered. Browning skillfully emphasized the improbability of this testimony by having the witness admit that these men talked about this secret arrangement in the presence of Daniels, a total stranger. This called for a further explanation, which took Daniels into ground not covered by the booklet. He claimed that after he overheard the plans he was arrested and kept under guard overnight in a tent. He said he was still a prisoner when he joined Davis's company for the march to Nauvoo, and that he was not released from arrest at that time. However, by the time the troops were disbanded at the shanties he was no longer under guard, and was then left free to go wherever he wished. Thus, Daniels was alone and unguarded when he arrived at the Carthage jail ahead of the mob. But he said he made no effort to warn the guards or anyone else in Carthage, since he supposed the Carthage Greys were part of the plot.[58] Browning concluded that line of inquiry, confident that Daniels had left the jury wondering why, if he was now speaking the truth, he had not told someone else of the murder plot. Each new detail which Browning had coaxed from the voluble Daniels was less believable than the last; the total effect of this testimony had precisely the discrediting effect Browning desired, without being so blatant as to warn the victim that these friendly questions were leading him into weakening his own credibility.

Next Browning exhibited the booklet bearing Daniels's name and asked him if he was the author and whether the facts related there were true. Daniels replied that "the facts as set forth in the Book are mostly correct as I stated them to Littlefield."[59] In response to Browning's gentle inquiry about what facts were incorrect, Daniels gave the easy reply Browning had wanted: "If I was going to tell the story off, the facts as set forth in the Book are as right as I could tell them."[60] By letting himself be identified more closely with the authorship of the pamphlet, Daniels destroyed the qualification Lamborn had introduced, thus facilitating Browning's impeachment effort.

Thus far, Browning had exposed the fact that Daniels was unable to give a satisfactory explanation of his presence in the murder mob, or of his relationship to Littlefield in the authorship of the pamphlet. He had regained the initiative. But perhaps overconfident because of this initial success, Browning moved hastily into a new line of questions on the noontime speeches at the shanties and the march to Carthage. He began by reading Sharp's speech, as reported in the booklet, and asked the witness if it was accurate. Daniels replied that it was given substantially as reported, "but the filling as published in the speech was put in by Mr. Littlefield."[61] Perceiving a new opportunity for showing discrepancies, Browning eagerly asked Daniels to describe exactly what Sharp had said. Daniels's reply lacked the journalistic embroidery of the booklet, but, to Browning's embarrassment, contained all the substance necessary to prove the conspiracy: "He urged them to kill the Smiths to get rid of the Mormons. He wanted them to kill the Smiths. . . . Sharp said the news would shock Nauvoo and they would kill the Governor. Sharp said if they killed Smiths the Mormons would kill Ford and they would get rid of Ford and the Mormons, too."[62] Daniels added that when Sharp finished his speech the men cheered him, but they did not seem willing to start out until Grover stepped forward.[63]

Shifting abruptly to a new line of attack, Browning questioned the witness about the march to Carthage. Daniels told how he came on with the troops until they were about four miles from Carthage; there a man dressed in a Carthage Grey uniform met them and gave Aldrich a written message. Daniels had told of this in his booklet. Apparently expected to highlight some inconsistency in his testimony, Browning read the jury the contents of the note as reported in the Daniels publication:

> Now is a delightful time to murder the Smiths. The Governor has gone to Nauvoo with all the troops — the Carthage Greys are left to guard the prisoners. Five of our men will be stationed at the jail; the rest will be upon the Public Square. To keep appearances you will attack the men at the jail — a sham scuffle will ensue — their guns will be loaded with blank cartridges — they will fire in the air.
>
> (Signed) The Carthage Greys[64]

Was this what you told Littlefield? Browning asked. "It is pretty much the same," Daniels replied. Browning persisted by asking how Daniels knew what was in the note. Here was the discrediting point of the inquiry — but this time Daniels slipped free with a believable answer, explaining that Aldrich read the note to himself and then read it aloud.[65]

This line of questioning had not helped the defense, but merely strengthened the evidence against Sharp and Aldrich. Daniels held fast to his original account, and each new detail only incriminated the defendants more completely. In respect to the speeches at the shanties and the march to the jail, Daniels apparently had none of the undisclosed personal secrets that had twisted his testimony about how he happened to join the Warsaw militia. Sensing this too late, Browning again abruptly abandoned his line of inquiry.

The full heat of the afternoon was now upon them, and the portly Browning's exertions must have turned his heavy Prince Albert coat into a steam room. Now he had ample use for the dandy pocket handkerchief, as a few less elegantly attired observers could note with satisfaction. Browning was respected, but not loved. One of his associates in the legislature observed that "I should have liked him better if he had been a little less conscious of his own superiority."[66]

Browning's next questions elicited details which Daniels had observed at the jail, interesting to round out the picture but not particularly helpful to prosecution or defense. This witness told how he counted eighty-four men as the mob arrived.[67] He saw three wounded men after the shooting. Daniels was acquainted with one of them, a man named Wills, whose "arm was shot all to pieces."[68] This man said in Daniels's presence that "Jo Smith shot him, that he was the first [attacker] shot through the door."[69] A man named Voras had blood on his shoulder but appeared to be only slightly wounded. A third man was wounded in the face. When the call came to go around to the window, the man who was wounded in the shoulder ran around to that side of the jail. There, Daniels said, "I saw him shoot Smith," holding the gun in both hands.[70] Daniels said he had not seen any of the wounded men since that day at the jail.[71]

Browning continued with the pattern of questioning the witness about the details of an event, and then reading a contradictory passage from his booklet. Immediately following Daniels's testimony about the wounds received by the three men, Browning asked about the truthfulness of the pamphlet's statement that Joseph Smith had mortally wounded two of his assailants. Daniels replied: "I told you I did not write that book — Littlefield wrote it."[72] Browning then had Daniels testify to the events of Joseph Smith's death, how (according to Daniels) Joseph Smith had hung in the jail window for a time, how Levi Williams had unsuccessfully called for someone to shoot him there, and how Joseph had finally fallen to the ground stunned. When he fell, many of the mob rushed over to him. A young man picked him up and set him against the south side of the well, saying "this is old Jo, I know him." Four persons then shot him in that position from a distance of ten or twelve feet.[73] "Were Smith's eyes open when they shot him?" Browning asked. When Daniels testified that he did not know, Browning read him the passage from the booklet that describes how Joseph Smith's "eyes rested upon them with a calm and quiet resignation." Was this correct? Daniels replied that he did not claim authorship of that statement. It was "more of Littlefield's filling." Somewhat sharply the tired young witness snapped at Browning: "I told you before, I do not claim the authorship of all as it is printed in that Book."[74]

Now Browning came to what he anticipated would be one of the most discrediting subjects in his entire cross-examination. He was sure that the miraculous light that sold books in Nauvoo would alienate jurors in Carthage.

Q: At what time did you see this marvelous light?

A: I saw it at the place after the shooting.

Q: How long after?

A: A short time after.

Q: Well tell us about that light.

A: It was like a flash of lightening [*sic*] there at the moment.

Q: It was not like a streak then?

A: It was like a flash.

Q: Was it where his body lay?

A: It passed right by his body at one side.

Q: When he was shot, did any person go up to him?

A: Yes, a young man attempted to get to him.

Q: Had he anything in his hand?

A. IIᵤ liad a pewlei flule iⅱ liis liaiid.

Q: Had he a bowey knife in his hand?

A: I did not see any.

Q: Did he get up to Smith?

A: No.

Q: What stopped him?

A: That light.

Q: How did it affect him?

A: He did not go any further.

Q: Did he look frightened?

A: I don't know. I was very much frightened myself.

Q: Then you did not see him stand like a marble statue?

A: No.[75]

Browning countered by reading the version of this incident from the booklet, including the ruffian's attempt to sever Smith's head with a bowie knife, the chain of light from heaven, and the immediate paralysis of the knife-wielding attacker and the four who had shot Smith against the well curb. Were these facts true as related in the booklet? "I did not write that," Daniels responded, "neither did I authorise it to be written."[76] Daniels insisted that he had given the correct facts to Littlefield, and had even "told him after the book was written of the mistakes it contained."[77] That statement of course invited Browning to elicit further details that would discomfort both Daniels and Lamborn. Did you tell Littlefield that the reference to the ruffian using a "bowie knife" was a mistake? Daniels admitted he had not corrected Littlefield on that point. How about the four paralyzed men? "I have said that after they shot him, they stood there," Daniels replied lamely, adding that Colonel Williams had halloed to them to come back and carry off these four men, which they did.[78]

Browning now entered upon the final phase of his cross-examination, leading the witness into areas not touched on by Lamborn's direct examination. His obvious purpose was to lay a foundation for impeachment by having Daniels testify to facts that would later be contradicted by defense witnesses. The first set of questions brought out that on the evening of the murder Daniels had stayed overnight at the home of an acquaintance, Larkin Scott. Daniels denied telling Scott or anyone else that he had assisted in killing Smith or in holding the guards while they were killed.[79] (Earlier, Daniels had denied ever entering the enclosure around the jail.)[80] When Browning asked where Daniels had had the vision recounted in his book, Lamborn objected, apparently successfully, that this question was foreign to the case.[81]

In response to Browning's next question, Daniels admitted that he had told Thomas English of Quincy that "I could get $500 for attending this trial." I didn't tell him "I was to get $500," Daniels clarified, "I told him I had been offered $500, but not by the Mormons."[82] Browning asked if anyone else had offered him money. Daniels replied that a man named Southwick at Quincy had told him he was a fool for filing his affidavit at Nauvoo, and that "if he was me he could make money out of it. . . . He told me he would give me $500 to clear out." A tavernkeeper by the name of Conyers told him "if he was in my place he would clear out, as the mobocrats would kill me if I staid." In response to Browning's persistent questions Daniels admitted "I told him I could get $500 for attending this trial."[83] Daniels also admitted having conversations with George Seabold and George McLean about this matter. Browning queried whether Daniels had told them he didn't know who killed the Smiths but he would "get $500 for swearing in this case." "No, I didn't," Daniels insisted.[84]

Speaking with a trace of sarcasm, Browning asked whether there was anyone else. Daniels testified that two strangers had stopped him on the street in Quincy the preceding summer and had offered him $1,500 in money and $1,000 in land in New York if he would not appear and testify against these defendants. "I wheeled around and went off," Daniels added, "[I] give them to understand I would not take it." Browning sought a description of these men, but Daniels could not provide one, except to say that they were young and of moderate size.[85]

Next Browning asked a question that would remind the jury of a fact whose relevance was questionable but whose persuasive effect was clear. In response to the inquiry about when he had joined the Mormon Church, Daniels replied: "Not a great while before the last court at this place,"[86] which was during October, 1844.

Browning was winding up his cross-examination, and his courteous manner, already frayed by fatigue and irritation, was giving way to a relentless and scornful tenor of questioning that urged the jury to adopt his conclusion of disdain for this witness. Now his questions were designed to lay a foundation for impeaching Daniels, and at the same time to furnish theories and innuendo upon which the jury would discredit the witness even without the anticipated contradictions. "Did you ever tell Tom English that you had written a book and expected to make a great sum of money out of it [or] that you had joined the Mormons for the purpose of making a speculation out of it?" Perhaps tired and discouraged after hours of hammering by the skilled advocate, Daniels either dropped his guard or failed to see the damaging implications of this question. "I don't know that I did or did not," he replied.[87]

Quick to exploit this damaging admission, Browning asked what Daniels had been doing in Nauvoo. Had he been following his trade of cooper? Daniels responded that he had been exhibiting a painting representing the death of the Smiths, which had the light delineated upon it. Calling attention to an important discrepancy between the representation of the miraculous light in the painting and the description the witness had just given in his sworn testimony, Browning asked the witness to explain. Daniels's answer reflected just the note of casual indifference to truth that Browning must have been seeking to demonstrate in the testimony of this key witness: "Since I have lived in Nauvoo I have exhibited a painting in Nauvoo representing this light and when asked I have told that it was not correct but when not asked I said nothing."[88] Well satisfied with his conclusion, Browning returned to his seat. His cross-examination was over.

On re-direct examination Lamborn had an opportunity to clarify aspects of his witness's testimony that had been clouded by the cross-examination, or to rehabilitate him where his credibility or truthfulness had been besmirched. Despite the apparent need for clarification and rehabilitation, Lamborn's examination was astonishingly brief. Owing to lack of time, or to fatigue or indifference, Lamborn contented himself with merely asking Daniels if all he had testified to was true and if the painting was by other persons without any participation by Daniels. Receiving the expected affirmative replies, the prosecutor concluded with the witness. It was then 6:15 on Saturday evening.[89] Judge Young announced that court was adjourned until seven on Monday morning, and that the jury was to be kept separate and in custody over the weekend.[90] The first day of trial was over.

It had been a remarkable afternoon. If the jury believed Daniels's testimony, it had enough evidence to convict all of the defendants except Davis. Sharp's speech at the railroad shanties had explained why the Smiths must be killed, aroused the mob to the effort, and sent them on their way. The firebrand Grover had been the first to volunteer and had carried a shotgun to the jail to aid in the killing. As the senior militia officer with the Carthage-bound mob, Aldrich had received the go-ahead message and the assurance of no resistance from the Carthage Greys, and he had communicated it to the mob. Colonel Williams was at the scene of the murder, issuing orders to the attackers. But Browning's cross-examination had exposed some of Daniels's testimony as questionable and had laid a foundation he hoped would bring impeachment by the testimony of defense witnesses. After the first day of the trial apprehensive observers still could not be certain what the final outcome would be.

1. Attachment in court files, *People* v. *Levi Williams; Circuit Court Record,* 276.

2. *Circuit Court Record,* 260, 276; copy of Ford subpoena in case file, *People* v. *Levi Williams;* "Minutes of Trial," 37.

3. *Missouri Republican,* May 27, 1845.

4. Watt Manuscript, 5. The opening arguments are also described briefly in "Minutes of Trial," 37.

5. Watt Manuscript, 6.

6. *Ibid.,* 7.

7. *Ibid.,* 7-8.

8. *Ibid.,* 9.

9. Deputy sheriff's May 21, 1845, certification on attachment for Henry Matthews, in case file, *People* v. *Levi Williams.*

10. Baxter, *Browning,* 11, 51, 288; Doyle, "Josiah Lamborn," 185-200.

11. *People* v. *Brennan,* 15 *Illinois Reports* 511, 517 (1854).

12. "Minutes of Trial," 37.

13. Watt Manuscript, 12; accord, "Minutes of Trial," 38.

14. Watt Manuscript, 11-12; "Documents," 1.

15. John Peyton owned a farm about three miles south of Warsaw. One of the earliest settlers in the county, he had come from Kentucky in 1830. His 2,500 acres made him one of the largest landowners in the county. He was also to become one of the first township supervisors of his area, and to be elected again and again to that position. Gregg, *History of Hancock County,* 648-49, 671; Hancock County Census, 1850, p. 442.

George Walker was also an early settler; he had come to Hancock County from Kentucky in 1833 with his wife and four children, settling on a farm about five miles southeast of Warsaw. The township of Walker was named for him. An ordained Baptist minister, he erected a log church building on his farm at his own expense. At the time of the trial he was an elected justice of the peace, and a few months after the trial he was the unanimously elected candidate for a three-year term as county commissioner. A Democrat, Walker was later elected to two terms in the legislature. Thomas Gregg, county historian, says Walker was "a man of deep religious convictions [and] of sterling integrity" (Gregg, *History of Hancock County,* 350, 450, 971-72; Scofield, *History of Hancock County,* 1102; *Election Returns,* 56:64; Hancock County Census, 1850, p. 295-A).

16. Since there were no completed railroads in Hancock County in 1845, the "railroad shanties" that figure prominently in this narrative were probably structures left over from construction work on the railroad that was to run from Peoria through Macomb to Carthage and thence to Warsaw along the Carthage-Warsaw road. Construction had been halted in 1839 due to lack of funds. Cochran, *History of Hancock County,* 584.

17. Watt Manuscript, 14.

18. *Ibid.,* 13; accord, "Minutes of Trial," 39; "Documents," 2.

19. "Minutes of Trial," 39; accord, Watt Manuscript, 15.

20. Watt Manuscript, 13.

21. *Ibid.,* 14-15; accord, "Minutes of Trial," 39.

22. Watt Manuscript, 16-17; accord, "Documents," 3; "Minutes of Trial," 39.

23. Smith, *History of the Church,* VI, 595.

24. *Ibid.,* 602.

25. Watt Manuscript, 18; "Documents," 3-4; "Minutes of Trial," 41.

26. "Minutes of Trial," 41; accord, Watt Manuscript, 18-19.

27. "Documents," 3; accord, "Minutes of Trial," 41; Watt Manuscript, 17-19.

28. "Minutes of Trial," 41; accord, Watt Manuscript, 19.

29. Hay, "The Mormon Prophet's Tragedy," 669, 675. John Hay had grown up in Warsaw. His father, Charles Hay, was the surgeon of Colonel Levi Williams's regiment of militia. (See "Muster Roll.") John was a boy of seven years when this trial was held. After receiving a legal education, Hay began a law practice in Springfield. There he came to the attention of Abraham Lincoln, who took him to Washington as his private secretary during the war years. After a succession of minor diplomatic and military posts, Hay embarked upon a literary career at about the time this article was published. (Gregg, *History of Hancock County,* 662-63.) He rendered distinguished service in diplomacy, serving as secretary of state from 1898 through 1905.

30. Subpoenas in case file in *People* v. *Levi Williams;* "Minutes of Trial," 42-44; "Documents," 4-6; Watt Manuscript, 19-26. The Watt Manuscript identifies these three witnesses as "Mr. Baldwin," "Lawyer Backman," and "Eli H. Wilson," errors probably attributable to their unfamiliarity to the Mormon scribe.

31. "Minutes of Trial," 44; accord, Watt Manuscript, 25. The Hancock County Census, 1850, p. 272-A, shows that the witness was young.

32. "Minutes of Trial," 42; "Documents," 5. The Watt Manuscript makes no mention of this witness, perhaps because his testimony was meaningless. The witness's age and occupation appear in Hancock County Census, 1850, p. 318-A.

33. "Minutes of Trial," 43; accord, "Documents," 5; Watt Manuscript, 22.

34. "Minutes of Trial," 34-35; Watt Manuscript, 26.

35. Documents in the probate file of Franklin Worrell's estate, filed in the Hancock County Courthouse after his death in the summer of 1845, copied and in possession of Graceland College, Lamoni, Iowa, show that Worrell had $2,287 worth of accounts receivable from over 400 individuals for the sale of shoes, muslin, calico, sugar, peaches, flour, coffee, tobacco, castor oil, Wrights Indian Vegetable Pills (purgative), vegetable balsam, etc.

36. "Minutes of Trial," 34-35; Watt Manuscript, 26.

37. Ford, *History of Illinois,* 368.

38. Snyder, "Forgotten Statesman," 324.

39. Watt Manuscript, 26.

40. *Ibid.;* "Minutes of Trial," 44; "Documents," 6.

41. Ford, *History of Illinois,* 368.

42. "Minutes of Trial," 44. Reliance on the privilege against self-incrimination was rare but not unknown. Just a few years after this trial the Illinois Supreme Court ruled that the privilege would not excuse a person from testifying in a civil case where the feared criminal prosecution was barred by the statute of limitations. *Weldon* v. *Burch,* 12 *Illinois Reports* 373 (1851) (no prior cases cited).

43. "Documents," 6; "Minutes of Trial," 44; accord, Watt Manuscript, 26. A few months after the trial, Thomas C. Sharp published a long account of the testimony at the trial, but he omitted this whole episode of Worrell's recall to the witness stand and his refusal to testify about the use of blank cartridges, even though the event was detailed in the "Documents," which were apparently Sharp's source material. Cf. Sharp, *Trial of the Persons,* 6, 7, with "Documents," 6. Sharp may have omitted the incident because Worrell was dead by that time, or perhaps because the incriminating inferences to be drawn from the episode were discomforting to one who had been a defendant at the trial.

44. Gregg, *History of Hancock County,* 755.

45. Watt Manuscript, 26.

46. "Minutes of Trial," 45; accord, "Documents," 7; Watt Manuscript, 27.

47. "Minutes of Trial," 45; "Documents," 7. In a rare deviation from the general harmony of the three sets of minutes, the Watt Manuscript, 27, attributes this comment to Davis rather than his detractors: "Davis said he would go home, and called them damn cowards, and said they would never elect him Captain again."

48. "Minutes of Trial," 45; "Documents," 8; Watt Manuscript, 28.

49. Watt Manuscript, 29; "Minutes of Trial," 46; "Documents," 8.

50. Watt Manuscript, 30; "Minutes of Trial," 46.

51. "Minutes of Trial," 46; "Documents," 10; Watt Manuscript, 31.

52. In 1882 Littlefield authored a small book, titled *The Martyrs,* that reproduced the content of the Daniels pamphlet. In introducing the Daniels material Littlefield describes it as "an account given by Wm. M. Daniels, which was written out carefully by the author of this volume, and printed in a pamphlet, at Nauvoo." He asserts that Daniels "evinced the fullest sincerity while relating the incidents of his narrative," and "as regards the flash of light described by him, which is illustrated in our engraving, he averred most emphatically that it occurred as related" (Littlefield, *The Martyrs,* 71). Littlefield's authorship of Daniels's booklet is more candidly described in his biographical notes, published in 1888, where he states that the Daniels eyewitness account "was written by me and first published in pamphlet form at Nauvoo. . . ." Lyman Omer Littlefield, *Reminiscences of Latter-day Saints* (Logan: Utah Journal Co., 1888), 172. Littlefield was a long-time member of the Mormon Church. In 1834, as a boy of 15, he had marched to Missouri with "Zion's Camp." In 1843 and 1844 he served short missions for the Church in Alabama, Illinois, and Ohio. (Smith, *History of the Church,* II, 184; V, 347; VI, 339, 485.) In February, 1842, his printing activities apparently went to some excess. Joseph Smith's journal notes that he "plead in an action of slander before the mayor, in behalf of the city, against Lyman O. Littlefield, and obtained judgment of $500 bonds to keep the peace." *Ibid.,* IV, 514.

53. "Minutes of Trial," 47; accord, "Documents," 10; Watt Manuscript, 31.

54. Watt Manuscript, 31-32. Thomas Sharp's publication of the testimony also refers to the possibility that the light could have been a reflection from a musket, but it puts the issue in more emphatic terms: "Possibly it might have been the reflection from the muskets. I was some excited." Sharp, *Trial of the Persons,* 8. The other two sources omit a reference to the musket: "I saw a light, but it was a shorter light than that described in the book, and right at the body of Joseph Smith." "Minutes of Trial," 47; accord, "Documents," 10.

55. "Minutes of Trial," 47; accord, "Documents," 10; Watt Manuscript, 32.

56. "Minutes of Trial," 47.

57. Here is what Daniels, the barrel-maker, was supposed to have written about what he saw and thought in Warsaw as the militia prepared to march toward Nauvoo: "All was commotion and turmoil through Warsaw and its vicinity. The scenery had become insipid and irksome to me, and I longed for relief and [to] be where my mind could be at rest. Passing through such continual bustle, watching the movements of the rabble, who, like a horde of impetuous barbarians, seemed impelled on, by the blind infatuation of priests and shallow zealots, in hopes of booty, disgusted and sickened me and fired me with contempt. My mind reverted to the time when the dark and bloody Attila led on the ignorant Huns to conquest, plunder and extermination, applying the torch of conflagration to pleasant villages and sequestred [*sic*] homes." Daniels, *Correct Account,* 6.

58. "Minutes of Trial," 47-49, 51; "Documents," 11-13, 15; Watt Manuscript, 32-36.

59. "Minutes of Trial," 48; accord, Watt Manuscript, 35.

60. "Minutes of Trial," 48; accord, "Documents," 12. "The facts I stated to Littlefield [but] the composition is his," Daniels explained a few minutes later, adding, however, that "there is some mistake about the light as I have already explained." "Minutes of Trial," 49.

61. "Minutes of Trial," 50; accord, "Documents," 14; Watt Manuscript, 36.

62. "Documents," 13; accord, "Minutes of Trial," 50; Watt Manuscript, 36. When Sharp published his account of the trial from the "Documents," he altered this portion to dilute the evidence of his own involvement: "He spoke of the necessity of killing the Smiths, or I took it in that sense. I understood him to advise killing the Smiths." Sharp, *Trial of the Persons*, 9.

63. "Documents," 14; "Minutes of Trial," 50; Watt Manuscript, 37.

64. As quoted in "Minutes of Trial," 50-51. This passage appears in Daniels, *Correct Account*, 9.

65. "Minutes of Trial," 50; accord, "Documents," 14.

66. Quoted in Baxter, *Browning*, 52.

67. "Minutes of Trial," 50; "Documents," 14.

68. "Minutes of Trial," 52; "Documents," 16; Watt Manuscript, 38.

69. "Minutes of Trial," 52; accord, "Documents," 16.

70. Watt Manuscript, 39; accord, "Documents," 16; "Minutes of Trial," 52. The Watt Manuscript attributes this shooting to Wills, who was shot in the arm, but the other two sources name Voras or Voorhees, who was slightly wounded in the shoulder. The Watt Manuscript says that one man was "hurt in the leg."

71. "Documents," 16; "Minutes of Trial," 52.

72. "Minutes of Trial," 52. The passage in question is Daniels, *Correct Account*, 11.

73. "Minutes of Trial," 52; Watt Manuscript, 39-40.

74. "Minutes of Trial," 52-53; accord, Watt Manuscript, 40. The quoted statement appears in Daniels, *Correct Account*, 14.

75. Watt Manuscript, 40. Note that the text passage is quoted from the Mormon source. The other two sources are in general accord with this account, with these differences on the specific description of the light. The "Minutes of Trial," 53, contains this summary: "The light looked just like a flash right there, just like a flash of lightening, and it disappeared again immediately — it was a flash right by his body rather to one side." The "Documents," 17, refer to this briefly, saying: "The light was like a flash poping [*sic*] by his body."

76. Watt Manuscript, 41.

77. "Minutes of Trial," 53; accord, Watt Manuscript, 41.

78. *Ibid.* In its brief reference to this testimony, "Documents," 17, refers to them as "wounded men."

79. "Minutes of Trial," 53; "Documents," 18; Watt Manuscript, 41.

80. "Minutes of Trial," 51; "Documents," 15; Watt Manuscript, 38.

81. Watt Manuscript, 42.

82. "Minutes of Trial," 54; "Documents," 18; accord, Watt Manuscript, 42. In what may have been an effort to discredit, Sharp omitted the words "but not by the Mormons" in his published account (Sharp, *Trial of the Persons*, 12), though the words appear in both the "Documents" and the "Minutes of Trial," which were probably his source material. But these words are also missing from the account in the Mormon source (Watt Manuscript, 42).

83. "Minutes of Trial," 54; Watt Manuscript, 42-43; accord, "Documents," 18.

84. "Minutes of Trial," 54; accord, "Documents," 19; Watt Manuscript, 43.

85. "Documents," 19; "Minutes of Trial," 54; accord, Watt Manuscript, 43-44.

86. "Documents," 20; "Minutes of Trial," 54; accord, Watt Manuscript, 44.

87. "Minutes of Trial," 54; accord, "Documents," 20; Watt Manuscript, 44.

88. "Documents," 21; accord, "Minutes of Trial," 54. The Watt Manuscript, 45, gives a slightly different and less damning account: "Did you give instructions to the painters [about the light]?" "Nobody told them about it. I told them when exhibiting it that the light was wrong."

89. "Minutes of Trial," 54.

90. *Circuit Court Record*, 277.

∞ 9 ∞

"Suppositions Ought Not to Hang Anyone"

Saturday evening and Sunday offered the court participants their first leisure in a week. The extraordinary evening court sessions had disrupted the socializing that normally broke the drudgery for the circuit riders, so a diversion was particularly welcome. The jury was compelled to spend the long, hot, idle hours of Sunday in close confinement under the watchful eye of the deputies, but the judge and lawyers made companionable association in the Hamilton House. The masters at drinking, story-telling, and other merriment were Dick Richardson and Archie Williams. Only Browning and Lamborn remained distant. Lamborn was isolated by the unpopularity of his cause and by his gloomy, foreboding manner. Browning's aloof personality, religious austerity, and abstinence from alcohol kept him from mingling easily with the crowd. Browning passed his Sunday with the Bible; Lamborn spent his with a bottle.

Court convened at seven on Monday morning, but Judge Young had to give initial attention to some civil cases, so it was nine o'clock before the jury filed into the courtroom and the murder case resumed.[1] Four prosecution witnesses testified before noon. The first two were Thomas L. Barnes, a thirty-three-year-old Carthage physician, and John Wilson, a forty-nine-year-old tavernkeeper who was captain of a ranger company in the militia.[2] These two men had been part of a group of three or four who rode out of Carthage at about three o'clock on the day of the murder to maintain a lookout on some high ground about four miles north. They were mostly watching in the direction of Nauvoo because, as Barnes told the jury, "it was expected that the Mormons would come up to rescue the Smiths that evening."[3] From their vantage point during three or four hours they saw several groups of men about a half-mile apart, "like distinct companies," coming to Carthage on the road from Warsaw and then leaving by the same way. "Did Barnes and Morrison know what that meant?" Lamborn asked Wilson. "They thought it was a company to exterminate the Mormons," was the witness's significant reply.[4]

Lamborn pressed both witnesses as to what they had observed in Carthage before they left at three. Barnes admitted that he had seen Aldrich, Sharp, and Williams in Carthage at this time, but when Lamborn pursued this subject he denied seeing any of them talking to Captain R. F. Smith or to any of the guards at the jail. Lamborn asked whether the witness knew of any conspiracy or understanding to kill the Smiths that evening. "I may have supposed something," Barnes replied, "but my suppositions ought not to hang anyone."[5] The jury was not to hear what Barnes supposed, but it was probably what he revealed many years later when he wrote his daughter that the mob had an "understanding" with some of the citizens of Carthage who were "partey to the hole matter." One of the guards later told him that they fired blank cartridges over the heads of the mob.[6]

Wilson was even more reluctant to testify. When Lamborn asked him if he had ever "heard any of these defendants say anything about a conspiracy to murder the Smiths," Wilson replied: "I did not want to hear anything, and would not have heard it if they had wanted to tell me." As if that were not sufficient evidence of this witness's attitude toward the Mormons, Wilson spiced his testimony by referring to the Mormons as "hell-hounds" and by declaring that he had "wanted them exterminated and do yet."[7]

Lamborn got a little helpful evidence from Thomas Dixon, a fifty-three-year-old Pennsylvania-born farmer from Dallas Township in the northern part of the county.[8] Dixon, who had been a witness before the grand jury, testified that he had seen Thomas Sharp in Carthage at about ten or eleven o'clock in the morning on the day of the murder. That afternoon, as he was riding out of Carthage for home, Dixon saw the sun glistening on the guns of a group of men approaching Carthage from the west. He turned back, left his horse at Hamilton's, and ran for the jail. On the way he saw Colonel Williams walking north across the courthouse square. Arriving at the jail just ahead of the armed mob, Dixon stood at the southeast corner and saw the same events that other witnesses had described. After a few of the guards fired, some of the attackers wrestled them to the ground, where they lay until after the Smiths were killed. Although the Greys had a shorter distance to march from their tents than Dixon had to run from Hamilton's Tavern, they still did not arrive until after the mob departed. When Dixon first saw them, they had halted along the way, some distance from the jail. Dixon told the jury that he knew Aldrich, Davis, Sharp, and Williams by sight, but he insisted that he had not seen any of them at the jail. In fact, although he had lived in the county for ten or eleven years and knew a good many of its citizens, he didn't see anyone he knew at the jail except the guards.[9]

Browning's cross-examination of this witness elicited some important testimony on the controverted circumstances involving Joseph Smith's plunge out of the window and his alleged firing-squad execution at the well curb:

Q: Did you see Smith fall out of the window?

A: Yes.

Q: Had he been shot before he fell out of the window?

A: He was shot or hurt some little for when he first came into the window there was blood on his pantaloons.

Q: Did you see him set up against the well curb?

A: I saw him raise up himself against the well curb and die immediately.

Q: Did you see four men shoot him?

A: No.

Q: Did you see anything about a marvalous [*sic*] light?

A: No.

Q: Did you see four men parallized [*sic*]?

A: No.

Q: Did you occupy a possition [*sic*] from which you could see him plainly?

A: He was about 10 steps from me [as] I stood on the southeast corner of the jail.

Q: How long did he hang before he fell?

A: He hung but a short time.

Q: What was his position in the window?

A: His head was out, right arm, and one leg.[10]

Having been conspicuously unsuccessful in trying to buttress his case from the testimony of witnesses who had been in Carthage around the time of the murder, Lamborn next elected to make another try with a witness from the Warsaw militia. Eli Walker, a well-to-do middle-aged farmer,[11] had marched with the militia from Warsaw to the railroad shanties. Lamborn obviously wanted this witness to supply the missing details and precise conversation that took place at the shanties. His hopes were in vain; despite searching questioning, Eli Walker was "unsure" or "could not recall" when questioned about any subject that might have incriminated any of the defendants. In contrast, he had a clear recollection of information that exonerated himself and defendant Davis. Thus he testified that soon after Colonel Williams read the disbanding order, Captain Davis had called for "all that were in favor of going to Warsaw and eating dinner at the tavern to come on."[12] Walker, Davis, and others thereupon returned to Warsaw.

On the potentially incriminating subjects, Walker admitted that he had heard some person at the shanties say "that he would blow the jail to hell," but he insisted that he did not know who it was.[13] He said he "heard a call made for volunteers," but he couldn't say who made it. He admitted Sharp was at the shanties, but said he did not recollect hearing him make a speech. He said he "might have" heard someone speak of going to Carthage, but he couldn't recollect who it was.[14] He admitted that someone spoke to the troops while they were still in ranks, declaring "that those who would go to Carthage should advance some paces in front," but he testified that he couldn't say who said it. He said he heard Colonel Williams say something about raising volunteers, but he couldn't recollect "whether he was in favor or against it."[15] He testified that he was "not prepared to say what number volunteered." Finally, after a series of questions concerning what Colonel Williams had said about volunteering, the frustrated Lamborn asked Walker: "Are you willing to say that you do not recollect anything he said?" "No," the witness replied cagily, "but I do not recollect it sufficiently to state what it was."[16]

It was perfectly apparent that Walker knew more than he told. His unwillingness to incriminate his fellow citizens is apparent in his sworn testimony that "It would be impossible for me to tell what I heard that day."[17] The farmer had been more than a match for Lamborn, who gave up in disgust. There was no cross-examination.

When court resumed at two o'clock, Lamborn called his second key witness of the trial. His morning witnesses had provided very little helpful testimony, their principal effect being to reinforce the impression that many responsible Hancock citizens who had not participated in the murder were nevertheless involved to the extent of being unwilling to give testimony against those who had. The prosecution could not afford to have the jury further infected by that impression, and Lamborn sought to counteract it with the testimony of a witness who had not appeared before the grand jury.

Eliza Jane Graham was a thirty-three-year-old Mormon[18] from Nauvoo. Her appearance was a surprise to many; Lamborn himself had become aware of her knowledge of events only a few days before. As the defense and the crowd regarded Eliza with apprehension and hostility, this lone Mormon woman probably looked on them with a fear bordering on panic. Lamborn must have done his best to put her at ease, inviting her to ignore the courtroom crowd and speak directly to the jury.

In response to Lamborn's encouragement Miss Graham told the jury about her employment in the Warsaw House, a tavern then being managed by a Mrs. Fleming, her aunt. Just before dark on the day the Smiths were murdered, Thomas Sharp and James Gregg arrived at the tavern in a two-horse carriage. Sharp came into the hallway and asked for a glass of water. He said he had come from Carthage in less than an hour, and he was very dry. Mrs. Fleming met him in the hall and asked him "how they came on at Carthage." Lamborn directed the witness to repeat his reply. "He said, 'We have finished the leading men of the Mormon Church.' "[19]

Eliza Graham testified that both Davis and Grover boarded at Fleming's, but neither had been there for supper that evening. At about midnight they came in together and said they wanted supper for about twenty men, but before the last of the men were served there were about sixty. She said that all talked openly about the events of the day. Lamborn asked her to relate their conversation to the jury. "Someone said he had killed Old Jo," Eliza replied, but another man insisted that "he had killed him." She testified that she heard Grover say "he had killed Old Jo," and Davis say "they had finished the men."[20] It was "general talk amongst the crowd" that they had killed the Smiths.[21] All around the house men were rejoicing and bragging about their work. At about two in the morning some of the men went upstairs to bed and others stood guard.

Eliza testified that she had seen two injured men that evening, one wounded slightly on the cheek and the other in the arm. The one with the face wound was a youth of fourteen or fifteen whom she did not know. The man with the wound on his arm was brought into the kitchen by Grover, who got Mrs. Fleming's permission for him to sit by the stove for about an hour. Eliza said his name was William Voras, and that he lived at Bear Creek. She said she did not hear anyone say how he came to be wounded.[22]

Lamborn was obviously well pleased with this testimony. To drive it home to the jury, he concluded his direct examination by having Eliza repeat the parts that had been most incriminating of defendants Sharp, Davis, and Grover. In response, she testified that Davis and Sharp had said, "we have finished the leading men of the Mormon Church,"[23] and "Grover and all the rest talked in the same way."[24]

Eliza Graham's testimony was seriously incriminatory of Sharp and Grover, and it was the first evidence of any sort against Davis. Consequently, it is not surprising that Browning conducted a lengthy cross-examination for the defense. Browning saw all women on a pedestal; as he approached the awkward task of publicly challenging Eliza Graham's testimony, he may have thought of his own beloved Eliza. Tall and portly, Browning's Kentucky-born Eliza was not a beautiful woman, but she was an intelligent, cultivated person who enjoyed life, won friends easily, and made him an ideal wife. Like some other southern women of this period, Browning's Eliza enjoyed puffing on a pipe and drinking "mint slings," in striking contrast to her Puritan husband. But Browning was devoted to his wife, and he wrote to her with the deepest affection at each separation.[25]

Browning's initial questions gave Graham an opportunity to testify that she supposed Sharp referred to killing the Smiths because the Smiths were the leading men in the Mormon Church. She had often heard Sharp threaten that he would kill the Smiths, most recently that morning at Fleming's before he started for Carthage in his carriage. Next he secured her admission that Sharp lived almost across the street from Fleming's, and that as he came from Carthage he had to pass his own home to get to the tavern.[26] Eliza seemed unaware that this part of Browning's cross-examination was inviting the jury to consider the improbability of Sharp's driving his carriage past his own home to the tavern for no apparent purpose other than to ask for a drink of water and make an incriminating admission.

Browning next turned to the witness's testimony regarding Davis and Grover. Eliza said that about half of the men in the dining room were claiming to have killed the Smiths. "One would say, 'I killed Old Jo,' [and] another would say 'No, you did not, I did.' "[27] But despite the fact that most of these men lived in Warsaw and the vicinity, Eliza claimed she did not recall the name of a single person who said he killed "Old Jo" except Grover. What about Davis? When Davis arrived, he said, "We have finished the men."[28] Why had she paid such close attention to what these two said? "Because I had no idea they would have done any such thing," Eliza replied, but then she was quickly forced to admit that she didn't think the others would have done it either.[29] In truth, the witness could not give a sufficient reason why she had paid such close attention to the statements of the defendants. With this line of questioning, Browning made this part of the witness's testimony seem like a recent fabrication.

Browning's next tactic was to draw from the witness's own lips an admission that she had earlier confessed that she knew nothing about the case. After close questioning Eliza acknowledged that she had made such a statement at Quincy, but denied that she said this in the presence of Warren and Reynolds. She explained her later denials on the basis that "I always denied it while I was in Warsaw because I was afraid of being called as a witness." Probing further, Browning asked her who had heard her denial in Warsaw. Flustered under close questioning, she replied, "I did not deny it to anyone in Warsaw because the question was never asked me and I had no occasion to deny it."[30]

As he drew toward the close of his cross-examination, Browning bore down harder on the witness. His questions jumped back and forth across the details of her testimony, probing for inconsistencies or improbable or embarrassing circumstances. He also sought to capitalize on the fact that the witness was a Mormon, implying that her willingness to testify and her incriminating recollections about Davis and Grover were prompted by her associations in Nauvoo.

Despite her fatigue and fear, however, Eliza held her ground. She testified that about six weeks after the murder she went to live with her parents in Nauvoo, where she had resided since that time. She admitted that she had stopped denying any knowledge about the killing when she went to live in Nauvoo, explaining that this was because she had no further idea she would be called as a witness. She had not heard she was to be a witness "until last Wednesday." Since that time she had discussed her testimony only with Lamborn. Hoping to catch the prosecutor in some impropriety in the preparation of his witness, Browning asked her what the gentleman had told her. "He told me to tell the truth," the witness responded, "and to tell all that I knew about it."[31]

Having gotten nowhere with that line of questioning, Browning came to his final point of inquiry — the witness's membership in the Mormon Church. Yes, she was a member, having joined the Church about five years ago. No, she did not know Littlefield, Judge Phelps, Mr. Taylor, Brigham Young, or any of the Twelve, except by sight, and she had had no conversations with them about the case. She knew the widows of Joseph and Hyrum Smith by sight, but was not acquainted with either of them.[32] Apparently unable to make anything favorable out of this testimony, Browning announced that he had no further questions. The ordeal of Eliza Jane Graham was over, and she stepped down from the witness stand.

Eliza Graham's testimony had given the participants much to ponder. If believed, the admissions of Sharp, Grover, and Davis were highly incriminatory. The cross-examination had cast doubt on the credibility of the witness's selective recollection of the Davis and Grover statements and the probability of Sharp's admission, but the testimony had at least placed these three defendants among a group of men who were bragging that they had killed the Smiths — a point upon which Lamborn might build a case with the help of subsequent testimony.

It was 4:15 P.M. when Miss Graham concluded her testimony.[33] Some judges would have found that a convenient time to adjourn for the day, but this lengthy trial had already used more than its share of the twelve days of court time which the fifth circuit allotted to the spring term in Hancock County. Despite the heat and the inevitable restlessness in the courtroom crowd, Judge Young signaled for Lamborn to call his next witness. If any spectator was hoping for brevity as he sat cramped on the hard wooden benches, he was to be disappointed. The next witness was the third of Lamborn's key witnesses, and his testimony was not to conclude until four hours later, well into the evening.

Lamborn's final witness on this second day of trial was Benjamin Brackenbury, an eighteen-year-old who had driven a baggage wagon with Captain Davis's company of Warsaw militia. Though not a Mormon himself, Brackenbury lived in Nauvoo with his mother and stepfather, Jabez Durfee, who were Mormons. Like Daniels, this young man was well known to everyone in the courtroom. His alleged perjury in his testimony to the grand jury had touched off his pre-trial arrest and release on habeas corpus, amid charges that the defense was trying to intimidate or kill him. The grand jury had recently refused to indict him for perjury. Now he would serve as the last key witness for the prosecution.

Lamborn's first few questions caused Brackenbury to relate the now familiar details about how three companies of militia (Davis's, Grover's, and a third from Green Plains) had been disbanded at the railroad shanties after their morning march from Warsaw. All five of the defendants were present at this time. Unlike some of the other witnesses, however, Brackenbury testified that he had not heard any speeches, and that he heard nothing about killing the Smiths. Brackenbury said Grover had called for volunteers "to go to Carthage to see the Gov[ernor]" to ask him why he had dismissed the men "with public arms in their hands."[34] Some of the troops then returned to Warsaw, but Brackenbury and others came on toward Carthage. Someone told the witness they were going to take the

Smiths to Missouri and hang them, which was the first he knew that the group had any such object in view. A man in a Carthage Grey uniform met the group on the way to Carthage and gave Aldrich a letter. After Aldrich read the letter, he instructed the troops to spread out "a little apart" as they went into the town. Like Daniels, Brackenbury next related how the troops turned off the road into the timber about three or four miles from Carthage, apparently seeking cover for their final approach to the town. The baggage wagons, including Brackenbury's, continued on the road.[35]

Brackenbury said he saw Aldrich, Grover, Sharp, and Williams at the point where the troops left the wagons. Lamborn inquired whether he had seen Davis in or near Carthage, probably knowing that Brackenbury was going to add some significant evidence linking Davis with the crime. Yes, the witness responded, when he was within a half-mile of the jail Davis and several other men overtook and passed him in a lumber wagon. Brackenbury continued on until he was about a quarter-mile southwest of the jail, where he remained in his wagon during the shooting.[36]

The men who came back from the jail were running. "They said they had killed the Smiths," Brackenbury told the jury. The first one he heard was a man named Gregg from Warsaw.[37] Lamborn asked if Grover was among them. "Yes." Did he say anything? "Yes, he said he had killed Smith, that Smith was a damned stout man, that he had went into the room where Smith was, and that Smith had struck him twice in the face. Grover said he was the first man that went into the house."[38]

The group then made their way back toward Warsaw. On the way Brackenbury saw Wills, Voras, and Gallaher. Voras was wounded in the shoulder, Wills in the arm, and Gallaher in the face ("in the cheek, like as if a ball had taken the skin off").[39] He also saw Aldrich, Sharp, and Williams, who passed his wagon on horseback about a half-mile west of Carthage. He didn't hear them say anything about the event. When he arrived in Warsaw, some of the group had gotten there first and were crowded around the Warsaw House; others were still coming.[40]

Obviously satisfied, Lamborn elected to terminate his direct examination. Brackenbury's testimony was of great importance. He was the first witness to place defendant Davis in the vicinity of the jail, he had corroborated Daniels's testimony about Aldrich and the Carthage-bound mob receiving a message from the Carthage Greys, and he had also corroborated Daniels's statement that Grover was a direct participant in the shooting. He had reinforced earlier testimony about the identity of the mob by tracing them from Warsaw to the shanties, to the Carthage jail, and thence back to Warsaw, showing also that defendants Aldrich, Sharp, and Williams, who accompanied the troops to Carthage, had returned with them. Finally, he had corroborated Eliza Graham's testimony about the mob's return to the Warsaw House and the men who were wounded on shoulder, arm, and face.

Browning's lengthy cross-examination of this witness was a mixture of success and failure. His attempt to shake the content of Brackenbury's testimony was unsuccessful, resulting only in the addition of vivid details to the incriminating evidence against the defendants. But his attack upon Brackenbury's personal credibility was effective in raising doubts, and he also laid a foundation for later impeachment.

One of Browning's first questions backfired, producing additional incriminatory evidence on some important subjects. In an apparent effort to have Brackenbury contradict Daniels, Browning asked whether Aldrich read the Carthage Grey's note to the men. "No," Brackenbury responded, but the messenger had spoken to the men. "Now is the time to rush on," he said, "the Governor is gone to Nauvoo and there is nobody in Carthage but what you can put dependence in."[41] Though apparently caught off guard by this unexpected corroboration of the conspiracy, Browning was nevertheless able to draw the force of the testimony somewhat by getting Brackenbury to admit that he was about fifty yards away when this was said in a conversational tone, and that he would not recognize the Grey if he saw him again.

Brackenbury next made a damaging concession. Under Browning's persistent questioning he admitted: "I had something to drink that day and had taken enough to make me feel nice."[42] Browning returned and exploited that subject a few minutes later when the witness explained that he could not recall how one of the defendants was dressed on that day. Brackenbury admitted that "my recollection is not very distinct of the events of that day,"[43] and "I should have remembered things better if I had not felt so [nice]."[44]

Browning scored a temporary advantage by getting Brackenbury to admit that he had not seen Grover go to the jail. But the young witness soon incriminated Grover anyway by testifying that he did see a man at the jail who appeared to be hunting something, and when Grover came up to his wagon, "he said it was him hunting his gun, a double barrel shot gun."[45] Browning also erred by giving the witness sufficient latitude to incriminate Grover further with this testimony: "When Grover got into my wagon he was talking to Mr. Williams about killing the Smiths. Grover told some one in the wagon that he was the first man who went into the jail and that Jo Smith struck him twice in the face."[46] Again, Browning partially discredited this testimony by having the witness admit that it was strange that Smith, who had been armed with a pistol, would strike Grover in the face instead of shooting him.

The cross-examination was successful in exonerating Davis from the incriminating effect of the earlier direct examination. Under Browning's questioning Brackenbury explained that the wagon with Davis and five or six others that passed him in sight of the jail "did not go to the jail at all," but stopped after a short ways.[47]

Browning's cross-examination also included a number of leading questions about whether the witness had made various statements to the grand jury, an obvious foundation for later impeachment. Brackenbury denied telling the grand jury that the messenger from the Carthage Greys had taken Colonel Williams and Henry Stephens to one side and spoken to them, denied saying that he saw Colonel Williams sitting on his horse at the jail during the entire time the men were there, and denied saying that Sharp had said as he passed his wagon that the Smiths were dead for he had hold of one of them.[48]

Browning now inquired about the witness's personal life. Brackenbury said he had resided in Nauvoo for six years. What business did he follow? "Loafering," the witness answered. How long had he done that, Browning inquired, obviously enjoying the effect these answers would have on a jury of hard-working farmers. "The most of this winter," the witness replied. When did he commence that trade? "A little before last court here."[49] Browning clinched this effort by leading the witness into admitting that he had boarded at Mr. Deming's at the last term of court and did not know who paid for his board, thus raising a question in the jury's mind as to whether Brackenbury had been paid for his testimony.

Browning concluded his cross-examination by asking the witness whether he had ever said that he would leave Nauvoo if they did not feed and clothe him. He denied this, but admitted that he did "complain of their treating Daniels better than me."[50] Satisfied that he could not end on a more favorable note, Browning announced that he had no further questions and sank wearily into his chair.

Apparently attempting to rehabilitate his witness from the discrediting effect of the last series of replies, Lamborn conducted a brief redirect examination. Although Brackenbury admitted that he did not know who paid for his board at Deming's, he solemnly testified that "I was never offered or paid anything for swearing here."[51] The witness was then allowed to step down. It was 8:30 P.M. After cautioning that the jury should again be kept separate, Judge Young adjourned court until seven Tuesday morning.[52]

Though it would not be announced formally until an hour after court convened Tuesday morning, the jury had now heard virtually all of the prosecution's case. All that remained was the brief reappearance of two previous witnesses. Canfield Hamilton came back at his own request to correct an inadvertent but minor error in a date cited in his prior testimony. While he was on the witness stand, Lamborn got him to admit that he thought he had seen Sharp in conversation with Governor Ford in Carthage on the morning of the day the Smiths were killed.[53]

Lamborn next called Franklin Worrell for his third appearance on the witness stand. Browning again opposed, but the judge allowed the testimony after Lamborn pleaded that he "had been disappointed in the getting of his witnesses."[54] Under questioning, Worrell testified that he thought he saw Sharp in Carthage at about eight in the morning on the day the Smiths were killed. But he denied knowing anything about any Carthage Grey or anyone else being sent out as a messenger that day.[55]

When Worrell stepped down from the witness stand at 8:15 Tuesday morning, Lamborn announced that he had no further witnesses. The prosecution's case was over, and Judge Young declared a one-hour adjournment.[56]

Here was a time for judge and jury to reflect on the strengths and weaknesses of the prosecution's case. If the case had gone to the jury at this point, and if the jury had believed the prosecution witnesses, there was sufficient evidence to convict Aldrich, Grover, Sharp, and Williams, but not Davis. Concerning the first count of the indictment, which charged that each of the defendants had personally shot Joseph, there was no evidence whatever that Aldrich, Davis, Sharp, or Williams had fired a gun at the jail. But there was evidence of Grover's guilt under this count — Daniels and Brackenbury had seen him at the jail with a gun, and Brackenbury quoted him as admitting immediately after the shooting that "he was the first man that went into the house" and that "he had killed Smith." Graham corroborated the later admission.

All of the defendants except Davis[57] could be found guilty of murder on the second count, which charged that the person or persons who shot Joseph Smith did so pursuant to a conspiracy or common design in which each of these defendants had participated. The mosaic of conspiracy was assembled in sufficient clarity to include Aldrich, Grover, Sharp, and Williams in the picture. The mob that killed Joseph and Hyrum Smith had been traced from the militia's bivouac outside Warsaw, north to where they were dismissed at the railroad shanties, east across the prairie to Carthage, and then back to Warsaw, where they took their midnight supper at the Warsaw House. Williams, Aldrich, and Grover commanded various units in this militia. Numerous witnesses agreed that these three and Sharp were present when the disbanding order was read, and that about a hundred of the disbanded militiamen were then persuaded to go to Carthage, rather than to return to their homes in and around Warsaw. Peyton and Walker testified that Aldrich and Williams called for volunteers to go to Carthage. Sharp, who had been in Carthage that morning according to Dixon, Worrell, and Hamilton, had joined the troops by this time. Peyton, Walker, and several other witnesses testified that Sharp gave a speech in favor of going to Carthage. Daniels said that Sharp spoke of "the necessity of killing the Smiths." Other witnesses were less specific on this subject, but several agreed that he sought to arouse the troops and send them to Carthage. Even some witnesses who were evasive on the exact purpose of the proposed ten-mile walk to Carthage agreed that it was associated with the mob's grievances against the Mormons and their hatred of Joseph Smith.

Daniels said that Captain Grover was the first to volunteer, and that he said he would go alone if no one else would go. Numerous witnesses agreed that about a hundred men started for Carthage, including Aldrich, Grover, Sharp, and Williams. Several witnesses saw them in Carthage around three o'clock, and just before and just after the five o'clock shooting at the jail. There was little evidence of what these leaders actually did in Carthage prior to the mob's arrival at the jail, except such as could be inferred in the circumstances. Daniels and Brackenbury both testified that a man in the uniform of the Carthage Greys met the mob about four miles west of Carthage and gave them a message that this was a good time to murder the Smiths, since all was arranged and the guards would not resist. Aldrich was present with the militiamen when this message was read, and the other three defendants were also seen there at about this time.

During the shooting two witnesses saw Grover at the jail with a gun. Williams was there also, according to several witnesses, but he was standing by observing the scene, though Daniels said that he shouted orders to the attackers. The sentries at the jail were totally ineffectual. When the shooting commenced, the reserve companies of guards marched deliberately to the jail, some seven hundred yards, arriving after the mob departed. They made no pursuit. After the shooting the men ran past Brackenbury's wagon, saying they had killed the Smiths. He heard Grover brag that "he had killed Smith."

That night in Warsaw Eliza Graham heard Sharp say, "We have finished the leading men of the Mormon Church." The wounded men whom Brackenbury saw coming from the jail came back to the Warsaw House, where, according to Eliza, Grover was caring for one of them. At the midnight supper Eliza heard members of the group, including Grover, bragging about killing the Smiths.

The mob had not acted spontaneously. Aldrich, Grover, Sharp, and Williams were the acknowledged leaders of these men — a leadership confirmed as to this specific deed by the speeches and actions at the railroad shanties, which had aroused the disbanded militiamen and sent them toward the Carthage jail. Sharp's presence in Carthage that morning, his appearance at the shanties where the troops were disbanded, his return to Carthage with the other leaders, the timely message to Aldrich from the Carthage Greys, and the subsequent behavior of the jail guards and the larger contingent of Carthage Greys suggest that Sharp and Williams were in Carthage preparing the way for the mob. Sharp's admission that evening at the Warsaw House confirms this interpretation.

Although there was probably sufficient evidence to convict four defendants at the conclusion of the prosecution's case, the three key prosecution witnesses had been somewhat discredited by the cross-examination, and there was promise of a thorough-going impeachment effort during the presentation of the defense. The prosecution's case was insecure, and more evidence would obviously have been desirable. Why didn't the prosecution provide more evidence?

There was nothing in Josiah Lamborn's style to lead one to conclude that he was a merciful, indifferent, or indolent prosecutor. He was not backward when it came to pouring in all the evidence at his command. His tendency was rather to err on the side of excessive zeal or even downright unscrupulousness. These tendencies had been evident in a celebrated trial in Springfield in which Lamborn prosecuted two brothers named Traylor for the murder of an old man named Fisher. Although Fisher's body had not been found, he was generally believed to be dead. When last seen, he was in the company of the Traylors. In a private conference Lamborn convinced one of the Traylors, who was said to be somewhat weak-minded, that the only way to save his life was to make a full confession. He did so, giving the particulars of a killing and subsequent robbery. Using this confession and a wealth of other circumstantial evidence, Lamborn built a case that pointed unmistakably to the conclusion that the defendants had murdered the missing man. Even though the Traylors had previously been regarded as good and reputable men, the citizens of Springfield were persuaded of their guilt. As Lamborn's vindictive denunciation of the defendants concluded, it appeared that he had his victory and that the Traylors would hang. At that dramatic moment the defense counsel, E. D. Baker and Stephen T. Logan, announced that the defense would have but one witness. The door to the courtroom opened, and in walked Fisher, the supposed victim. The crowd's angry reaction against Lamborn was almost uncontrollable, and if it had not been for the saving efforts of Baker and Logan, Lamborn might have been lynched on the spot.[58]

It would obviously have been desirable for Lamborn to have had more witnesses and to have drawn out and exploited his witnesses's testimony more effectively. Nevertheless, the prosecutor's preparation may have met the standards of that day, at least as related to routine criminal cases. Abraham Lincoln, one of the most successful Illinois trial lawyers of this period, apparently did not go over his witnesses's testimony before putting them on the stand — in fact, he is said to have gone into his trials without any advance preparation.[59] This pattern of spontaneous rather than advance trial preparation was probably a consequence of the circuit system, in which lawyers often had to be engaged and cases put to trial within a few hours after the legal caravan rode into the county seat. In contrast, three successive prosecutors (McConnell, Elliot, and Lamborn) had spent almost a year seeking to locate and assure the appearance of prosecution witnesses in this case.

It is possible to identify additional evidence that the prosecution could have used to strengthen its case. In an address to the public in the *Warsaw Signal* Thomas Sharp had defended the murders committed two weeks earlier as a justifiable "execution" that had been advocated by "some of our most respectable citizens." Sharp wrote that "our citizens have regretted and still regret the necessity that existed for taking the law in this particular instance, into their hands," but he argued that this course "was inevitable, and the only question was as to the proper time." Apparently including himself among those responsible for the decision, Sharp reviewed the anti-Mormon's grievances against the Mormon leaders and asked:

> Should we have laid quietly down, and suffer [sic] the tyrant to rivet the chains that had already galled us to madness. . . . No man through whose veins courses one drop of that noble blood which prompted our forefathers to throw off the yoke of British oppression, will ask his fellow freemen to kneel at the nod of any tyrant, nor condemn him for asserting his liberty, even if in so doing he is obliged to commit a daring violation of law.

There was no charge here that the act was done by Missourians. Referring to reports that all the troops had been disbanded "except four small companies," Sharp wrote: "It is certain that these troops were highly dissatisfied — that they thought the Governor had trifled with them — that they thought furthermore, that the evils under which they were laboring, had not been reached, and could only be removed in one of two ways: either by expelling the body of the Mormons, or by cutting off their leaders." Asserting general agreement that the Smiths deserved death, Sharp declared that the only questions were as to the appropriateness of "the time and manner." Reminding his readers of the likelihood that the Mormon leaders would otherwise have escaped any penalty, Sharp concluded, "we plead the necessity of the case."[60] Such implied and expressed admissions further implicated Sharp at least, and could also have been used to reinforce the prosecution's other evidence of conspiracy.

In addition, there were other witnesses who might have provided valuable testimony for the prosecution; foremost among them were Worrell's fellow guards at the jail. But in most instances the additional prosecution witnesses may have been unavailable as a practical matter. For instance, subpoenas were out for Levi Street and William Baldwin, who were among the guards at the jail, but deputies reported that they were unable to locate them.[61] We know nothing of the three or four other jail guards whom Lamborn neglected to have Worrell identify. Also sought as witnesses were John Morrison, Warsaw militiaman William Houck, and Henry Stephens, a Warsaw lawyer who was the adjutant of Major Aldrich's Warsaw battalion. Writs of attachment were issued for these three men, but none could be found.[62] Henry Mattias or Mathews, who had willingly given important testimony before the grand jury in October, was arrested on May 21 on a writ of attachment issued in December. But, as already indicated, he was not brought into court as a witness because, the deputy reported, he "resisted with deadly weapons and thus escaped my custody."[63] The list of attachments issued in December also included the name of John Taylor, who had originally signed the criminal complaint upon which this prosecution was based. He was never served because he and other Mormon leaders hid from the deputies who were trying to arrest them and take them to Carthage to testify. Mormon records contain the name of at least one witness who was willing to testify about events at the jail,[64] but he apparently was not called.

In the months preceding trial the prosecution's attachments and subpoenas had gone out across the state, and many were successful. During the winter Governor Ford was served with a subpoena in Springfield, and William Daniels received one in Quincy. Lamborn had the court issue other subpoenas or attachments after he arrived in Carthage just before the trial. Jonas Hobert and Thomas Dixon were among the witnesses arrested on writ of attachment who appeared either in custody or under bond given to secure their appearance. Over a dozen other potential witnesses, such as George W. Thatcher, Thomas Morrison, and Robert F. Smith, were served with prosecution subpoenas[65] but were never called to the witness stand. In view of the intransigence of other Hancock County citizens whom Lamborn did bring before the jury, it is easy to imagine why he chose not to hear the testimony of such notorious anti-Mormons as these.

Of course there were yet in the county many uncommitted non-Mormons. During the "Mormon War" that erupted a few months after the trial, there were non-Mormons of courage and objectivity who tried to stand between the warring parties and restore order in the county. Some of these people must have known facts that would have helped strengthen the prosecution, but the prosecution had obtained little helpful evidence when it had succeeded in locating such witnesses and calling them to the stand. George and Eli Walker, Thomas Barnes, and Thomas Dixon were relatively detached citizens who obviously knew facts that would have helped the prosecution's case, but could not bring themselves to incriminate the defendants when sitting in the witness chair facing their belligerent fellow citizens of Hancock County. Lamborn interrogated them carefully, but without success. It is difficult to blame him for not multiplying his embarrassment by calling other citizens of like mind.

Lamborn's difficulties were magnified by the Mormon leaders' refusal to assist in locating witnesses in order to avoid jeopardizing the public peace. If peace was so important to the Mormons that they wouldn't press for convictions, why should the non-Mormons risk their future accord with powerful groups in the county in order to convict men like Thomas C. Sharp, especially when a conviction would almost surely shatter the uneasy peace in Hancock County? Indeed, Lamborn might have wondered, why should the prosecution press harder than it had already? In the world of practical politics, there were limits to the risks one should assume to vindicate the honor of the state.

1. *Circuit Court Record,* 278; "Minutes of Trial," 55.

2. Hancock County Census, 1850, pp. 273-B, 276-A.

3. "Minutes of Trial," 56.

4. Watt Manuscript, 46, 49; "Minutes of Trial," 57.

5. "Minutes of Trial," 57; Watt Manuscript, 48-50.

6. Thomas Barnes to Miranda Haskett, November 1, 1897, in Keith Huntress, *Murder of an American Prophet* (San Francisco: Chandler Publishing Company, 1960), 146, 150-51.

7. "Minutes of Trial," 55; accord, Watt Manuscript, 46.

8. Hancock County Census, 1850, p. 428-A; Scofield, *History of Hancock County,* 1071.

9. "Minutes of Trial," 59-60; accord, "Documents," 25-26; Watt Manuscript, 55-58. The Hamilton House was one block east of the courthouse square; the jail was northwest of the square. Cochran, *History of Hancock County,* 212.

10. Watt Manuscript, 57-58; accord, "Minutes of Trial," 60; "Documents," 26.

11. Hancock County Census, 1850, p. 376-A.

12. "Documents," 23; accord, "Minutes of Trial," 58; Watt Manuscript, 52.

13. "Documents," 23; accord, Watt Manuscript, 54.

14. "Minutes of Trial," 54; accord, "Documents," 23; Watt Manuscript, 51.

15. "Minutes of Trial," 58-59; accord, "Documents," 23; Watt Manuscript, 52-53.

16. "Minutes of Trial," 58-59; accord, Watt Manuscript, 53, 55.

17. "Minutes of Trial," 58; "Documents," 23.

18. "Early Church Information File," Genealogical Library of the Church of Jesus Christ of Latter-day Saints, Salt Lake City, Utah.

19. "Documents," 26-27; "Minutes of Trial," 61; Watt Manuscript, 59.

20. "Minutes of Trial," 61; accord, "Documents," 27; Watt Manuscript, 60.

21. "Documents," 28.

22. "Minutes of Trial," 61; "Documents," 28; Watt Manuscript, 60-61. The "Minutes of Trial" spells his name "Voras"; the "Documents" gives it as "Vorees"; the Watt Manuscript refers to him as "Boarus."

23. "Minutes of Trial," 62; accord, "Documents," 28-29; Watt Manuscript, 61.

24. "Documents," 29; accord, "Minutes of Trial," 62; Watt Manuscript, 61.

25. Baxter, *Browning,* 12, 52, 60.

26. "Minutes of Trial," 62; "Documents," 29; Watt Manuscript, 61-62.

27. Watt Manuscript, 65; accord, "Minutes of Trial," 63-64.

28. "Documents," 32; "Minutes of Trial," 63-64; Watt Manuscript, 63, 65.

29. "Minutes of Trial," 63; accord, "Documents," 31; Watt Manuscript, 64.

30. "Minutes of Trial," 64-65; accord, "Documents," 33; Watt Manuscript, 67.

31. "Minutes of Trial," 65; Watt Manuscript, 68.

32. "Minutes of Trial," 66; accord, "Documents," 33; Watt Manuscript, 68, 70.

33. "Minutes of Trial," 66.

34. "Documents," 34; accord, "Minutes of Trial," 66; Watt Manuscript, 70-71. On cross-examination the witness quoted Grover as being concerned about the state arms because he was responsible and had given bond and security for them. "Documents," 36; "Minutes of Trial," 67.

35. "Minutes of Trial," 67; Watt Manuscript, 71-72.

36. "Minutes of Trial," 67; "Documents," 34; Watt Manuscript, 71-72.

37. "Minutes of Trial," 67; Watt Manuscript, 72-73.

38. "Minutes of Trial," 67; accord, "Documents," 34-35; Watt Manuscript, 72 (except the latter source has Grover saying that "they" had killed Smith).

39. Watt Manuscript, 79.

40. "Minutes of Trial," 67; "Documents," 35; Watt Manuscript, 72-73.

41. "Minutes of Trial," 68; Watt Manuscript, 74-75.

42. "Minutes of Trial," 68; accord, Watt Manuscript, 75-76.

43. "Minutes of Trial," 69.

44. Watt Manuscript, 78.

45. "Minutes of Trial," 69.

46. *Ibid.;* accord, Watt Manuscript, 77-78.

47. "Minutes of Trial," 70; accord, Watt Manuscript, 79.

48. "Minutes of Trial," 68-69; Watt Manuscript, 76-77.

49. "Minutes of Trial," 70; accord, Watt Manuscript, 79-80.

50. "Minutes of Trial," 71; accord, Watt Manuscript, 81.

51. "Minutes of Trial," 71; Watt Manuscript, 81.

52. *Circuit Court Record,* 278.

53. "Minutes of Trial," 71.

54. Watt Manuscript, 81.

55. "Minutes of Trial," 71; Watt Manuscript, 82.

56. "Minutes of Trial," 71-72. During this adjournment Judge Young called in the grand jury, which returned 2 indictments for larceny and 1 for riot, reported the conclusion of its business, and was discharged. *Circuit Court Record,* 279.

57. There was insufficient evidence to include Davis in this conspiracy. His refusal to accompany the mob to Carthage "to kill a man who was confined in prison" established his disavowal of participation in any arrangement, even though Brackenbury testified that he later rushed to the jail, arriving just as the shooting ended, and accompanied the mob back to Warsaw.

58. Moses, *Illinois Historical,* II, 967-68; Doyle, "Josiah Lamborn," 192.

59. Frank, *Lincoln as a Lawyer,* 34, 169.

60. *Warsaw Signal,* July 10, 1844.

61. Smith, *History of the Church,* VII, 142; subpoenas in case file in *People* v. *Levi Williams.*

62. Returns on subpoenas in case file in *People* v. *Levi Williams;* Scofield, *History of Hancock County,* 758; "Muster Roll."

63. Returns on subpoenas in case file in *People* v. *Levi Williams;* list of witnesses on grand jury indictment, *People* v. *Levi Williams.*

64. Jeremiah Willey, whose August 13, 1844, statement is in Brigham Young's correspondence in the Church Archives, was willing to testify that William Voras, Wills, and Charles Gullien [probably Gallaher] were wounded by Joseph at the jail.

65. Returns on subpoenas in case file in *People* v. *Levi Williams.*

∾ 10 ∾

To "Tranquilize the Public Mind"

The examination of defense witnesses took a little over one court day, commencing at 9:15 on Tuesday and concluding just before lunch on Wednesday.[1] The defense effort was predictable. All sixteen defense witnesses focused on impeaching the prosecution's key witnesses, Brackenbury, Daniels, and Graham. There was no alibi evidence. None of the defendants took the stand.

The first two witnesses were used to impeach the truthfulness of Brackenbury. New Hampshire-born William Smith and Pennsylvanian James Reynolds were residents of La Harpe, in the northeast part of the county.[2] Reynolds had been the foreman and Smith a member of the grand jury that had returned the indictments in this case. Both testified to differences between what Brackenbury had said in this trial and the testimony he gave to the grand jury. Their recollection of the grand jury testimony was strengthened by reference to the memorandum of Daniels's and Brackenbury's testimony that Reynolds had written and signed within a few days after the grand jury hearing in October. Browning was allowed to read this memorandum to the jury "by common consent" of counsel.[3]

Consistent with the written memorandum, Reynolds and Smith testified that Brackenbury had told the grand jury that Colonel Williams had been at the jail on horseback during the shooting.[4] In this trial Brackenbury had denied giving such testimony. This same contradiction had just been presented to the May grand jury in support of the perjury charge against Brackenbury, but the grand jury, with its Mormon foreman, had refused to indict.[5] Now the same testimony was being used to impeach Brackenbury.

Reynolds and Smith also described how Brackenbury had told the grand jury that the messenger in the Carthage Grey uniform had spoken with Colonel Williams and Henry Stephens. In the current trial Brackenbury had testified that Williams was not present, and that it was Aldrich who got the message. Contrary to his denial in the present trial, Brackenbury had also told the grand jurors that when Sharp rode past his wagon after the shooting he said that the Smiths were dead, for he "had hold of them."[6] Reynolds and Smith thus identified at least three significant contradictions in Brackenbury's testimony to different juries.

Lamborn's brief cross-examination of William Smith sought to retrieve Brackenbury's damaged credibility. He succeeded in having the witness concede that "most of his statements which I heard him make on yesterday corresponded pretty generally with what he said before the [grand] jury."[7] Nonetheless, the inconsistencies identified by the defense, though isolated, remained unexplained.

In contrast, it is significant that neither Reynolds nor Smith testified to any contradictions between Daniels's lengthy trial testimony and what he told the grand jury. This was no oversight. Comparison of the memorandum of grand jury testimony with the various accounts of the trial shows that Daniels's testimony was essentially the same on both occasions. The impeachment of Daniels would have to take a different form.

Nine witnesses gave testimony to discredit Daniels. The first four contradicted his trial testimony, and the other five sought to discredit his integrity and truthfulness generally.

Three young farmers who lived south of Carthage, Larkin Scott, Derrick Fuller, and John Pike,[8] all described the same events. Fuller and Pike were southbound on the Quincy road just outside Carthage when they heard gunfire. Daniels overtook and joined them about a mile farther on and told them the Smiths had been killed. Near dark the trio stopped at Larkin Scott's farm, eight miles south of Carthage. Here Daniels told the three men that he had been with the first group of men who jumped the fence around the jail and struggled with the guards. He marveled over the strength of Worrell, who waved his sword about and had to be held down by two or three men. "I am the man who took his sword out of his hand and threw it over the fence,"[9] Daniels told them. Fuller and Pike testified that Daniels had asked them "if we saw Worrell before he did to tell him where his sword was."[10] All of this of course flatly contradicted Daniels's statements during cross-examination, where he denied telling these men that he helped in the struggle with the guards at the jail. Scott quoted Daniels as saying that it did not affect him to see the Smiths killed, "as they richly deserved it."[11]

As this trio of witnesses quoted Daniels in supposed additional contradictions, they got into some minor contradictions of their own. Fuller said Daniels told them that Smith was set up against the well curb; Scott and Pike did not hear him say this. Scott and Fuller said Daniels mentioned nothing about any marvelous light, but on Lamborn's cross-examination Pike remembered Daniels saying "there was a flash [of] lightning come down then at the jail house, at the time the murder was committed."[12] All three agreed that Daniels said nothing about men being paralyzed and having to be carried away.[13]

Like so many of their fellow citizens of Hancock County, these three witnesses were anxious to minimize their knowledge of the crime. Whether they approved it or not, they didn't want to be involved. A short series of questions which Lamborn asked Larkin Scott on cross-examination illustrates the typical attitude:

Q: Why did you stop [Daniels] from telling the names of those engaged in killing the Smiths?

A: Because I did not want to know the men that did it.

Q: Why did you not want to know the men that did it?

A: Because I felt that I did not want to know anything more about [it].

Q: You stopped him before he mentioned any others?

A: Yes.[14]

Lamborn's cross-examination was particularly skillful, reminding the jury that none of these witnesses had identified any contradictions between Daniels's testimony and what he told them earlier on the key fact that these five defendants were involved in the murder. One of his questions suggested that Daniels's account of being in the struggle with the guards was just bragging "to make himself appear a big man." He also secured an admission that except for the differences noted, the balance of Daniels's statement to Fuller "was about as he told it here."[15]

Browning's attempts to get direct contradictions of Daniels's testimony duplicated evidence he had already brought out in his cross-examination of a prosecution eyewitness, Thomas Dixon. In contrast to Daniels's account, Dixon had testified that Joseph Smith did not hang in the window before he dropped. He did not see anyone take hold of Smith or raise him up, and he did not see four men shoot Smith after he raised himself against the well curb. Finally, Dixon saw no marvelous light about his body and no one paralyzed so that he could not move.[16]

The testimony of the fourth witness in this group, John Carlisle, was hopelessly confused and meaningless, and Browning hustled him off the witness stand as soon as he could.[17] Apparently even the large battery of defense counsel occasionally had insufficient advance review of their witnesses' testimony.

The five witnesses in the second group were used to attack Daniels's character and credibility generally, rather than to contradict specific details of his testimony. Charles Andrews, a carriage painter, was Daniels's brother-in-law. He told how Daniels came to his house in Quincy, just after his July visit to the Mormons in Nauvoo, and flashed around ten dollars in bills which he said he had received from Emma Smith for his expenses. Later Daniels told Andrews that Mr. Bedell of Warsaw had offered him $500 to go away, but that he intended to stay and testify, since he could get $1,000 from the state.[18]

The four other witnesses, Coleman Garrett, Thomas L. English, George Seabold, and George McLean, all testified to a more discrediting story. Three of these men were coopers, like Daniels. He had worked with them in Quincy during the summer following the murder and had confided in them as "brother chips."[19] Browning skillfully directed each witness into revealing Daniels's boasting about his part in the trial. Garrett told the jury how Daniels had bragged to him that he "had quit coopering and never expected to do any more hard work."[20] McLean quoted Daniels as saying "there was no use in working so hard when a man could make plenty of money without working."[21] Seabold and McLean both told the jury how Daniels had bragged that he would get $500 from a "speculation," which he did not identify.[22]

Three witnesses quoted Daniels as saying that he was to be paid

$500 for giving evidence against the men who were charged with killing the Smiths.[23] According to witnesses English and Seabold, he did not identify the person who made him this offer. Daniels told Garrett that "the Mormons" were paying him $500 or $600 to testify, and that he had already gotten some of it.[24] Daniels also told this witness that Governor Ford was going to pay him $300 in addition.

English testified that when he first asked for news about the Mormons, Daniels told him he knew nothing about the killing of the Smiths. McLean told the jury the same thing. Later, according to English, Daniels went to Nauvoo. When he returned in August or September, he told English "he had made a great speculation in writing a book" about the murders in Carthage.[25] Browning questioned the Irishman about what he said then. "Why, says I, you told me you know nothing about it. Well, says he, as long as I can make a speculation I will and do you say nothing about it." Daniels also told English that he had not gotten any money, but he had gotten $100 in trade, which suited him just as well. English said he then told Daniels he thought he "was not intelligent enough to write a book,"[26] or, as another source puts it, "He was not a man of any great figures as I had tried him." Daniels replied that "he had friends to aid him in it."[27]

Lamborn's cross-examination of English was notably unsuccessful, serving only to strengthen the impression that here was a man who spoke forthrightly, honestly, and completely.

Q: And you get nothing for coming here?

A: Not a cent, sir.

Q: Who paid your expenses?

A: No one but myself.

Q: I suppose you thought it right to kill Jo Smith?

A: I don't think it right to kill any man.

Q: What made you so peculiar anxious in volunteering your services [in testifying]?

A: I thought I was in duty bound to do so.[28]

Lamborn's cross-examination gave McLean an opportunity to affirm that Daniels had told him he was in Augusta the night of the murder, which would place him far from the events he claimed to have witnessed.[29]

While the testimony of these impeaching witnesses was not entirely consistent, its overall effect was surely discrediting. Lamborn probably winced inwardly at hearing his key witness portrayed as a cheap opportunist. Not only was there evidence that Daniels had a corrupt pecuniary motive for his testimony, but Seabold and McLean had made Daniels seem a liar by contradicting his denial on direct examination that he had told these men that he had been offered $500 to testify. The only bright spot was the admission secured on cross-examination from one witness that Daniels didn't "say anything about coming here to swear to anything that was not true."[30]

Daniels was apparently paid or promised some money by someone in Nauvoo for his contribution to the booklet, and some of his bragging could doubtless have been related to that arrangement. Immediately after the Carthage trial·Lyman O. Littlefield would publish a notice in Nauvoo that no one should purchase the two fifty-dollar notes he had given to William M. Daniels, dated November 23, 1844, since Littlefield "has not had value" and also had valid counterclaims against Daniels.[31] The total of these notes may have been the $100 in trade for his "speculation" that Daniels described to English.[32] Lamborn's failure to bring out this redeeming explanation on cross-examination or by rebuttal witnesses may have resulted from insufficient preparation; or, like other deficiencies, his performance may have been attributable to mental deterioration from the excess drinking that was soon to cause his death.

Browning's impeachment effort had been effective, and as court adjourned at 4:30 P.M. on Tuesday the defendants could feel reassured that their prospects for acquittal had been noticeably improved.

In a letter apparently sent on Tuesday evening, the correspondent of the *Missouri Republican* gave this account to his readers: "The testimony on the part of the State has been very lame, and that of the witnesses so very contradictory, and the fact that improper influences have been brought to bear upon them, so very apparent, that it is not within the bounds of probability that the jury will hesitate for one moment in honorably acquitting the prisoners." The writer also referred particularly to his belief that witness Daniels, the "most important on the part of the State, has been proven to have acknowledged that he was to get $500 from the Mormons and $300 from Gov. Ford, for testifying in the case."[33]

The last trial testimony commenced at seven o'clock on Wednesday, May 28. John W. Williams, an elderly Carthage farmer,[34] began with the brief testimony that he had been in Carthage on the morning when the Smiths were killed, and that he had seen Sharp in company with Governor Ford at Hamilton's just after breakfast and before the governor's council with the militia officers. The obvious purpose of this testimony was to contradict Eliza Graham's statement that she had seen Sharp in Warsaw that same morning. But Lamborn's lengthy cross-examination ignored this testimony and struck out in a new direction in an apparent effort to elicit additional evidence helpful to the prosecution. That effort was soon aborted by Browning's objection and Judge Young's ruling that the prosecutor had to limit his cross-examination to matters in the witness's earlier testimony. He could not use cross-examination "for the purpose of making out his case."[35]

The last four witnesses for the defense were used to impeach Eliza Jane Graham by contradicting numerous other details of her testimony. Abraham I. Chittenden, a sixty-four-year-old farmer[36] who owned the land where the militia bivouacked just east of Warsaw and who had two sons in the militia unit, testified that Grover had eaten breakfast at his home that morning,[37] contradicting Graham's testimony that Grover and Davis took their breakfast at Fleming's. Her testimony on that point was also countered by E. W. Gould, a Warsaw merchant boarding at Fleming's, who could not recall seeing either man at breakfast that morning.[38] Graham had testified that Sharp arrived at Fleming's Warsaw House in a two-horse carriage with James Gregg just before sundown on the day the Smiths were killed. Parts of this testimony were contradicted by these witnesses, but their testimony was itself somewhat inconsistent. Chittenden swore that James Gregg rode into Warsaw on horseback just before sundown — alone. Gould testified that Gregg rode into Warsaw on horseback at about sundown — with Sharp.[39] Neither of these witnesses saw any two-horse carriage. Neither did Edward A. Bedell, a young Jack Mormon and prosperous Warsaw merchant,[40] who testified that he saw Sharp ride into Warsaw on horse-back alone about twenty minutes before sundown. Lamborn easily exploded this supposed inconsistency with Eliza Graham's testimony by securing concessions on cross-examination that Sharp and Gregg could have gone to Fleming's in a carriage after their arrival in Warsaw on horseback.[41] Nonetheless, these damaging contradictions could linger in the minds of the jury.

Lamborn's cross-examination secured a partial corroboration of one aspect of Graham's testimony. Chittenden admitted that when Gregg rode by him he said, "The Governor has not whipped us yet — the Smiths are dead."[42] More important, Gould testified that when Sharp dismounted after his arrival in Warsaw, someone asked him the news; he replied, "Jo and Hyrum Smith are no more."[43] Gould also admitted that he saw two wagonloads of men arrive at the Warsaw House that evening, including a man named Wills who was wounded in the arm or wrist. Between forty and sixty took supper at Fleming's that night.[44]

The final defense witness was thirty-two-year-old Ann Fleming,[45] wife of the proprietor of Fleming's Warsaw House. Lamborn had originally subpoenaed her as a prosecution witness, but she had failed to appear. On Tuesday Browning obtained an attachment to compel her presence in support of the defense. Her husband, Samuel Fleming, who was acting as a deputy in this case, brought her into court on Wednesday morning,[46] and now the reluctant lady was called to the stand.

Ann Fleming's direct testimony was brief, pointed, and flatly contradictory of Eliza Graham's. She had no conversation with Sharp on the evening the Smiths were killed. She had no recollection of Sharp or Gregg coming into the hall that evening and calling for a drink of water. She remembered that a number of men came there after dark and took supper, but Captain Grover was not among them. She said she didn't hear the men say anything "about what they had been doing at Carthage that day or about the killing of the Smiths." She couldn't recall seeing Sharp or Grover that evening. There was a wounded man sitting by the kitchen fire that night, but Grover had not come and asked permission for him to sit there.[47]

Having achieved the strong conclusion he sought, Browning had the Daniels booklet admitted as evidence, so the jury could compare its account with Daniels's testimony on the witness stand. The defense then rested its case. Lamborn said he had no rebutting witnesses. Court was then adjourned until two o'clock.[48]

As the crowd reassembled to hear the closing arguments, they may have felt some degree of apprehension, despite the fact that the defense had concluded this four-day trial with an effective attack on the credibility of the prosecution's three key witnesses. Lamborn had a reputation for winning impossible cases. With easy flow of words and superb voice control, he was a master of courtroom dramatics. One of Judge Young's colleagues on the Supreme Court later said he "knew of no lawyer who was his equal in strength and force of argument."[49] Lamborn could explain the evidence and redirect the thinking of even a hostile jury by his understanding of human nature and his ability to communicate on intimate terms with the fears, prejudices, and aspirations of each juror.[50]

A well-known example of Lamborn's mastery of the closing argument occurred in a murder case he had prosecuted near Springfield. After the evidence was in, defense counsel E. D. Baker delivered a brilliant and stirring closing argument that seemed to assure acquittal. Sensing that he had no oratorical match for Baker's plea for mercy, especially in the mood this advocate had created, Lamborn seized upon the lateness of the hour and his own supposed indisposition to persuade the court to adjourn until that evening, when he would deliver his closing remarks. Leaning on the arm of a friend, Lamborn limped to the home of the sheriff to request that the only illumination in the courtroom that night be a candle, positioned so that its rays would strike full in the jury's face. That evening the jury and a courtroom filled with spectators anxiously watched Lamborn standing before them, stooped and silent, as the single candle cast ghostly shadows on the walls and turned Lamborn's face into a grotesque mask. All thoughts of Baker's eloquent appeal were erased by that gloomy and foreboding presence. A lawyer who witnessed the scene left this description:

Every eye was fixed upon him, when, with awful deliberation, in a cold and sepulchral voice, he said, "Whoso sheddeth man's blood, by man shall his blood be shed!" Straightening himself up and again pausing for half a minute, the shadows around him seeming to grow darker, he again repeated the verse from Holy Writ. Then he was once more silent. Spectres seemed to hover around him. The audience held its breath to hear what he would say next. Rising to his full height, with another awful pause, in tones as solemn as the grave, he for a third time repeated, "Whoso shed-deth man's blood, by man shall his blood be shed!" Raising his arm and pointing his quivering finger toward the jury, he exclaimed with a voice like a trumpet, "Such is God Almighty's awful decree! Disobey it if you dare!" He sat down and said no more; but it was enough. The verdict of guilty had been secured.[51]

The lawyer who recorded the event concluded: "I have seen in my lifetime some wonderful actors, have witnessed some extraordinary scenes on the stage, but never have I seen anything to equal that night's work in that humble courtroom."[52] The courtroom crowd in Carthage was doubtless eager to see what an advocate of Lamborn's ability could do in this difficult situation.

As Lamborn stood to begin his argument, he must have known that only the greatest good fortune could save his case against any of these defendants. The crowd may have expected some courtroom dramatics, but they can hardly have been prepared for the extraordinary maneuvers Lamborn employed.

Walking painfully with the assistance of his cane, the tall but crippled prosecutor skillfully used his physical disability to underline his helplessness in being arrayed against four distinguished lawyers for the defense. He called upon the jury's sympathy for his plight as a stranger who had to conduct his case alone in the face of such odds.[53] Then, moving with sudden speed and boldness, Lamborn stunned his listeners with a series of daring concessions that altered the entire posture of the prosecution's case.

No doubt Daniels was in Carthage when Smith was killed, Lamborn began, and "no doubt the substantial features of his evidence are true." "But he has made statements which ought to impeach his evidence before any court." His book, Lamborn conceded, was ridiculous, "a tissue of falsehoods from beginning to end." Therefore, it is "impossible to rely on his testimony." "I intend to be fair and candid," Lamborn declared, "and therefore exclude Daniels' evidence from the consideration of the jury."[54] Having made this concession, Lamborn went still further, dismissing Brackenbury's testimony in similar fashion. "Brackenbury was drunk, is a loafer and perjured himself before the grand jury. I am satisfied that his evidence can be successfully impeached, and therefore withdraw it from the jury."[55] Turning to Eliza Jane Graham, his other major witness, Lamborn declared that he was "sincerely of the opinion that she spoke the truth, and that the other witnesses were mistaken. But she is contradicted, and I therefore give her up."[56]

In a few moments' time Lamborn had completely surrendered on the issue of the credibility of his three major witnesses. But there were more concessions to come. In short order Lamborn effectively dropped the charges against Davis and Grover: "I have no doubt in my own mind, not a particle, that Davis cooperated in the murder, but there is no legal evidence to convict him. Nor is there evidence to convict Captain Grover, although I verily believe he was at the jail with his gun."[57] Suddenly, after this bewildering change of direction, the prosecution's case stood without the testimony of its three key witnesses, Daniels, Brackenbury, and Graham, and consisted of charges against only three persons — Mark Aldrich, Thomas C. Sharp, and Levi Williams — as to whom the remaining evidence was diffuse and circumstantial.

What could have motivated Lamborn to make such unexpected and devastating concessions? There are at least three possibilities: logic, fear, and favor.

The prosecutor's action can be explained at least in part on logical grounds, as an attempt to win the jury's respect for his impartiality and encourage their reliance on other prosecution witnesses by candidly disavowing the questionable ones. This explanation could account for Lamborn's dropping the case against Davis, which was entirely insufficient. The case against Grover, on the other hand, was strong if the prosecution witnesses were believed, since they had testified that he had led the mob to Carthage, that he was the only defendant seen at the jail with a gun, and that he had bragged that he had killed Joseph Smith. But this testimony was almost solely that of Daniels, Brackenbury, and Graham, so Lamborn's disavowal of these three witnesses left the evidence against Grover on the same insufficient basis as that against Davis. Thus, if Lamborn's strategy was to demonstrate his impartiality, and if that demonstration required disavowal of the controverted prosecution testimony, then Grover's case was just as appropriate for dismissal as Davis's.

But the strategy of disavowing the testimony of controverted

173

witnesses was highly questionable as a basis for repudiating Eliza Graham. Unlike Daniels and Brackenbury, she had not been impeached. True, several defense witnesses had contradicted her testimony in important respects, but that common phenomenon of courtroom experience — witnesses with different perceptions or recollections — was hardly a sufficient justification to withdraw her testimony. More likely she was disavowed because, once Daniels and Brackenbury were excluded, she was the only remaining Mormon witness. By excluding her, Lamborn would give up some usable evidence, but he might counter the anti-Mormon feelings of the jury. Making certain that his concessions would be seen in that light, Lamborn later reminded the jury that he had not asked "that a Mormon should be put upon the jury," and emphasized that "we use no Mormon witness."[58]

The correspondent of the anti-Mormon *Burlington Hawkeye* gave Lamborn the credit for candor and fairness he may have been seeking by these concessions. Writing from Carthage on the day of Lamborn's speech, he said: "The evidence for the prosecution has been very positive and to the point nominally, but never were witnesses more thoroughly ridiculed in the cross-examination. So completely and effectually were they discredited, even from their own mouths, that the Prosecution Attorney felt himself obliged to declare three of them perjured scoundrels."[59]

Second, the prosecutor's concessions might have been at least partly attributable to fear that the armed and hostile courtroom crowd would take reprisals against him if he appeared to press this unpopular case with too much diligence. Lamborn could not have forgotten how angry spectators in Springfield had nearly lynched him for his excessive zeal in prosecuting the Traylor case. So far as the current trial was concerned, Governor Ford later reported to the legislature that Lamborn prosecuted this case "at the constant peril of his life."[60] His fee for the entire prosecution was only $100.[61] How much risk could a man be expected to run for that amount of money?

Of even less credit to Lamborn is the third possibility: that his concessions might have been motivated by corrupt favors or the hope of such favors from the defense. In most prosecutions such concessions — even by a prosecutor of Lamborn's assertiveness and partisanship — could be seen as tactical moves that raised no ugly doubts of impropriety. But Lamborn's background does not allow one to ignore the possibility of corruption. Usher Linder, one of Lamborn's contemporaries at the Illinois bar, charged in a posthumous biographical note that Lamborn "was wholly destitute of principle, and shamelessly took bribes from criminals prosecuted during his administration." Writing of a period just a few years before the Carthage trial, Linder says: "I know myself of his having dismissed forty or fifty indictments at the Shelbyville Court, and openly displayed the money he had received from defendants. He showed me a roll of bills amounting to six or eight hundred dollars, which he acknowledged he had received from them — the fruits of his maladministration of his office as Attorney-General of the state."[62]

Whatever motivated Lamborn's startling concessions, he pressed forward with his argument that Aldrich, Sharp, and Williams should be convicted upon the remaining testimony. He spoke for over an hour. The evidence was only circumstantial, Lamborn acknowledged, but circumstantial evidence could be "the most conclusive." Since this was a case of conspiracy, Lamborn reminded the jury, the prosecution was "not bound to prove that these men struck the blow, or were at the jail."[63] It was sufficient that they were part of the plot to kill the Smiths and that they had committed acts in aid of that plan.

Speaking of the circumstantial evidence against these three defendants, Lamborn told the jury that the men who murdered Joseph Smith could easily be traced from the railroad shanties to Carthage and back to Warsaw. Sharp was in Carthage on the morning of the day of the murder, opposing the disbanding of the troops and fanning the flame of rebellion and mobocracy. When the governor discharged the troops, Sharp "inflamed them at the railroad." Another point of evidence against Sharp, which Lamborn made with great emphasis, was the fact that "Sharp did not inform the Carthage Greys that a mob was coming." Finally, "Sharp carried the news to Warsaw." So far as is revealed by the only source on his argument, Lamborn said very little about the evidence against Williams and

Aldrich. "Col. Williams knew that volunteers were called for, for Carthage. . . . He saw it all done, and sanctioned and approved of it." As for Aldrich, he "was at the railroad."[64]

Lamborn concluded his argument by entreating the jury not to say they "have no legal evidence." It is true that these defendants "put others forward," but "these men were the soul of the movement."[65]

That was all. A master of the dramatic gesture and the surprise tactical thrust, Lamborn was less expert at marshaling scraps of evidence from the mouths of nearly a score of witnesses and bringing them to focus on the guilty involvement of the defendants. The evidence Lamborn had referred to in his argument was predominantly the evidence given on the last day of the trial, on cross-examination of defense witnesses. This was the evidence most easily recalled, but it was only a fraction of the evidence available against the remaining three defendants. There is no record of his mentioning a multitude of other undisputed incriminatory facts proved from witnesses other than Daniels, Brackenbury, and Graham. Aldrich had attempted a speech, and Sharp had made a full speech at the railroad shanties. Sharp had damned the Mormons and their power in the county. Aldrich had made a call for volunteers to go to Carthage. Levi Williams had also said something about volunteers. Someone spoke about "blowing the jail to hell." Davis had indicated his knowledge of what was being proposed when he withdrew from the group because he said he'd be damned if he'd kill men in jail. After these statements a crowd of men, including Aldrich, Sharp, and Williams, had started for Carthage. These three, who were on horseback, arrived in Carthage before three o'clock. The jail guard fired into the mob, but no one was hit. The Carthage Greys, called out when the shooting began at the jail, marched to the jail so slowly that the mob had departed toward the west before they arrived. The guard made no attempt at pursuit. Just before sundown Sharp rode into Warsaw, which had been almost deserted during that day, and announced that the Smiths were dead. That night between nine and midnight a group of forty to sixty men, including two who were wounded, arrived in Warsaw and took supper at the Warsaw House.

This additional evidence may have been insufficient to convict any of the three defendants. Nevertheless, it is strange that Lamborn, whose voluntary exclusion of the testimony of Daniels, Brackenbury, and Graham can only be justified as a tactical maneuver intended to reinforce the strength of his remaining evidence, so conspicuously failed to marshal and utilize that remaining evidence.

Perhaps the prosecutor deliberately pulled his punches. Governor Ford had sent him to vindicate the honor of the state, and that objective could be served by a prosecution that resulted in acquittal. A conviction would surely heighten domestic strife and perhaps cause a civil war. To many, the prosecutor's effort appeared satisfactory. The correspondent of the *Missouri Republican* said that Lamborn "managed the prosecution with much ability, and must have convinced all parties — especially the Mormons — that everything was done that it was possible to accomplish by a faithful and indefatigable discharge of his duty to the state."[66]

Although acquittal seemed the most likely result following Lamborn's argument, the defense counsel could not take any chances. Since death by hanging was the single mandatory penalty for the crime of murder,[67] the defendants' lives were in jeopardy and no effort could be spared in their defense.

Three lawyers spoke for the defense; their speeches concluded the day on Wednesday and occupied most of Thursday as well. Calvin A. Warren spoke first. The *Burlington Hawkeye* reporter observed that Warren was "an able and effective speaker, and his biting sarcasm and keen wit had every chance for display."[68] A correspondent for the *Missouri Republican,* writing two days later, was somewhat more reserved in his praise. After heaping compliments on the other two defense counsel, Skinner (speech "marked with much ability") and Browning ("able"), the correspondent withheld praise and merely observed that "Mr. Warren also made a speech in a vein and a manner which is peculiarly his own."[69] A Mormon source termed Warren's speech the "most inflammatory" of the trial.[70]

Warren's dominant theme was an appeal to anti-Mormon prejudice by attacking the dead Mormon leaders and by suggesting that whoever killed them had acted in the best interest and with the approval of the non-Mormon citizens of the county. He sounded his dominant theme at the outset: "If these men are guilty, then are every man, woman and child in the county guilty. The same evidence that has been given against the defendants could have been given against hundreds of others."[71] Time after time Warren reminded the jury that the defendants were strongly identified with the predominant interest of the county: "These men were with the whole country enraged at the audacity and conduct of the Smiths. They dared complain of their grievances, and because the Smiths were murdered on the same day[,] you are asked to believe that they did it." Next, Warren accused Lamborn of trying to prejudice the jury by suggesting that "it is necessary [that] there should be a conviction in order to restore peace to the county and quiet the excitement," or that "a curse would rest upon the county until a victim should be offered up." Almeron Wheat, Warren's law partner, who took notes on the address, omits any details of how Warren enlarged on this subject, only observing caustically: "Then Warren gets religious and talks about the Bible, truth, God &c &c."

After quoting a sentiment from Jefferson about oppression caused by public excitement, Warren gave the jury this characterization of the ruling legal principle in this prosecution for murder: "What is the law? It is based upon public opinion, and is worth nothing without it." Here Warren was apparently attempting to imply that the law did not require the jury to punish a murderer where the public approved of the killing.

In commenting on the evidence against individual defendants, Warren seized upon Lamborn's dismissal of charges against Davis and Grover and urged that the evidence against the other three was no stronger. "You can't let these men off without letting all off," he cried. "All are equally guilty. The transaction is over, and whatever was going on, one of these defendants is as guilty as the rest." Warren then concluded by returning to his dominant theme: "If you believe that these defendants are not as clear of the murder of the Smiths as all the rest of the people in the county, hang them. If you do hang them, it will be for not participating in this matter, for all the evidence except the three Mormons show they had nothing to do with it."[72] Once again Warren had told the jury that the defendants were simply accused of doing what the old citizens of the county wanted. On that note, Warren's ninety-minute argument concluded, and court adjourned until Thursday.

On Wednesday evening a person with the initials of J. T. M. wrote a letter to the *Burlington Hawkeye* which speaks derisively of the whole affair.

> The Jury will probably retire tomorrow night, to make up their verdict, but there seems to be no doubt of the result. It is generally thought that the Jury will not be out half-an-hour, and that a verdict of "not guilty," will be rendered for each defendant. Two of them, Davis and Grover, are virtually clear, as the prosecution admit that there is no evidence against them.
>
> The whole appears more like a farce than a solemn trial, involving the lives of five men. The defendants are at large without bail, the most unconcerned men of any engaged in the proceeding. This fact itself shows plainly what the general opinion is as to their guilt, and how certain is their acquittal.[73]

On Thursday morning, May 29, the jury heard young Onias C. Skinner in the major forensic effort for the defense. This speech was to have been given by the senior defense counsel, Colonel William A. Richardson, but Skinner told the jury that Richardson was ill and it devolved upon him to make the argument.[74]

Skinner commenced by alerting the jury to Lamborn's "remarkably shrewd" purpose in excluding the evidence of the three witnesses and conceding the acquittal of Davis and Grover. "The object and design of all this anxiety on his part is, to impress upon & deceive the jury — to throw the case into a new channel . . . and having obtained your ill-placed confidence, to triumph in this prosecution by, in his concluding speech, wringing and weaving in with the slight circumstances against the defts, the testimony of his abandoned and perjured witnesses." Why did he do this? "I do not wish to charge the gentleman with corruption or improper motives," Skinner declared.

> I am willing to attribute all these efforts at conviction through management, trick and chicanery to his inordinate ambition — his pride of success and love of fame. He comes here with a reputation for criminal prosecution unparalleled in our country, and, perhaps, he would not have had a rival among the great champions of state trials in any other country; and such has been his success throughout this state that it seems to be understood that when Lamborn prosecutes conviction follows, guilty or innocent! It is this enviable reputation — the glory of his highest ambition he desires to sustain by the conviction of these defendants.[75]

Skinner then referred to the "three Mormon witnesses, Daniels, Brackenbury and Graham," as "witnesses legally and conclusively impeached — witnesses that no honest Mormon would for a moment credit — witnesses whose absurd and stultifying statements while on the stand sent successive sensations of mirth and disgust through this audience and shocked the jury and every spectator at their utter depravity and degradation."[76] Skinner was obviously an advocate of considerable skill, who concentrated his fire upon the prosecution's case, not upon the anti-Mormon or anti-Smith prejudices of the jury.

Skinner next analyzed and ridiculed the testimony of the remaining witnesses, piece by piece. It was true that Sharp rode out and met the Warsaw troops at the railroad shanties, but he merely delivered the news about the governor disbanding them. In his speech he just informed his friends, including Williams and Aldrich, of what had taken place in Carthage and of his conversation in trying to persuade the governor to march to Nauvoo. Considering the circumstances, there was "nothing sinister" about Sharp's speech. Hundreds of others had also recited grievances against the Smiths. Eli Walker's lack of recollection that Sharp made a speech suggests that his so-called speech was nothing more than a private conversation with those around him. The same was true of Aldrich and Williams. In view of the anxious condition then existing in the county, no one could go from place to place without being compelled to make at least a small speech to convey what information he possessed. That was all the evidence against Aldrich, Skinner contended, and now Lamborn "asks you to convict a man for using language that anybody used."[77] Peyton said Williams was at the shanties, but he did not have him say one word, and he didn't even know whether Williams was there at the time the volunteers stepped out. If Williams had been trying to raise mobs and urge them on to murder, wouldn't Peyton have known it?

"Before you can find any of the defendants guilty," Skinner told the jury, "you must believe from the evidence that a conspiracy was found and entered into to kill the Smiths."[78] Was there a common design? Skinner then proceeded to challenge the idea of conspiracy by characterizing the actions at the railroad shanties as just the behavior one would expect when a military force was disbanded suddenly, with the removal of military discipline and vigor. Some were saying they would go to Carthage to see why they were disbanded, some were cursing the governor, some were abusing the Mormons as the cause of their miseries, some were speaking of returning to Warsaw for dinner, and some were shooting at marks. Where was the common design?

"In order to do justice to this case," Skinner told the jury, "you should have a clear understanding of circumstantial evidence."[79] Before the jury found the defendants guilty it would have to be clearly proved that there was a conspiracy to kill the Smiths; that this conspiracy did kill them; and that these defendants were part of the conspiracy and planned, aided, and abetted its design. Skinner contended that the evidence was insufficient on all of these points.

The Smiths could have been killed by men with whom the defendants had no connection, Skinner argued. Since the area was full of men who had threatened Joseph Smith's life, many of whom had just been discharged in or around Carthage with weapons in their possession, couldn't "the murder have been committed by some of these men?" Skinner asked. He reminded the jury that witnesses Hobert, Worrell, and Dixon, all well acquainted with the residents of the county, were at the jail when the act was committed, and "they did not know any of the men, although they were not disguised." If the mob that numbered from 60 to 150 had been from Warsaw, wouldn't some of the witnesses have known some of them? The inference from this fact, Skinner concluded, is that "the mob was not composed of the Warsaw men, but of strangers."[80]

Skinner concluded his argument with the charge that the whole case against the defendants amounted to nothing more than the fact that certain men were thirsting for blood and desired to have "some victim offered up upon the gallows to appease the [name] of the prophet, the idol of a powerful faction."[81]

Skinner had spoken for three hours, and it was almost noon. Buoyed by the effectiveness of their counsel's arguments, the defendants and their friends must have been relaxed and confident of the outcome. A newspaperman described the trial at this point as "orderly and decorous," and observed that "the interest in the case, though deep, has not manifested itself in any undue form."[82]

The final spokesman for the defense was Orville H. Browning.

His argument, which began immediately after lunch, was a thoroughly professional attack upon the prosecution and its case. It began in a manner familiar to every trial lawyer. He sympathized with the jury that had been "close confined for many days" on its tedious task, promised "not to detain you longer than necessity demands," and spoke in reverent terms of the "peculiar responsibility" of a jury when "the matter at stake [is] not property nor liberty — but life."[83]

Proceeding to the substance of his argument, Browning first ridiculed Lamborn's statement that "he came here a stranger without sympathy." "Who brought him among strangers?" Browning asked. "The people of Hancock did not send for him. He thrust himself among them." Then Browning complained about the efforts of certain newspapers to arouse public prejudice against these defendants, and about a "crusade commenced against these defendants" based on "witnesses so foul and corrupt that even Mr. Lamborn withdraws their testimony from your consideration, and tells you they are not worthy of belief."[84]

Browning skillfully turned Lamborn's concession on Davis and Grover to the defendants' advantage by declaring that "it destroys his case against the other defendants" because "there is as much evidence against Grover as against Williams, as much against Davis as against Aldrich and as much against either as against Sharp."[85] If the evidence given by the other witnesses was sufficient to convict the defendants, as the prosecutor had said, then, Browning asserted, "he has been at an immense amount of labor for nothing. If he really believed it he would not have put himself to the trouble of bringing these perjured witnesses."[86] In one of his few appeals to popular prejudice, Browning shrewdly played upon the jurymen's fears of civil war in the county: "Mr. Lamborn says convict Williams, Aldrich and Sharp and peace will be restored. I say acquit these men and peace will be restored. But let a sentence of conviction be attempted to be carried into execution and the gallows will be a beacon around which to rally a more terrible armed force than you or I have ever seen. It would be the commencement of a more bloody and terrible war than you or I would want to see."[87]

At the outset, Browning had stated his intention to "confine myself to what Mr. Lamborn wishes us to be confined." Anticipating a strong jury bias against the Mormon witnesses, however, Browning soon told the jury that he "propose[d] speaking a few words about the witnesses whose testimony Mr. Lamborn has thrown out."[88] He then devoted a major part of his argument to an attack on the three forfeited witnesses: "No human mind can doubt but Daniels has been bribed. He cares for neither God nor man. He was in the market, and no man can doubt but some hell-defying scoundrels in Nauvoo have bought him up. I do not charge the Mormons as a body."[89] Browning reminded the jury that Daniels had "fared sumptuously" ever since joining the Mormon Church, "though he neither toils or spins yet he is a cooper by trade." Brackenbury had also found it convenient to go to Nauvoo about the same time, "And he too fares sumptuously. He is fed by an unseen hand. He follows no business for a living. Is, to use his own language, professionally a loafer and has followed loafing ever since he went to Nauvoo."[90] After criticizing Eliza Graham for inconsistencies between her testimony and that of other witnesses, challenging her "with reluctance," he said, "because she belongs to the gentler sex," Browning concluded this point by reading from a legal treatise to the effect that if there is reason to suppose that a witness's lying is the result of deliberate encouragement by one of the parties, this affords a reasonable ground, in a doubtful case, for suspecting the testimony of other witnesses offered by the same party.[91]

Speaking candidly to a jury partial to his cause, Browning said: "Although the defendants be guilty, yet all you can look at for the purpose of determining that question is the evidence and unless you are satisfied of the guilt of the defendants beyond any reasonable doubt you must acquit them." Reviewing and dismissing as nonincriminatory all of the remaining evidence against the defendants, Browning said scornfully, "Why, you would not hang a dog on such evidence." In his final moments Browning reminded the jury of the dire consequences that would follow from a conviction: "Find a verdict whatever it may be," he said, "but do not hang — that would be the greatest calamity that could befall your county — or these defendants."[92]

By time-honored tradition, the prosecutor had the last word. Lamborn's second and concluding argument may have been given Thursday afternoon, following Browning, but it was probably delivered Friday morning. Its content is unknown; the various trial records and newspapers are silent on the subject.

Judge Young gave the jury their instructions just before noon on Friday.[93] In his *History of Illinois* Governor Ford states that trial judges in early Illinois courts were adverse to deciding questions of law if they could possibly avoid it, and "they never gave instructions to a jury unless expressly called for; and then only upon the points of law raised by counsel in asking for them."[94] Judges never commented upon the evidence or undertook to show the jury what inferences or presumptions might be drawn from it. Judge Young was an experienced and able jurist; it was doubtless through custom and the expectation of the lawyers rather than through any lack of judicial ability that his jury instructions in this case were very brief.[95]

Most of Judge Young's instructions mirrored points of law already adverted to in the closing arguments of defense counsel. All were clearly instructions tailored for the benefit of the defense. There is nothing out of the ordinary about the content of the instructions that were given, but the absence of instructions favorable to the prosecution is striking. Lamborn apparently made no requests for instructions. There were no instructions on inferences that could properly be drawn from evidence. Despite the fact that the prosecution's case depended upon an application of the complicated legal theory of conspiracy, there were no instructions on the defendants' legal responsibility for the acts of others pursuant to their common design. The total absence of jury instructions to explain the theory of the prosecution's case is among the most obvious and the most serious of the prosecution's mistakes at the trial.

Judge Young finished instructing the jury at 11:30 on Friday, May 30, 1845,[96] just six court days after the jury had begun hearing testimony. Court then adjourned for lunch, and the jury filed out to the room set aside for their use. No one was apprehensive about their verdict, and little excitement accompanied its delivery. The trial that began with fears and preparations for armed conflict was drawing quietly to an end. On the second day of the trial, during the choosing of the jury, a newspaperman had written of a "bad state of things," where "everybody almost . . . attending court comes armed to the teeth."[97] Two weeks later, after the trial was concluded, this same paper (and probably the same correspondent) published the following euphoric description of the event:

> During the whole progress of this trial, Judge Young has presided with a dignity and an impartiality which has commended him to all parties in the county, and which did more towards tranquilizing any ascerbity of feeling which may have been entertained by any portion of them.
>
> The whole trial passed off quietly, nothing occurring during its progress to reflect upon the character of the citizens of the county; and upon the announcement of the verdict, no feeling either upon one side or the other, was manifested.[98]

At two o'clock, when court reconvened, the jury reported that they had reached their verdict:

The trial of the indicted assassins of Joseph Smith had ended in acquittal.[99]

It is impossible to determine the extent to which the jury's verdict was attributable to the weakness of the prosecution's case in view of Lamborn's concessions or to the jury's unwillingness to convict whatever the evidence. It was probably a combination of both. Defense counsel argued the weakness of the evidence, but they also urged acquittal because conviction could bring civil war, and because the community in fact approved of the crime.

Aside from the Mormons, the people of Hancock County were generally satisfied with the verdict. John Hay declared: "There was not a man on the jury, in the court, [or] in the county, that did not know the defendants had done the murder. But it was not proven, and the verdict of NOT GUILTY was right in law. And you cannot find in this generation an original inhabitant of Hancock County who will not stoutly sustain that verdict."[100]

The *Nauvoo Neighbor* carried a brief notice of the acquittal, observing that if the jury had convicted it would have been "a violation of all the rules of the world in all martyr cases before." The Mormon paper "referred the case to God for a righteous judgment."[101] Brigham Young recorded in his journal that the defendants had been acquitted "as we had anticipated."[102] But the jury's verdict still stung the Mormon leaders. Three times during the week following the trial the Twelve met and prayed "that justice might overtake the murderers of Joseph and Hyrum,"[103] "that Judge Young might be afflicted for joining hands with the murderers," and that "the judge and jury be afflicted."[104]

Thoughtful members in all parties rejoiced that the trial had concluded without bloodshed or other provocation for civil war. If some were doubtful that the trial had achieved justice, most were satisfied that it at least had preserved peace. For the state, the defendants, and even the Mormons, the effect of the trial was just as Josiah Lamborn had predicted when he told the jury in his closing argument that this trial "will . . . tranquilize the public mind."[105]

1. "Minutes of Trial," 72, 86.
2. Scofield, *History of Hancock County*, 1080-81; Hancock County Census, 1850, pp. 389, 433.
3. "Minutes of Trial," 74. For a copy of this memorandum see *ibid.*, 4-7.
4. *Ibid.*, 72, 74; accord, "Documents," 37, 39; Watt Manuscript, 82.
5. Original copy of proposed indictment in case file in *People* v. *Brackenbury*.
6. "Minutes of Trial," 72-74; "Documents," 38-39; Watt Manuscript, 83, 85-86.
7. "Minutes of Trial," 73; accord, Watt Manuscript, 83, 85.
8. Scott was 34 years old and had a wife and five children. He had come to the county from Tennessee in 1834 (Hancock County Census, 1850, p. 419; Scofield, *History of Hancock County*, 1078, 1358). Fuller was 29 (Hancock County Census, 1850, p. 420). The elisors had called him for jury service, but the prosecution excused him by peremptory challenge ("Minutes of Trial," 2). Pike lived in Bear Creek Township, south of Warsaw (Gregg, *History of Hancock County*, 508).
9. "Documents," 41; accord, "Minutes of Trial," 75; Watt Manuscript, 87 (testimony of Scott; Fuller and Pike testified to same effect; see note 10, below).
10. "Documents," 42, 43; accord, "Minutes of Trial," 75, 76; Watt Manuscript, 88, 90.
11. "Minutes of Trial," 75; accord, "Documents," 41; Watt Manuscript, 87.
12. "Minutes of Trial," 76; accord, "Documents," 43; Watt Manuscript, 88, 90.
13. "Documents," 40-43; "Minutes of Trial," 74-77; Watt Manuscript, 87.

14. Watt Manuscript, 88.

15. "Minutes of Trial," 75-76; Watt Manuscript, 89.

16. "Documents," 26; Watt Manuscript, 57-58; "Minutes of Trial," 60.

17. "Documents," 44; "Minutes of Trial," 77; Watt Manuscript, 91.

18. "Minutes of Trial," 79-80; "Documents," 48; Watt Manuscript, 96-97. Sharp's published version of the minutes reports at this point that "Daniels said he was going to take the highest bid" (Sharp, *Trial of the Persons*, 29). There is no comparable statement in the three primary sources of this witness's testimony, so this may have been an addition by Sharp.

19. "Minutes of Trial," 78 (testimony of English).

20. "Minutes of Trial," 77; Watt Manuscript, 92; accord, "Documents," 45.

21. "Minutes of Trial," 80; accord, "Documents," 49; Watt Manuscript, 97-98.

22. "Minutes of Trial," 79-80; "Documents," 47-49; Watt Manuscript, 95-98.

23. "Minutes of Trial," 77-80; "Documents," 45-48; Watt Manuscript, 92-96 (witnesses Garrett, English, and Seabold).

24. "Minutes of Trial," 77; accord, Watt Manuscript, 92-93; "Documents," 45.

25. "Minutes of Trial," 78; Watt Manuscript, 94; accord, "Documents," 46. (Watt Manuscript, 93, mistakenly names this witness "James L. Gill.")

26. "Documents," 46; accord, Watt Manuscript, 94.

27. "Minutes of Trial," 78; accord, Watt Manuscript, 94.

28. Watt Manuscript, 95.

29. "Minutes of Trial," 80; Watt Manuscript, 98.

30. "Minutes of Trial," 78 (testimony of Garrett).

31. *Nauvoo Neighbor*, June 4, 1845. The publication of this newspaper notice seems to confirm the original Daniels-Littlefield financial arrangement and to date the falling-out between the two young venturers. Perhaps Littlefield sought to rescind payment of his obligation to Daniels just after the trial because he felt that Daniels's sworn disavowal of authorship and contradiction of details had ruined sales prospects for the booklet.

32. "Minutes of Trial," 79; Watt Manuscript, 94; "Documents," 46.

33. *Missouri Republican,* May 31, 1845.

34. Hancock County Census, 1850, p. 299; Scofield, *History of Hancock County,* 1059.

35. "Minutes of Trial," 82-83; "Documents," 51; Watt Manuscript, 100.

36. Hancock County Census, 1850, p. 315.

37. "Minutes of Trial," 81; "Documents," 50; Watt Manuscript, 98.

38. "Minutes of Trial," 85; "Documents," 53; Watt Manuscript, 104.

39. "Minutes of Trial," 83; "Documents," 51-52; Watt Manuscript, 101.

40. Bedell, who was quartermaster of the Warsaw militia, said he did not get as far as the shanties on the day of the murder. An elected justice of the peace, Bedell figured in this trial at many stages. He was chosen for the grand jury that indicted these defendants, but was excused for cause. In this May term of court he was selected on the third panel of petit jurors, but was again excused. He was appointed a deputy elisor in the case. Thomas Sharp's unpublished manuscript on the anti-Mormon disturbances (Yale University Library) called Bedell "the only notorious Jack Mormon in Warsaw," and describes how he had to flee to Nauvoo during the late summer of 1845. Thomas Barnes also referred to him as a Jack Mormon during this period; yet defense witness Charles Andrews testified that William Daniels had told him that Bedell was the one who offered him $500 to go away and not testify against the defendants. Bedell denied this in his testimony. See "Muster Roll"; *Election Returns,* 56:64

(1843); Barnes Letter in Huntress, *Murder of an American Prophet*, 154; "Minutes of Trial," 81; Watt Manuscript, 99.

41. "Minutes of Trial," 81-83; "Documents," 50; Watt Manuscript, 99-100.

42. "Minutes of Trial," 81; accord, "Documents," 50. The Mormon source is more incriminating: "The Governor has not wipt us yet for we have killed the Smiths." Watt Manuscript, 99.

43. "Minutes of Trial," 84; Watt Manuscript, 102.

44. "Minutes of Trial," 84-85; Watt Manuscript, 102-4.

45. Hancock County Census, 1850, p. 419.

46. Subpoena and attachment in case file in *People* v. *Levi Williams*.

47. "Minutes of Trial," 85; accord, "Documents," 54; Watt Manuscript, 105.

48. "Minutes of Trial," 86; Watt Manuscript, 106.

49. Linder, *Reminiscences*, 258-59.

50. Doyle, "Josiah Lamborn," 186-87, 189, 191.

51. Moses, *Illinois Historical*, II, 968-69; Doyle, "Josiah Lamborn," 187-88.

52. Doyle, "Josiah Lamborn," 188.

53. "Minutes of Trial," 22-23, contain summary notes on Lamborn's argument.

54. "Minutes of Trial," 22.

55. *Ibid.*

56. *Ibid.* Though abandoning the testimony of these witnesses because of their supposed perjury, Lamborn took care to emphasize that he made no charges against the Mormons, the defendants, or anyone else for trying to influence their testimony.

57. "Minutes of Trial," 22. Two days later a newspaperman wrote from Carthage that Davis and Grover declined Lamborn's offer to stop all further proceedings against them because they preferred to await the jury's decision of acquittal (*Missouri Republican*, June 7, 1845). Whether the charges were formally withdrawn from the jury's consideration or not, once Lamborn made his concession, these two defendants were effectively relieved from the prosecution and could not be tried again for the same offense.

58. "Minutes of Trial," 22.

59. *Burlington Hawkeye*, June 5, 1845, quoted in Cecil A. Snider, "Development of Attitudes in Sectarian Conflict: A Study of Mormonism in Illinois in Contemporary Newspaper Sources" (M.A. thesis, University of Iowa, 1933), 256.

60. *Illinois State Legislature, Report of the Select Committee Relative to the Sinking Fund*, H.R., 15th Assem., 1st sess., March 1, 1847, p. 8.

61. *Ibid.*, 5. This fee seems small for a week-long trial and preparation, when compared with the $25 fee Abraham Lincoln received for representing the state as special counsel in a typical criminal trial that was probably concluded in a matter of hours. Frank, *Lincoln as a Lawyer*, 66.

62. Linder, *Reminiscences*, 259.

63. "Minutes of Trial," 22.

64. *Ibid.*, 23.

65. *Ibid.*

66. *Missouri Republican*, June 7, 1845.

67. *Revised Statutes of Illinois* (1845), 155.

68. *Burlington Hawkeye*, June 5, 1845, quoted in C. Snider, "Development of Attitudes in Sectarian Conflict," 256.

69. *Missouri Republican*, June 7, 1845.

70. Smith, *History of the Church*, VII, 420.

71. All quotations from the Warren speech are taken from the 6-page typescript copy of the notes of Almeron Wheat from Columbia University Library.

72. *Ibid.*

73. *Burlington Hawkeye,* June 5, 1845, quoted in C. Snider, "Development of Attitudes in Sectarian Conflict," 256-57.

74. There are two sources on the content of the Skinner argument. Almeron Wheat made 11 pages of handwritten notes, which are now found in the Illinois State Historical Society Library, Springfield (hereafter cited as Wheat Notes on Skinner Argument). Shortly after the trial, Wheat gave these notes to Skinner. On June 20, 1845, Skinner returned the notes with a letter in which he says that he had used the notes and his memory to write out his speech ("Minutes of Trial," 102). The speech was apparently written out for publication, because Skinner requests Wheat to examine and correct the proof sheets before publication. Skinner's written version (which appears in the "Minutes of Trial,' 87-101) is almost three times longer than the Wheat Notes on Skinner Argument, and is of course much smoother. A comparison of the two sources shows that the manuscript Skinner prepared for publication polished and expanded the content of the notes, and also added some new material. The differences are what would be expected when an extemporaneous speech is revised for publication to a wider audience.

75. "Minutes of Trial," 87.

76. *Ibid.,* 88.

77. Wheat Notes on Skinner Argument, 8.

78. *Ibid.,* 5-6.

79. *Ibid.,* 9.

80. *Ibid.,* 10-11.

81. *Ibid.,* 11.

82. *Burlington Hawkeye,* June 5, 1845, quoted in C. Snider, "Development of Attitudes in Sectarian Conflict," 255-56.

83. "Minutes of Trial," 16. This is the only source for Browning's argument.

84. *Ibid.,* 18.

85. *Ibid.*

86. *Ibid.,* 20.

87. *Ibid.,* 18.

88. *Ibid.,* 16-17.

89. *Ibid.,* 19.

90. *Ibid.*

91. Thomas Starkie, *A Practical Treatise on the Law of Evidence,* 8th American ed. (1860), 873, referred to in "Minutes of Trial," 20, 23.

92. "Minutes of Trial," 20-21.

93. *Circuit Court Record,* 291.

94. Ford, *History of Illinois,* 83.

95. "The Court is asked to instruct the jury for the Defendants that unless the circumstances and facts proven in this case satisfy them as fully and completely of the guilt of the Defendants, as they would have been satisfied by the positive evidence of eye witnesses, they will find the Defendants not guilty.

"That if all the facts and circumstances which the evidence in this case tends to prove may be true, and still the murder have been committed by other persons than the Defendants, and without the agency of the Defendants, that then it will be the duty of the jury to find the Defendants not guilty.

"That unless the evidence is of such a character as to establish conclusively the guilt of the Defendants, and to show that the murder must have been committed by them, and to satisfy the minds of the jury beyond all reasonable doubt that the murder could not have been committed by other persons than the Defendants, and without the agency of the Defendants, that then they will find the Defts. not guilty.

"That where the evidence is circumstantial admitting all to be proven which the evidence tends to prove, if then the jury can make any supposition consistent with the facts by which the murder might have been committed without the agency of the Defendants it will be their duty to make that supposition, and to find the Defendants not guilty.

"That before they can find the Defendants guilty they must be satisfied to the exclusion of every reasonable doubt that the murder was committed by the Defendants, and not by others without the agency of the Defendants.

"And that if they entertain any reasonable doubt of the murder having been committed by the Defendants, that then it will be their duty to find the Defendants not guilty.

"That in order to [find] a verdict of acquital [sic] it is not necessary that the jury should be able to say who committed the murder.

"That if they are in doubt as to who the persons are who actually committed the murder, and if it is possible, consistently with the facts proven, that the murder may have been committed by other persons than the Defendants and without their consent that then they must find a verdict of not guilty.

"That in making of their verdict in this case they will exclude from their consideration all that was said by Daniels, Brackenburg [sic] and Miss Graham.

" 'Whenever the probability is of a definite and limited nature, whether in the proportion of one hundred to one, or of one thousand to one, or any other ratio, is immaterial, it cannot be safely made the ground of conviction, for to act upon it in any case would be to decide, that for the sake of convicting many criminals the life of one innocent man might be sacrificed.' I Starkie, 508." Jury instructions in case file in *People* v. *Levi Williams,* partially published in Gregg, *History of Hancock County,* 330. The last paragraph is a direct quote from Starkie, *A Practical Treatise on the Law of Evidence,* 861.

96. *Circuit Court Record,* 291.

97. *Missouri Republican,* May 27, 1845.

98. *Ibid.,* June 7, 1845.

99. Jury verdict in the case file, *People* v. *Levi Williams; Circuit Court Record,* 291.

100. Hay, "The Mormon Prophet's Tragedy," 678. Thomas Gregg in his *History of Hancock County,* 330, charges Hay's article with "abounding in extravagant and sensational statements and surmises," and calls the above accusation "extremely unjust."

101. *Nauvoo Neighbor,* June 4, 1845, reprinted in Smith, *History of the Church,* VII, 422.

102. Smith, *History of the Church,* VII, 420.

103. *Ibid.,* 425.

104. "Journal of Willard Richards," June 1, 5, and 8, 1845, Church Archives.

105. "Minutes of Trial," 22.

❧ 11 ❧

"Away to a Land of Peace"

Exonerated of the charge of murdering Joseph Smith, the Carthage defendants now demanded that their trial for the murder of Hyrum begin immediately. However, the prosecution asked for more time to collect evidence since the witnesses used in the first trial had been so thoroughly discredited. Judge Young responded by ordering a special term of court to commence on Tuesday, June 24. The defendants gave bail of $5,000 and were set free.[1]

Preparations for the special session went forward routinely. On June 5 the county commissioners selected the names of twenty-four persons to serve as petit jurors.[2] Apparently following the precedent of the elisors, they selected not a single Mormon. On the same day Lamborn gave the clerk of court a list of sixty-one persons whom he wished to subpoena as witnesses for the prosecution; on June 18 he added thirty-two more, making a total of ninety-three. This was the sort of advance work that should have been done for the first trial. By trial time forty persons had been served with subpoenas, including some who were not participants in the first trial. George and Mrs. Stigall, the jailers at Carthage, were served with subpoenas, as were Henry Stephens, militia adjutant who reportedly received the message from the guards at the jail; William Baldwin, who was one of those guards; and Michael Barnes, Jr., and other members of the Carthage Greys. A subpoena was also issued for John Taylor, but he could not be found.[3]

Judge Young returned to Carthage for the trial on June 24, but no one appeared for the prosecution. Young adjourned court until the next day, but to no effect. Neither Lamborn nor any other prosecutor appeared. Judge Young accordingly ordered that the case be "dismissed for want of prosecution and that the said defendants be discharged."[4]

There is no direct evidence to explain why the state failed to proceed with the prosecution for the murder of Hyrum, especially after extensive preliminary preparations seemed to promise new testimony. The single source touching on this matter is a letter which Lamborn wrote to Governor Ford on June 11 in which he incidentally mentioned the trials at Hancock and asked for the governor's views on whether he should go to Carthage for the special term of court.[5] In light of this inquiry, it seems doubtful that Lamborn stayed away and discontinued the prosecution solely on his own initiative. Ford probably decided that the honor of the state was sufficiently vindicated by the trial in May and that the possible new testimony made no difference for that purpose. Ford had little faith that the Mormons had a future in Illinois in any case. In April, before the first trial, Ford had recommended to Brigham Young that the Saints migrate to a far distant country. Given your enemies, he said, "I confess that I do not foresee the time when you will be permitted to enjoy quiet."[6]

Ford's anticipation of further conflict proved justified. On the day set for the trial for the murder of Hyrum Smith, violence broke out against Minor Deming, the county sheriff who had been elected with Mormon support in August, 1844. Deming, a sensitive and deeply religious man, had settled on a farm in St. Mary's Township in eastern Hancock County in 1838 and worked his way up to brigadier general in the state militia. Opposed to mob activities, he said in the fall of 1844 that his election as sheriff had put him at the "head of the party in the county that contends for the *rights* of the Mormons against robbery and extermination."[7] But the polarization of politics in the county made it extremely difficult for any neutral voice to be heard; a pacifist like Deming could not speak for Mormon rights without being viewed as an enemy by the anti-Mormons. In a letter to his brother in July, 1845, Deming protested that "these men have declared they will not regard the law." Deming said considerable pressure was put upon him to join the anti-Mormon cause: "Would I be the instrument of their designs for agitation, violence & crime, I could escape their wrath."[8]

When Deming entered the lower hall of the courthouse on June 24, he was quickly "surrounded by the men that were engaged in

the murder of the Smiths, & who were armed with pistols & knives."
One of the crowd, a man of violent temper named Samuel Marshall,
began to argue with Deming over a contested land sale.[9] Deming,
who until recently had never worn a gun, had come to court armed,
maintaining that his life had been previously threatened. In Deming's account of the incident, Marshall grasped him by the collar
and "assailed me in a fit of passion from whom I retreated while
he was beating & attempting to throttle me."[10] In the struggle Deming shot Marshall in the stomach.[11] Deming believed that Marshall's
attack was premeditated, that the anti-Mormons wished to involve
him in an incident to disqualify him as sheriff.[12] The *Quincy Whig*,
however, took a typical anti-Mormon view, labeling Deming "an
instrument of Ford and his right hand friends the Mormons." The
editor said the county could expect such violence until the cause
is removed.[13]

On the day after the killing Deming was indicted by a non-
Mormon grand jury, hastily assembled by coroner George W. Stigall
(whom Judge Young had appointed to perform the sheriff's duties
during his disability).[14] Young set bail at $5,000, which was
promptly furnished with the aid of some Mormons.[15] Deming's
trial was set for the October term. In July he resigned as sheriff.
According to his wife, he did this "so it could not be said that he
used his official station to prejudice his trial."[16] This made necessary
a special election, which was held in early August.[17]

The new political campaign sharpened Hancock County antago-
nisms to the point of further violence. The Mormons lent their support for sheriff to Jacob Backenstos, a non-Mormon of shrewdness
and easy manners who was an intimate friend of Stephen A. Douglas.[18] H. W. Miller was the Mormons' choice for coroner, but they
supported no one for county commissioner, leaving unopposed the
non-Mormon candidate, George Walker, who had been a witness
at the trial.[19] The anti-Mormons, with no apparent chance for victory, ran John Scott and David Bettisworth for sheriff and coroner,
primarily, as the *St. Louis Reveille* noted, to harass the Mormons.[20]
On election day a fight nearly broke out at Warsaw between the
two groups. Commenting on the situation a former resident of Warsaw, the Reverend B. F. Morris, wrote in the *Warsaw Signal* that

the anti-Mormons were awaiting some Mormon atrocity as an excuse to drive them from the state. He said, "Every tie which binds man to his fellows seems broken."[21]

When Backenstos defeated Scott by 2,334 votes to 750, the largest majority ever in the county, the anti-Mormons were infuriated. Thomas Sharp published an attack on the new sheriff, describing him as "a despicable puppy."[22] The Mormons seemed to gain some moral lift from the political victory; Brigham Young wrote to Wilford Woodruff in England, "The mobocrats begin to tremble, and make preparations for leaving this county and we pray the Lord to speed their flight."[23] But a week later Young instructed the Council that three thousand men should start for upper California in the spring.[24]

On September 10 Minor Deming died suddenly of consumptive fever at his home in St. Mary's. His death marked more than the end of a man's life, for on that same day news reached Nauvoo that attacks had begun on an outlying Mormon community. The uneasy peace had terminated. Whatever commitment may have remained to maintaining law and order and resolving Mormon and non-Mormon differences with customary legal procedures was now without a voice or a leader. Between the Mormons and anti-Mormons, with their sharply divergent views of social and political pluralism, warfare alone would settle the issues.

The renewed violence began on September 9, when shots were fired at a schoolhouse in Green Plains, where the anti-Mormons were holding a meeting.[25] The anti-Mormons blamed the Mormons, and the following day, under the leadership of Levi Williams, they attacked the Mormons at Morley's settlement and burned several houses.[26] Before the burning of outlying Mormon communities had ceased a month later, the antis had destroyed about a hundred Mormon homes. When Solomon Hancock, the leader of a Mormon settlement, sought counsel from Brigham Young, he was told to sell out to the mob for cattle and wagons and emigrate to Nauvoo "and perhaps next Spring some further."[27]

Young sent instructions to Sheriff Backenstos to "quell the mob" and urged him to inform Governor Ford and obtain assistance.[28] He wrote to Solomon Hancock, "Let the Sheriff of Hancock county attend to the mob & let us see whether he and the 'Jack Mormons' so called, the priests of law & order, will calmly sit down & watch the funeral procession of Illinois liberty."[29] To the elders he said he would let the mob continue "until the surrounding counties should be convinced that we are not the aggressors."[30] But when Backenstos advised Young on September 14 that he was not able to secure the support of neutrals at Warsaw, Young commanded General Charles C. Rich to have all "quorums" of the elders ready for any military emergency.[31] On September 15 Backenstos wrote Young that Levi Williams had ordered out his militia and "we must whip them," but Young told Backenstos to wait a few days.[32]

On the sixteenth Sheriff Backenstos, threatened with violence at Carthage because of his close tie with the Mormons, began to move his family to Nauvoo. Seeing that he was followed by armed men, he took refuge overnight with a friend in Warsaw. The next morning, as he hurried north out of Warsaw in a buggy, ten or twenty men gave chase on horseback. Franklin Worrell of the Carthage Greys, commander of the guard at the jail and a key witness at the trial, was one of four men who, in an attempt to intercept Backenstos, separated from the main body after a two-mile chase. As these pursuers closed to within 150 yards, Backenstos reached the railroad shanties north of Warsaw, where some members of the Mormon militia were escorting to Nauvoo some Mormon families who had been burned out of their homes. Backenstos shouted to the Mormons for help and got an instant response from Orrin Porter Rockwell, close friend and former bodyguard of the dead prophet. Rockwell reassured Backenstos that his men had fifty rounds of ammunition and two fifteen-shot rifles. Backenstos immediately commanded his pursuers to stop, but they kept riding toward him. At Backenstos's command Rockwell singled out Worrell, took careful aim, and shot him squarely in the belt buckle, knocking him out of his saddle.[33] The other pursuers reined in, put Worrell in a wagon, and rode hard for Warsaw. Worrell died en route. He was buried in a ten-dollar coffin beneath a wooden headboard bearing the epitaph: "He who is without enemies is unworthy of friends."[34]

The Worrell shooting produced a new wave of anti-Mormon excitement. The *Warsaw Signal* issued another call to arms,[35] and E. A. Bedell, the Jack Mormon postmaster of Warsaw, was driven out of town by an armed mob and took refuge in Nauvoo. Brigham

Young, who had already seen the drift of events, on September 16 urged the Twelve to propose a settlement with their enemies, either to buy out the old citizens of Hancock County or to sell out and launch a general Mormon exodus in the spring.[36] A document to this effect was drawn up and sent to the anti-Mormons at Warsaw.[37] On September 18 the old citizens appointed a committee consisting of Levi Williams, George Rockwell, and others to consider the Mormon offer, but Williams rejected the preamble, which was addressed to "the mob engaged in burning Mormon houses."[38]

Meanwhile, Jacob Backenstos collected a large contingent of Mormon militia and moved toward Carthage to arrest Levi Williams and his men. One of Backenstos's aides informed Young on September 18 that Williams had but three hundred men and might easily be arrested if the sheriff's force were large enough. Backenstos asked Young for six hundred of the Nauvoo Legion. For a time Young entertained the idea,[39] but on the nineteenth he told Backenstos that if the mobbers moved toward Missouri the sheriff should not cut them off but should post enough men to prevent their return. Young promised that "when we can we will bring them to justice, for the time will come that they may be dealt with according to the law of God and not endanger the lives of the Saints." He ordered the militia to return to Nauvoo but to leave forty or fifty men east of Warsaw to keep watch.[40] At this point many of the anti-Mormons fled the state, believing that their enemies had military control of the county.[41]

From the Missouri side of the river the *Republican* began to beat the drum for a war of extermination. The editor observed that "the excitement exceeds anything of which I had any conception."[42] An incident that heightened anti-Mormon feeling was the killing of a house burner, McBradney, and the reported mutilation of his body by Backenstos's men.[43]

By this time news of civil war had reached Governor Ford. He hurried to Jacksonville to confer with leading Whigs and called for volunteers for an expeditionary force, citing evidence that ninety houses had been burned by the anti-Mormons. Ford asked a Whig, John Hardin, to take command and march toward Carthage, where Sheriff Backenstos had set up temporary headquarters after driving the anti-Mormons out.[44] Ford wrote to the sheriff on September 21 that he should surrender to Hardin and submit himself for trial before Judge Purple for the murder of Worrell. Ford told Backenstos that there would be a large meeting at Carthage with representatives from many surrounding counties and all would demand the sheriff's arrest.[45]

On September 22 a delegation of citizens of Macomb, Illinois, came to Nauvoo to investigate whether the Mormons were willing to leave the state according to the proposition that had been sent to the Warsaw troops. Brigham Young replied that Levi Williams had not complied with the Mormon terms, but if the people of the surrounding counties would help the Saints sell their land, it would hasten their departure. Young indicated that all payments for land must be made beforehand in cash or goods, all house burnings must cease, and vexatious indictments must be stayed.[46]

Many in the surrounding counties were irate at the Mormons' alternative suggestion that the non-Mormons should sell out to them. The citizens of Macomb urged that non-Mormons wage war on the Saints, rather than sell their land.[47] At Quincy on September 22 citizens met and resolved that all Mormons must go.[48] Thomas Gregg informed Young, however, that there were enough people in western Illinois who wanted peace that violence could be stopped if the Saints would guarantee their departure. Young replied to Gregg on the twenty-third that the Saints would sell out at a fair price or offer the old citizens such if they preferred. On the same day officer Michael Barnes came to Nauvoo with writs for several Mormon leaders. The anti-Mormons were determined to put as much pressure as possible upon the Mormon leaders to force them to a decision. Barnes took several Mormons, including Willard Richards, John Taylor, and Orson Spencer, to Carthage on the twenty-third, but the complainant withdrew the charges he had made against them for participation in the *Expositor* affair, saying he had no first-hand evidence. The Mormon expression of willingness to leave the state had brought a wait-and-see attitude on the part of some of the anti-Mormons of Carthage.

Still, other citizens maintained the pressure to leave. On the twenty-fourth a committee from Quincy, headed by Henry Asbury, requested a statement of Mormon intentions. Brigham Young replied that his people could not promise to leave within six months, but when "grass grows and water runs." Young made an important concession at this point — the Mormons would be the ones to sell out, and they would plant no more crops in Nauvoo.[49] Irene Hascall, a young Mormon, recorded the decision: "The Twelve will go where they will not trouble [the] United States with the Mormon religion." Irene said that they would "cross the rocky mountains to the healthier climate," and added, "What a good time we will have journying and pitching our tents like the Israelites."[50] Young had apparently been influenced by the objections of the substantial citizens of counties adjoining Hancock that for the old citizens to sell out to the Mormons would leave those in the surrounding areas still with a "Mormon problem."[51]

While the difficult negotiations were underway, John J. Hardin crossed the Illinois River at Beardstown on September 26 en route to Carthage with a small contingent of downstate militia. Accompanied by Stephen A. Douglas, W. B. Warren, and Attorney General J. A. McDougal as special representatives of Governor Ford, Hardin was to restore order in Hancock County and urge the Mormons to leave the state.[52] On the twenty-eighth Hardin issued a proclamation that no armed force in the county was to exceed four men.[53] When Hardin arrived at Carthage, he found Jacob Backenstos and his men in control of the town and thirty men bivouacked in the courthouse. Hardin gave Backenstos twenty minutes to leave town.[54]

On the thirtieth Hardin, along with Douglas and McDougal, came to Nauvoo and searched for the bodies of two anti-Mormons allegedly hidden there. The Mormons bitterly resented the intrusion of armed troops into their city, but Hardin's main purpose was to put pressure upon the Mormons to hurry their exodus. The *Sangamo Journal* stated on October 1 that public sentiment throughout the state was decidely against the Mormons, and that they must go.[55]

Brigham Young wrote to Hardin on the first that plans were already underway at Nauvoo so that a thousand families would depart in the spring. Young said they would leave regardless of whether or not sufficient land sales had taken place, but others would remain until their property was sold, which included hundreds of farms and two thousand houses. Young said his people would not sacrifice this property or give it away.[56]

At Carthage on October 1 and 2 a convention of citizens from several counties surrounding Hancock met to consider terms for peace with the Mormons. After debating whether the Mormons must exodus now or in the spring, they agreed to accept the Mormon propositions, provided the Saints would adhere to them. They stipulated that the old citizens should be allowed to return to their homes without any legal proceedings being initiated against them and without any harassment by Sheriff Backenstos. They demanded that Mormon lawlessness cease and recommended that a small body of state militia be kept in the county until spring. They warned that, should any outrages occur in the interim, their troops would march en masse on Nauvoo and summarily end all disturbances. They requested that Judge Purple hold no sessions of the circuit court in October, when proceedings against the house-burners had been scheduled, and demanded that Mormon officers in the county — Backenstos, Miller, Coulson, and Perkins — resign.[57]

John J. Hardin attended the meetings in Carthage and wrote to the leaders of the Mormons on October 2 that he had conferred with the representatives of nine counties at Carthage and learned of their acceptance of the Mormon proposal. He warned that if the Mormons did not go, expulsion would follow. Governor Ford wrote Hardin on October 13, praising him for getting the Mormons to go "voluntarily" and without bloodshed.[58]

Brigham Young wrote to Wilford Woodruff that Hardin and Stephen A. Douglas "told us plainly that the prejudice of the people was such that the state cannot possibly protect us and that it is therefore advisable for us to remove as the only conditions of *peace*." After coming to an understanding with the Mormon leaders, Hardin and his men went into the field to try to arrest the mobbers who were still burning some Mormon homes. But Brigham Young told Wilford Woodruff that Hardin had accomplished "nothing as yet against the house burners and they never will."[59]

Hardin was able to establish sufficient order for the October session of the circuit court of Hancock County to be held at Carthage. Some Mormons accused of riot in the *Expositor* affair were scheduled for trial, and an attempt was to be made to have a grand jury indict the mobbers who had participated in the September burnings. The anti-Mormons were countering with an attempt to indict Jacob Backenstos for the murder of Worrell.

The county commissioners numbered two to one in favor of the Mormons, with Mormons Andrew H. Perkins and George Coulson standing against George Walker, who had been elected in August. On September 17 the commissioners chose a grand jury, as well as two panels of petit jurors.[60] The twenty-three selected as grand jurors included at least eight Mormons, while there were twelve among the two panels of petit jurors.[61] It seemed that there was a chance for justice to be done if cooperation were possible — but the politics of the situation overrode all other considerations, and the anti-Mormons soon maneuvered to remove Mormon jurors from their cases.

As soon as court convened on October 20, Michael Barnes, who had been charged with being one of the "grain and house burners," filed an affidavit claiming that the county commissioners were prejudiced against him and asking that the grand jury be set aside and elisors be appointed to select replacements. Following Judge Young's precedent from the May term, Judge Purple granted the motion and appointed Thomas H. Owen and James D. Morgan as elisors.[62] These men selected a new grand jury with only four Mormons.[63] This jury indicted Backenstos for the murder of Worrell. The judge authorized the coroner, acting as sheriff, to dispatch troops if necessary to protect Backenstos. To escape trial before a hostile Hancock jury, Backenstos obtained a change of venue to Peoria and later to Knox County, where he was tried and acquitted in December.[64] Non-Mormons testified that Worrell knew he was following Backenstos and that he planned to kill him.[65] In early May, 1846, Orrin Porter Rockwell was taken into custody in Nauvoo by six heavily armed riflemen who took him to Quincy to be held for the Worrell killing. After a change of venue to Galena, Rockwell was indicted by a grand jury in June and tried and acquitted in August, after Sheriff Backenstos testified that he ordered Rockwell to shoot Worrell.[66]

The forty or so Mormons who sought a hearing on the house burnings could get no consideration from the grand jury. They knocked at the door of the jury room and even made supplications to individual jurors, but the jury refused to admit them or hear their testimony.[67] In contrast to their difficulty with the elisor's grand jury, the Mormons had things their own way with a petit jury selected from the panels chosen by the county commissioners. Eleven Mormons had previously been indicted for riot in the destruction of the *Expositor,* but only two were arrested and brought to trial. These men — Jesse P. Harmon and John Lytle, law enforcement officials in Nauvoo — seemed doomed to conviction when Judge Purple told the jury to disregard their defense, that they had acted under the order of the city council. Purple instructed the jury that if they found that the defendants participated in the suppression of the *Expositor,* they must find them guilty. Fortunately for Lytle and Harmon, each had a brother who was also a policeman in Nauvoo, and the witness for the prosecution said he could not determine which Harmon or Lytle he had observed. The jury took this opportunity and brought in a verdict of not guilty.[68] This may have been another instance of jury "nullification," but if so it was at least administered by a jury representing a cross-section of the principal groups in the county.

In describing the unique situation prevailing at this time, Governor Ford said that the law had provided a means for giving each party a jury to their liking. As a result, "no one would be convicted of any crime in Hancock; and this put an end to the administration of the criminal law in that distracted county."[69] While there is some truth in this observation, it constitutes an overstatement, for examination of the court records from 1844 through 1846 shows that grand juries continued to indict accused persons, and voluntary dismissals of the prosecuting attorney continued to account for far more people going free than acquittals by a jury.

Despite the establishment of a military and legal equilibrium in Hancock County by October, feelings remained agitated. On October 23 Orson Spencer wrote to Governor Ford, affirming that Hardin's troops had achieved nothing against the burners but were harassing the Mormons at Nauvoo with frequent visits.[70] Governor Ford answered this letter on October 30 by claiming that while Backenstos had driven the burners out, he had aggravated the anti-Mormons to the point that they were ready for an armed invasion of Nauvoo. Ford warned the Saints against any retaliation against the burners by stealing. These activities could lead to expulsion before spring.[71]

In Iowa Dr. Abitha Williams swore out a writ against the Twelve for the making of bogus money. Almon W. Babbitt informed Brigham Young of this on October 26 and said that Major Warren, with downstate militia, was coming to Nauvoo the next day to aid the sheriff in making arrests. The Twelve went into hiding in the night.[72] On October 27, amidst great excitement, Brigham Young was indicted by the Hancock County grand jury. Abitha Williams, himself under suspicion for counterfeiting, testified at the hearing that he could show where the bogus money was being made in Nauvoo.[73]

Major Warren came to Nauvoo the following evening but told the Mormons that although he had writs against the Twelve, he would not serve them, since he believed they were of a vexatious sort. Warren said he feared that if the writs were served it would prevent the exodus. George Miller, who visited Governor Ford in behalf of the Mormon leaders, reported Ford as saying that "if he were to exert the executive influence in your behalf, as ought to be done in justice to us, it would result in his overthrow and ours also." Ford said that "the whole state were mob and that he could not trust them to act in any emergency where we as a community were a party."[74] When Ford wrote to Backenstos, he informed him not to be concerned over the writs from Iowa, for he and the leaders of the antis believed that attempts to serve them would impede the exodus. Should the governor of Iowa request extradition, Ford said he would encourage him to withdraw it. But Ford added that an impending federal indictment of the Twelve was another matter, and that President Polk might call out the army to prevent the Mormons from going to the Rockies. Ford speculated that federal officials feared that, once out of the United States, the Mormons might attach themselves to the British during the war that seemed impending over the drawing of the Oregon boundary.[75] Ford's letter was apparently intended to add an additional reason for the Saints to hasten on their way.

In early November federal writs were issued against Brigham Young for counterfeiting. Federal officers came to Nauvoo accompanied by the Quincy Rifles, a contingent of the state militia from downriver. Nauvoo was immediately in an uproar, its citizens believing that the terms of the compromise settlement of October had been violated. The *Quincy Whig* reported that the Mormons vowed they would honor no more writs, and that armed resistance might be resorted to.[76]

Violence broke out again on November 15. A fire was set near the barn of Edmund Durfee, a Mormon at Camp Creek in the southern part of the county, and when he went to put it out he was shot and killed by a mobber who boasted that he could down the Mormon with one shot.[77] The *Quincy Whig* deplored the burnings and murder and maintained that it was the act of a drunk,[78] but an anti-Mormon magistrate at Carthage would hear no Mormon witnesses, and charges were dismissed.[79]

The Mormons intensified their preparations for exodus, urging the faithful to gather at Nauvoo and make ready for the trek west. Orson Pratt, who had been chosen to administer the church affairs in the East, wrote to the Saints: "Let every branch in the East, West, North and South be determined to flee out of Babylon . . . Judgment is at the door."[80] The *Nauvoo Neighbor* announced on November 19 that 2,500 wagons were ready. Blacksmiths were working night and day in the Mormon town, preparing wagons and handcarts.

Concern in the Mormon community mounted in mid-December, when Samuel Brannan wrote to Brigham Young from New York that the secretary of war was determined not to allow the Mormons to leave the United States. The elders in Nauvoo prayed that they might "be led out of this ungodly nation in peace."[81] On December 12 the *Illinois State Register* ran a piece from the *Washington Union,* urging the federal government to look into the Mormon exodus. In a somewhat ironic request, the editor of the *Register* advised the Saints to publish why they were leaving. The editor said it would be foolish for the Mormons to establish their own government in the West — that after the impending war with the United States the British would abandon the Mormons.

Perhaps to offset fears of Mormon alienation, Brigham Young wrote to Secretary of War William L. Marcy on December 14 and to Stephen A. Douglas three days later, seeking a government contract to build federal forts in Oregon. He told Douglas that the Mormons would remember him when their territory became a state.[82]

In late December a grand jury of the U.S. Circuit Court at Springfield returned indictments against the Twelve for counterfeiting, and federal marshals came to Nauvoo to arrest Brigham Young. They were without a detachment of state militia which they had sought from Governor Ford, who insisted that militia would first have to be called out by the president.[83] Taking into custody a man they thought to be Young, the marshals escorted their prisoner to Carthage — only to find that the Mormons had dressed William Miller in Brigham's clothes and perpetrated a hoax. Young and the Twelve went into hiding once more.[84] None were ever arrested, and the case against Brigham and ten others was "dismissed on motion of the District Attorney" in 1848.[85]

During this time the execution of legal process in Hancock was crippled by hostile feelings between Mormons and non-Mormons. County commissioners refused to pay the expenses that George Stigall said he incurred during the special June term, and he brought suit against them in the circuit court.[86] In January, 1846, the anti-Mormon clerk of the county commissioners court, George Thatcher, refused to pay a claimant who had furnished provisions to a posse led by Sheriff Backenstos. The county commissioners judged Thatcher in contempt and ordered that he be attached and confined for fifteen days or until he should comply. They also purported to remove him from office (which they apparently had no legal authority to do, since he was an elected official). The commissioners appointed a Jack Mormon lawyer, George Edmunds, as Thatcher's successor and swore him into office. Edmunds demanded the records; Thatcher refused to turn them over, appealing to the circuit court.[87] The issue was not settled until commissioners Coulson and Perkins abandoned their positions and left with the Mormons during their exodus in the spring.

Meanwhile, the Mormons intensified their work on the construction of the temple. By December they had completed certain rooms for a vital religious ceremony, the endowment. Thereafter they conducted these rituals night and day until their expulsion.[88] Thus by the narrowest of margins the Mormons attained their objective of keeping the peace and finishing the temple, a controlling consideration in the strategy of avoiding a confrontation with the anti-Mormons during the prosecution of the accused assassins.

The Mormon leaders attempted to counter the growing opinion that their loyalty to the United States was questionable by having the Nauvoo High Council write an epistle to the Saints which affirmed Mormon loyalty and promised that, if war should come with England, they would support the U.S. claim to Oregon. This pledge was redeemed within a few months, when five hundred elders left the main body of Mormons in Iowa and marched to California as the "Mormon Battalion," a contingent of the U.S. Army during the Mexican War.[89]

By early January non-Mormons in Illinois were confused and perplexed over the Mormon question. According to the *Sangamo Journal,* the Democrats in the state were planning for political purposes to encourage the Mormons to stay on in the state, but at the same time expressing fear that the federal government would not allow the Saints to immigrate to Oregon lest they help the British in a war that seemed imminent. The *Journal* itself criticized Ford bitterly for not sending state militia to arrest Brigham Young, apparently unconscious of the possible deterring effect this might have on emigration.[90]

On January 29 Samuel Brannan wrote to the Mormons that Amos Kendall had informed him of the federal government's intention to station troops west of Nauvoo and to take away Mormon arms.[91] This warning appears to have been decisive in persuading the Mormon leaders to begin their departure. They met on February 2 and agreed that they would begin the exodus as soon as possible, "for if we are here many days our way will be hedged up; our enemies have resolved to intercept us whenever we start." On the third Brigham Young told the Saints assembled at the temple that he was going to get his wagons ready and be off. The next day the first wagons crossed the ice-filled Mississippi and headed west.[92] On the eleventh the *Warsaw Signal* reported that a thousand people had left Nauvoo, including the Twelve and High Council.

Louis Barney, who rolled out of Nauvoo on the seventh, camped at Sugar Creek across the river for three weeks due to the severity of the weather. When at last his camp was ready to pull out once more, he wrote: "We . . . set our faces westward trusting in the

Providences of Almighty God for our deliverance." As the company reached a rise in ground between the Mississippi and the Des Moines rivers, they turned to look back at the temple. Its spire was "glittering in the bright shining sun. The last view of the temple was witnessed in the midst of sighs and lamentations, all faces in gloom and sorrow bathed in tears, at being forced from our homes and Temple that cost so much in toil and suffering to complete."[93]

The editor of the *Illinois State Register* wrote in March, 1846, that "the universal desire [at Nauvoo] seems to be to get away to a land of peace."[94] According to one of the persons who participated in the exodus in May: "I feel as if I narrowly escaped from Babylon with a mighty effort, it is not my wish to return."[95]

It was not until August, 1846, when a majority of the Mormons had left Nauvoo, that Thomas Sharp announced in the *Warsaw Signal* that the anti-Mormon ticket in Hancock had been uniformly successful. He told his readers, "Now we can defend our rights and property by legal means."[96] Sharp's comment was in its way something of a confession: that the anti-Mormons in their opposition to the Mormon kingdom had largely depended upon means above or beyond the written law; that political considerations and appeals to popular sovereignty had transcended commitments to legal procedures and legal rights.

1. *St. Louis New Era,* June 9, 1845; *Missouri Republican,* June 2 and 7, 1845; *Circuit Court Record,* 291-92.

2. *Hancock County Board Minutes,* 4:317.

3. See Smith, *History of the Church,* VII, 142; "Muster Roll"; subpoenas and returns in case file in *People* v. *Levi Williams;* Appendix herein.

4. *Circuit Court Record,* 302. See also *Missouri Republican,* June 30, 1845.

5. Josiah Lamborn to Thomas Ford, Governor's Correspondence File, 1840-45, Illinois State Archives, Springfield.

6. Smith, *History of the Church,* VII, 398.

7. Minor Deming to Stephen Deming, August 22, 1844. Deming's wife later wrote that his enemies "could bring no charge against him except he thought the Mormons should be treated like other people." Abigail Deming to Stephen Deming, September 23, 1845. The Deming letters are in the Illinois Historical Survey, University of Illinois Library, Urbana.

8. Minor Deming to Stephen Deming, July 1, 1845.

9. *Ibid.; Illinois State Register,* July 4, 1845; Scofield, *History of Hancock County,* 766.

10. Minor Deming to Stephen Deming, June 24, 1845.

11. Brigham Young to Wilford Woodruff, June 27, 1845, Young Papers, Church Archives; *Illinois State Register,* July 4, 1845.

12. Minor Deming to Stephen Deming, July 1, 1845.

13. *Quincy Whig,* July 2, 1845.

14. *Circuit Court Record,* 296-97, 308; Gregg, *History of Hancock County,* 339; and Appendix herein.

15. *Ibid.,* 311; and Smith, *History of the Church,* VII, 432. *Circuit Court Record* gives the bail at $5,000, rather than the $10,000 cited in the *History of the Church.*

16. Abigail Deming to Stephen Deming, June 28, 1845. See also Minor R. Deming to Thomas Ford, July 1, 1845, Executive File.

17. *Election Returns,* 65:87.

18. Ford, *History of Illinois,* 408.

19. Perhaps the Mormons relied on the fact that they would still control two out of three of the county commissioners.

20. Cited by *Warsaw Signal,* August 20, 1845.

21. *Ibid.,* August 13, 1845.

22. *Ibid.,* September 3, 1845; *Election Returns,* 65:87.

23. Brigham Young to Wilford Woodruff, August 21, 1845, Young Papers, Church Archives.

24. "Journal History," August 28, 1845.

25. Thomas Sharp's "Manuscript History," Chicago Historical Society.

26. Flanders, *Nauvoo,* 327, Gregg, *History of Hancock County,* 340, 374; Smith, *Hisory of the Church,* VII, 439-40.

27. Brigham Young to Solomon Hancock, September 11, 1845, Young Papers, Church Archives. Figures vary on the number of houses burned during September; Flanders may be too high in estimating 200 total. See *Illinois State Register,* September 26, 1845, for Ford's estimate, and that of the editors; cf. Flanders, *Nauvoo,* 328.

28. Brigham Young to Jacob Backenstos, September 11, 1845, Young Papers, Church Archives.

29. Brigham Young to Solomon Hancock, September 12, 1845, Young Papers, Church Archives.

30. "Journal History," September 14, 1845.

31. Young's order to Rich, September 14, Young Papers, Church Archives.

32. "Journal History," September 15, 1845; Smith, *History of the Church,* VII, 445.

33. Backenstos's account appears in "Journal History," September 16, 1845. Thomas Sharp maintained that Worrell did not know it was Backenstos, that he came to a full stop on Backenstos's command, with his gun strapped to his back. Sharp did not adequately explain why Worrell pursued the sheriff. See *Warsaw Signal,* September 17 and 24, 1845. For an account which varies slightly from Backenstos's, see Harold Schindler, *Orrin Porter Rockwell; Man of God, Son of Thunder* (Salt Lake City: University of Utah Press, 1966), 145.

34. Document in the probate file of Franklin Worrell's estate; Hay, "The Mormon Prophet's Tragedy," 675.

35. *Warsaw Signal,* September 17, 1845.

36. "Journal History," September 16, 1845.

37. *Ibid.,* September 18, 1845. By the 18th the proposition of the Mormons was already in the hands of the anti-Mormons at Warsaw.

38. A. B. Chambers to Brigham Young and Council, September 18, 1845, Young Papers, Church Archives.

39. "Journal History," September 18, 1845.

40. *Ibid.,* September 19, 1845.

41. *Quincy Whig Extra,* September 18, 1845, containing a letter dated September 20.

42. *Missouri Republican,* September 19, 1845.

43. *Illinois State Register,* September 26, 1845, for a letter from Warsaw dated September 18; *Missouri Republican,* September 20, 1845; Smith, *History of the Church,* VII, 145 for Backenstos's comment.

44. Ford, *History of Illinois,* 410, and *Illinois State Register,* September 26, 1845.

45. Thomas Ford to Jacob Backenstos, September 21, 1845, Ford Papers, Church Archives.

46. "Journal History," September 22, 1845, and Young's statement to the Committee from Macomb dated September 22, 1845, Young Papers, Church Archives.

47. *Illinois State Register,* October 3, 1845, which published the resolutions of these citizens dated September 24, 1845.

48. Josiah B. Conyers, *A Brief History of the Leading Causes of the Hancock Mob, in the Year 1846* (St. Louis: Cathcart and Prescott, 1846), 7-11. Cf. *Missouri Republican,* September 26, 1845, and Henry Asbury, *Reminiscences of Quincy, Illinois* (Quincy: D. Wilcox & Sons, 1882), 160-62.

49. "Journal History," September 23 and 24, 1845.

50. See Hascall's letter dated September 31 [*sic*], 1845, in "Letters of a Proselyte," *Utah Historical Quarterly* 25 (April, 1957), 135.

51. "Journal History," September 25, 1845.

52. *Missouri Republican,* September 27, 1845; Ford, *History of Illinois,* 410.

53. "Journal History," September 28, 1845.

54. Jacob Backenstos to John Hardin, September 29, 1845, Hardin Collection, Chicago Historical Society. See also report by *Missouri Republican,* October 3, 1845.

55. "Journal History," September 30, 1845; Ford, *History of Illinois,* 411; Smith, *History of the Church,* VII, 447-48; *Sangamo Journal,* October 1, 1845.

56. Brigham Young to John Hardin, Douglas, etc., October 1, 1845, Hardin Collection, Chicago Historical Society.

57. A typewritten copy of these resolutions dated October 2, 1845, is in Pioneer Collection, Brigham Young University.

58. "Journal History," October 2, 1845; Thomas Ford to John Hardin, October 13, 1845, Hardin Collection, Chicago Historical Society.

59. Brigham Young to Wilford Woodruff, October 16, 1845, Young Papers, Church Archives.

60. *Hancock County Board Minutes,* 4:350, 359.

61. See Appendix for classification of jurors.

62. *Circuit Court Record,* 334; Smith, *History of the Church,* VII, 483, 493-94; *Warsaw Signal,* October 22, 1845. The elisor first designated was William D. Abernethy, who had served in May, but Abernethy was objected to and the judge named Captain Morgan of Adams County, who was probably James D. Morgan, commander of the Quincy guards. See Gregg, *History of Hancock County,* 345.

63. See Appendix for classification of jurors.

64. *Circuit Court Record,* 369, 370, 374, 375; Smith, *History of the Church,* VII, 494, 541.

65. *Illinois State Register,* December 19, 1845.

66. Schindler, *Orrin Porter Rockwell,* 153-55.

67. Smith, *History of the Church,* VII, 486, 494.

68. *Circuit Court Record,* 346-47; Smith, *History of the Church,* VII, 484, 485.

69. Ford, *History of Illinois,* 369.

70. Orson Spencer to Thomas Ford, October 23, 1845, Orson Spencer Papers, Church Archives.

71. Smith, *History of the Church,* VII, 505-8.

72. "Journal History," October 26, 1845.

73. Pierpont Sperry to Anson Sperry, October 27, 1845, Mormon Collection, Chicago Historical Society.

74. "Journal History," October 28, 1845.

75. Thomas Ford to Jacob Backenstos, October 29, 1845, Ford Papers, Church Archives.

76. *Quincy Whig,* November 5, 1845.

77. *Nauvoo Neighbor,* November 19, 1845.

78. *Quincy Whig,* November 19, 1845.

79. "Journal History," November 24, 1845.

80. *Times and Seasons* 6 (December 1, 1845), 1043.

81. "Journal History," December 11, 1845.

82. Brigham Young to William Marcy, December 14, 1845; Young to Stephen A. Douglas, December 17, 1845, Young Papers, Church Archives.

83. *Davenport Gazette,* January 8, 1846; *Times and Seasons* 6 (February 1, 1846), 1114-15; *Quincy Whig,* December 31, 1845.

84. "Journal History," December 23, 1845.

85. "Records of the Solicitor of the Treasury," Record Group 206, National Archives, Washington, D.C.

86. *Circuit Court Record,* 360, 391.

87. *Hancock County Board Minutes,* 4:399-423; *Circuit Court Record,* 394; Gregg, *History of Hancock County,* 346; Berry, "The Mormon Settlement in Illinois," 97-98.

88. Brigham Young to David Hollister, January 1, 1846, Young Papers, Church Archives; Smith, *History of the Church,* VII, 570.

89. *Times and Seasons* 6 (January 20, 1846), 1096-97; Roberts, *Comprehensive History,* III, 60-90.

90. Cited and commented upon by *Illinois State Register,* January 2, 1846.

91. "Journal History," January 29, 1846.

92. *Ibid.,* February 2, 3, 4, 1846.

93. "Journal of Louis Barney," February 28, 1846, Church Archives.

94. *Illinois State Register,* March 13, 1846.

95. Ursula Hascall to Col. Wilson Andrews, May 2, 1846, in "Letters of a Proselyte," 151.

96. *Warsaw Signal,* August 11, 1846.

∽ 12 ∾

"The People Reign in the American Political World"

The murders and trial at Carthage exposed some basic issues that divided Mormon and non-Mormon in Hancock County. In its own way, each group was committed to the written laws of state and nation, yet each paid allegiance to another law they deemed higher than these. The source of the Mormons' higher law was the revelations of God; its spokesman was their prophet. But with source and spokesman vested in the same individual, the anti-Mormons feared a potential tyranny.

The anti-Mormons also appealed to higher law, but its sources were diffuse and its spokesmen many. Their sources were the Bible, reason, and individual conscience — reliance on God, but also on "nature." In justifying the murders, Thomas C. Sharp called upon the natural individual and group impulse to preserve life and property:

> The Law of God and Nature is above the law of man. There is an uncontrollable impulse in the human bosom, which prompted every man to prefer his own safety and property before the law of the land. . . . True he violates the law of the land by so doing; but nature teaches every one that he commits no crime by preferring his own safety to its provisions. . . . What is true of individuals in relation to this matter is applicable to communities.[1]

This reliance upon natural law and individual conscience was consistent with developing secularism in America, and also with ideals of popular sovereignty. Sharp said in defense of the murders that where the law is too slow or too weak to function (as he maintained it was in respect to the Smiths) it became a "mere mockery; such was the conviction of every sensible man."[2] The ultimate source for justifying the "summary execution" of the Smiths was the opinion of the community of "sensible men." The authentic voices for this justification were either the town meeting, which the anti-Mormons frequently called into session, or, when the matter was forced into the judicial system, the jury. When Calvin Warren, arguing for the defense, declared that the law was "based upon public opinion, and is worth nothing without it,"[3] he was reminding the Carthage jury of their role as the spokesman for the sovereign will of the people.

The idea of the sovereign authority of the jury dates from the jury's earliest appearance. During the Middle Ages the English jury replaced a system that included trials by battle or ordeal, by which the judgment of Heaven was thought to be manifest. The jury system put the responsibility of judgment squarely upon the representatives of the community.[4] Its sovereignty was emphasized by the familiar characterization of the jury as a "barrier . . . between the liberties of the people, and the prerogative of the crown.[5] Its almost plenary authority was evident in its familiar power to determine the law as well as the facts. When nineteenth-century judges began giving instructions on the law, formally limiting the jury's function to resolving disputed facts, juries nevertheless continued to exercise control over the law in certain cases by their acknowledged power to return a general verdict of guilt or innocence without stated reasons.[6]

Prominent legal theorists like Roscoe Pound and John H. Wigmore have praised the jury's power to disregard the law in certain cases. In their view, this was necessary "to enable a verdict to be rendered which will accord with the moral sense of the community"[7] and to remedy the inevitable conflict between law and justice by supplying "that flexibility of legal rules which is essential to justice and popular contentment."[8] Referring specifically to recent prosecutions for resistance to the war and for other forms of civil disobedience, another commentator has stoutly defended what he calls the "right of jury nullification," since it allows the jury to acquit apparently guilty persons in "situations in which violation of the law should be viewed as justifiable."[9]

The history of the jury system is replete with examples of criminal defendants who were probably guilty under the plain terms of the written law but who were acquitted because the jury, as representatives of the community, approved of their crimes or thought the prescribed punishment too harsh. English and colonial juries refused to convict persons accused of a large number of relatively minor crimes that carried a death penalty.[10] The communities of colonial Massachusetts "freely received the common law of England as the basis of their jurisprudence, but simultaneously reserved the unfettered right to reject [through the action of juries] whatever parts of that law were inconsistent with their own view of justice and morality or with their own needs and circumstances."[11] In the earliest days of the republic, Massachusetts juries invariably refused to convict persons accused of violating the Embargo Act, to which the citizens of the state were unalterably opposed.[12] A similar example from Mormon history is the alleged refusal of Mormon jurors in the Utah Territory to convict co-religionists who were accused of polygamy, a refusal countered with measures to exclude Mormon jurors in such cases.[13] One of the leading causes of the failure of prohibition in the 1930's was the unwillingness of jurors to convict persons accused of violating the laws against the use of alcoholic beverages.[14] A more recent and notorious example of jury nullification concerned the frequent failure of white southern juries to indict or convict whites shown to be guilty of crimes against Negroes or civil rights workers.[15] Jury acquittals of police officers guilty of unprovoked assaults on unpopular persons fit in the same category.[16] The leading scholarly study of the jury confirms that jurors "see themselves as on trial," and are readily moved to acquit a defendant when they are out of sympathy with the prosecution or with the law he is accused of breaking, or when they are hostile to the victim or easily identify with the acts of the accused.[17]

If the community opposes punishment in a particular case, an accused criminal can readily escape punishment because he has a constitutional right to a jury trial that will be conducted under procedures that will permit a jury to acquit him. Thus, a defendant has the right to change the place of trial to escape a community attitude that is prejudicial, but a prosecutor cannot change the place of trial to avoid a community attitude that is sympathetic.

The jury's sovereign power to nullify the written law can be used to shield a person who has committed a morally reprehensible act that is approved by the community from which the jury is drawn.

Calvin A. Warren was counting on that approval when he reminded the Carthage jury that the defendants were identified with the community interest in ridding the state of the Smiths. "If these men are guilty," he declared, "then are every man, woman and child in the county guilty."[18] Similarly, in the *Warsaw Signal*'s elaborate justification of the murders prior to the trial, Thomas C. Sharp referred to the Mormon leaders' "outrages on the rights of our citizens" and to the anti-Mormons' "burning desire to avenge individual wrongs." Sharp spoke of "the common street declarations of some of our most respectable citizens, that the act ought to be done, and that the perpetrators would not only be protected but honored."[19] Those who made these arguments were appealing for jury nullification, confident that the twelve non-Mormon jurors would identify with those who welcomed the death of the Smiths and would exonerate the men accused of their murder.

If the evidence was sufficient to convict the accused assassins of Joseph Smith, and if the jury acquitted them because they approved of the crime — matters that cannot be known with certainty — then the Carthage trial was a classic case of jury nullification, displacing the written law against murder with the higher law of community approval. But it is doubtful that the stoutest advocates of jury nullification would seek to justify the action of the Carthage jury as an application of that principle. First, the main theoretical justifications and historical examples of jury nullification have concerned crimes like smuggling, drinking, or other minor offenses. A deliberate public killing — even for political motives — is another matter.

Second, the case for jury nullification at least requires that the composition of the jury be reasonably representative of the entire community.[20] Otherwise, one segment of the community could gain control of the jury system and use that control to nullify the enforcement of laws enacted for the protection of all citizens. Southern juries that have acquitted persons who have committed crimes against blacks and civil rights workers have been notoriously unrepresentative because of deliberate exclusion of the black citizens of their communities. By the same token, the jury of Carthage "bystanders" that the elisors selected to sit in judgment on the indicted assassins of Joseph Smith was assembled in such a way as to exclude all Mormons, even though they comprised at least half the population of the county. If Judge Young had not set aside the legally constituted and representative jury and approved a procedure for choosing an unrepresentative one, the jury might not have exonerated the murderers by a verdict of acquittal. The most likely outcome, in view of the comparative weakness of the prosecution's evidence, would have been a stalemated or "hung" jury. Such a result would have been a fairer representation of the political and ideological dissension in Hancock County, and would at least have certified that the judicial system had not yet completed its task.

For the anti-Mormon defendants tried and acquitted at Carthage, the jury, as voice of the community, had provided a ceremonial cleansing by which the defendants could return to society absolved of the stigma of murder and fully qualified to function in a community soon to be rid of the Mormons. Many years later, when Thomas C. Sharp was asked after a long and creditable career in politics and government in Warsaw if he had murdered Joseph Smith, his only response was fully relevant — "Well, the jury said not."[21] The democratic version of the higher law — popular sovereignty — had been applied to his case; its spokesman, the jury, had fully exonerated him of any sense of guilt.

For the Mormons, the Carthage trial epitomized the deficiencies of popular sovereignty as higher law. Despite their electoral majority and formal control of the county commission, they could not enjoy the benefits of popular sovereignty in Hancock County. This was apparent from the judge's decision to have the jury selected by appointed officials rather than by elected commissioners. As a minority in the state, the Mormons had to respond to the will of the majority, subject only to the limited and remote guarantees of the written constitution. In their case those guarantees proved insufficient to preserve either their prerogatives as the elected majority or their rights as a participating minority.

1. *Warsaw Signal,* July 10, 1844.
2. *Ibid.*
3. Wheat Notes on Warren argument.
4. John Reeves, *History of the English Law,* 2nd ed. (New York: Augustus

M. Kelley, 1787), I, 20-21, 85-87; *Blackstone's Commentaries*, IV, 336-38. Blackstone refers to the criminal defendant who demands a jury trial as one who "hath put himself upon the country, which country the jury are." *Ibid.*, V, 349.

5. *Blackstone's Commentaries*, V, 349.

6. Mark DeWolfe Howe, "Juries as Judges of Criminal Law," *Harvard Law Review* 52 (1939), 582; Nelson, "The Legal Restraint of Power," 16, 23-25; *Revised Statutes of Illinois* (1845), 186.

7. Roscoe Pound, "Law in Books and Law in Action," *American Law Review* 44 (1910), 18-19.

8. John H. Wigmore, "A Program for the Trial of Jury Trial," *Journal of the American Judicature Society* 12 (1929), 170.

9. Joseph L. Sax, "Conscience and Anarchy: The Prosecution of War Resisters," *Yale Review* 57 (1968), 481, 487; see also "Trial by Jury in Criminal Cases," *Columbia Law Review* 69 (1969), 419.

10. Leon Radzinowicz, *A History of English Criminal Law and Its Administration from 1750* (London: Stevens & Sons, 1948), I, 91-97.

11. Nelson, "The Legal Restraint of Power," 26.

12. Charles Warren, *The Supreme Court in American History* (Boston: Little, Brown, 1926), 341-65; Worthington Chauncey Ford, ed., *Writings of John Quincy Adams* (New York: Macmillan, 1914), III, 284-88 (over 40 embargo cases prosecuted at the last term of court had failed to produce a single conviction).

13. Legal and administrative efforts to exclude Mormons from Utah juries in polygamy cases are described in Orma Linford, "The Mormons and the Law: The Polygamy Cases," *Utah Law Review* 9 (1965), 543, 553-56; Nels Anderson, *Desert Saints* (Chicago: University of Chicago Press, 1966), 263, 290, 321. Under judicial procedures approved by the Supreme Court and later embodied in the Edmunds-Tucker Act, persons who practiced or believed in polygamy — i.e., virtually all orthodox Mormons — were excluded from serving on petit juries in polygamy cases. *Reynolds* v. *United States*, 98 *United States Reports* 145, 147, 157 (1878); *Miles* v. *United States*, 103 *United States Reports* 304, 310-11 (1880); *Statutes at Large* 22 (1882), 30. The principle was even carried so far as to exclude Mormons from any grand juries who might consider polygamy indictments. *Clawson* v. *United States*, 114 *United States Reports* 477 (1885). It is interesting to note, however, that the grand jury that indicted and the petit jury that convicted George Reynolds, defendant in the leading Supreme Court case, were composed of about equal numbers of Mormons and non-Mormons. Linford, "The Mormons and the Law," 332-33.

14. Message from the President of the United States, *Enforcement of the Prohibition Laws of the United States*, House Document No. 722, 71st Cong., 3rd sess. (1931), 21-60. The reluctance of juries to convict in such cases is described in W. C. Durrant, ed., *Law Observance* (New York: Durrant Award Office, 1927), 216, 450, 474.

15. *Report of the United States Commission on Civil Rights* 5 (1961), 42, 107, 110; Harry H. Shapiro, "Limitations in Prosecuting Civil Rights Violations," *Cornell Law Quarterly* 46 (1960-61), 532, 537 n. 17; Ronald Goldfarb and Stephen Kurzman, "Civil Rights v. Civil Liberties: The Jury Trial Issue," *UCLA Law Review* 12 (1965), 486, 487; Paul Good, "The White Hand of Justice," *Nation* 201 (1965), 278.

16. Rudolph Unger, "Jury Absolves Policeman in Beating Case," *Chicago Tribune*, December 6, 1969, p. 10, col. 5-6.

17. Harry Kalven and Hans Zeisel, *The American Jury* (New York: Little, Brown, 1966), 296. Also see pp. 227-36, 247-49, 286-97.

18. Wheat Notes on Warren argument.

19. *Warsaw Signal,* July 10, 1844.

20. The American tradition of trial by jury, considered in connection with either criminal or civil proceedings, necessarily contemplates an impartial jury drawn from a cross-section of the community. *Glassner* v. *United States,* 315 *United States Reports* 60, 85-86 (1942).

21. Gay Davidson, "Early Mormon Days in Illinois," *Chicago Times,* February 12, 1887.

⟋ Afterword ⟍

A persistent Utah myth holds that some of the murderers of Joseph and Hyrum Smith met fittingly gruesome deaths — that Providence intervened to dispense the justice denied in the Carthage trial.[1] But the five defendants who went to trial, including men who had been shown to be leaders in the murder plot and others associated with them, enjoyed notably successful careers.

After losing his election for sheriff in Hancock County in 1846, Mark Aldrich left Illinois for California during the Gold Rush. By the 1860's he had settled in Tucson, Arizona, where he served as postmaster and was elected to three terms in the upper house of the territorial legislature, acting during the 1866 term as its president. He died in Tucson in 1874 at the age of seventy-three.[2]

Jacob C. Davis distinguished himself as one of Hancock's most successful politicians. He was reelected to the state senate in 1846, 1850, and 1854, making four successive terms. In 1856 he was elected to Congress, filling a vacancy created by the resignation of William A. Richardson, but he was defeated in his bid for reelection.[3]

William N. Grover ran last among four candidates for state representative from Hancock County in 1852; afterward he moved to St. Louis, where he practiced law. In 1863 he was appointed U.S. attorney for the eastern district of Missouri. He moved back to Warsaw prior to 1871 and was still living there in 1890, prosperous and respected.[4]

His political objectives toward the Mormons attained, Thomas Sharp gave up the *Warsaw Signal* in 1846. Thereafter he became an educator, lawyer, judge, and, again, a newspaperman. He was elected delegate to the state constitutional convention in 1847, was chosen justice of the peace in 1851, and in 1853 he began the first of three successful terms as mayor of Warsaw. He was unsuccessful as a Republican candidate for Congress in 1856, but in 1865 he was elected to a four-year term as judge of Hancock County, where he was "greatly esteemed." Still later he served as school principal. When he died in 1894, at the age of eighty, he owned the *Carthage Gazette,* which he left to his son.[5]

Levi Williams, psychologically a more violent man than the others, was active in raiding Mormon settlements as late as May, 1846. Nothing is known about his career after this, except that he served as postmaster of Green Plains, that the Mormons took routine notice of his death in 1858, and that he is buried beneath an imposing gravestone in the cemetery in Green Plains.[6] Captain Robert F. Smith, whose Carthage Greys failed in their guard duty at the jail, was a colonel of the Illinois militia in the Civil War. He participated in Sherman's siege of Atlanta and the march to the sea. At Savannah he was brevetted brigadier general, and he served for a time as military governor in that area.[7]

The subsequent careers of counsel for the defense were even more noteworthy. William A. Richardson served as a major in the Mexican War and was then elected to Congress for five successive terms. At the height of his power he was chairman of the House Committee on Territories which reported the Kansas-Nebraska Bill, and was the unsuccessful choice of the Democratic caucus for speaker of the House. In 1856 he left Congress to accept his party's nomination for governor. After he lost this election, President Buchanan named him governor of the Nebraska Territory. Back in Congress for his sixth term, Richardson was elected in 1862 to complete the remaining two years in the Senate term of the deceased Stephen A. Douglas.[8]

Onias C. Skinner served in the Illinois legislature, as a justice of the Illinois Supreme Court, and as a leader in the constitutional convention of 1869. Calvin A. Warren was a master in chancery for sixteen years and was three times elected states attorney for the fifth judicial circuit.[9] Archibald Williams served for four years as U.S. attorney for Illinois. In 1861 his close personal and professional friend, Abraham Lincoln, named him U.S. district judge for the district of Kansas.[10] Colonel E. D. Baker, who joined Browning in representing Sharp and Williams in their preliminary hearing in Quincy, commanded a regiment in the Mexican War and was then elected to Congress from the Galena district of Illinois. Later he moved to Oregon, where the legislature named him to serve in the U.S. Senate in 1859. He was killed in action at the beginning of the Civil War, at Ball's Bluff in October, 1861.[11]

Of all the participants in the trial, the one who made the greatest impact on the nation's history was Orville H. Browning, the leader of the defense. In 1856 he was one of the founders of the Republican party, and in 1860 he played a significant role in securing the Republican presidential nomination for Abraham Lincoln. In 1861 he served an interim appointment in the Senate until the state legislature filled the vacancy created by the death of Stephen A. Douglas, and he acted as "Lincoln's mouthpiece" in the Senate during this period. President Andrew Johnson named Browning secretary of the interior in 1866. He concluded his career as a leading member of the Illinois bar.[12]

The only principals involved in the Carthage trial who seem to have been stalked by tragedy in their later careers were the prosecutors, the sheriff, the judge, and the governor.

The first prosecutor, Murray McConnell, enjoyed continued success in the political arena, including a presidential appointment as auditor of the U.S. Treasury and a term as state senator. In 1869 he was murdered in his law office in Jacksonville, shot by a man who owed him money.[13] William Elliot, the prosecutor who obtained the indictment, served as quartermaster of an Illinois regiment during the Mexican War and died at home shortly after his return.[14] James H. Ralston, the states attorney pro tem during the trial, also served in the Mexican War. He moved to California, where he perished in the Sierra Nevada Mountains.[15]

Sheriff Minor Deming's sudden death soon after his indictment for the killing of Samuel Marshall has already been described. Colonel John J. Hardin, who had been instrumental in the arrest of Sharp and Williams, was killed in the battle of Buena Vista in the Mexican War.[16]

But no sequels were more tragic than those of the chief prosecutor, the judge, and the governor. Already in decline at the time of the trial, Josiah Lamborn continued his heavy drinking and lost any remaining respect among his colleagues at the bar. His biographer states that he abandoned his wife and child and consorted with gamblers. He died of delirium tremens at Whitehall, Green County, Illinois, in 1847, a miserable man who is remembered chiefly for his venality in office and for his association with contemporaries like Douglas and Lincoln, who rose to the great heights he sought but could not attain.[17]

Judge Richard M. Young sought the Democratic nomination for Governor in 1846 but was defeated. He took up residence in Washington, D.C., where a friend from his Senate days, President James K. Polk, appointed him commissioner of the General Land Office in 1847. Dismissed from that job in less than two years, when the Whigs came to power with Zachary Taylor, Young then persuaded the House of Representatives to elect him clerk of the House for a two-year period ending in 1851. Thereafter he practiced law in Washington, gradually descending the ladder of prominence which he longed to climb. In 1858 his reason failed him, and he was forced to retire. In 1860 he was admitted to the Government Hospital for the Insane. He was released after six months but died a year later, broken in fortune, body, and mind.[18]

Governor Thomas Ford, who had initiated the prosecution to vindicate the honor of the state, was turned out of office in 1846. He retired to his home in Peoria, where he was dependent upon the charity of the local citizens to provide him with necessities. While afflicted with the consumption that took his life in 1850, he wrote his excellent *History of Illinois,* by which he hoped to provide some support for his destitute children. In his history Ford lamented the possibility that the names of "Nauvoo, and the Carthage Jail, may become holy and venerable names, places of classic interest, in another age; like Jerusalem, the Garden of Gethsemane, the Mount of Olives, and Mount Calvary to the Christian. . . ." Ford wrote that, if this were to be the case, he felt "degraded by the reflection, that the humble governor of an obscure State, who would otherwise be forgotten in a few years, stands a fair chance, like Pilate and Herod, by their official connection with the true religion, of being dragged down to posterity with an immortal name, hitched on to the memory of a miserable imposter."[19]

1. See Lundwall, *The Fate of the Persecutors,* 292-358.

2. Gregg, *History of Hancock County,* 637, 653-54; Cochran, *History of Hancock County,* 155; *Acts, Resolutions and Memorials Adopted by the First Legislative Assembly of the Territory of Arizona* (Prescott: Office of the Arizona Miner, 1865), 4; *Acts, Resolutions and Memorials Adopted by the Third Legislative Assembly* (1867), 4; *Acts, Resolutions and Memorials Adopted by the Seventh Legislative Assembly* (Tucson: Office of the Arizona Citizen, 1873), 4.

3. Gregg, *History of Hancock County,* 450-54.

4. Hay, "The Mormon Prophet's Tragedy," 669, 673; Thomas Gregg to Mason Brayman, September 2, 1890, Mason Brayman Papers, Chicago Historical Society; Cochran, *History of Hancock County,* 598; Letter of Daniel J. Bartlett, Jr., U.S. Attorney for the Eastern District of Missouri, to Dallin H. Oaks, August 25, 1969.

5. Gregg, *History of Hancock County,* 756-57; Scofield, *History of Hancock County,* 760; Hay, "The Mormon Prophet's Tragedy," 673; Davidson, "Early Mormon Days in Illinois," *Chicago Times,* February 12, 1887; "A Mobocrat Dead," *The Latter Day Saints' Millennial Star* 56 (Liverpool and London: Anthon H. Lund, 1894), 349-50.

6. *Illinois State Register,* October 17, 1845; *Lee County Democrat,* May 16, 1846; St. Louis *People's Daily Organ,* May 14, 1846; Roberts, *Comprehensive History,* II, 330; Cochran, *History of Hancock County,* 605.

7. Roberts, *Comprehensive History,* II, 331; Gregg, *History of Hancock County,* 816; Hay, "The Mormon Prophet's Tragedy," 676.

8. Moses, *Illinois Historical,* I, 491; II, 601, 671; Holt, "The Political Career of William A. Richardson," 242-43, 262.

9. Bateman, *Historical Encyclopedia of Illinois,* 482, 577; Moses, *Illinois Historical,* II, 562, 788, 1146, 1149, 1184; Gregg, *History of Hancock County,* 452-55.

10. Bateman, *Historical Encyclopedia of Illinois,* 590; Moses, *Illinois Historical,* II, 554.

11. Linder, *Reminiscences,* 248-52; Arnold, "Recollections," 17-18; Conkling, "Recollections," 57-59.

12. Baxter, *Browning;* Moses, *Illinois Historical,* II, 600, 671, 788, 1198, 1205; Albert J. Beveridge, *Abraham Lincoln,* I (Boston: Houghton Mifflin, 1928), 180.

13. Bateman, *Historical Encyclopedia of Illinois,* 360; William K. Ackerman, *Early Illinois Railroads,* Fergus Historical Series, no. 23 (Chicago, 1884), p. 101n.

14. Gregg, *History of Hancock County,* 416.

15. *Ibid.,* 410; John M. Palmer, ed., *The Bench and Bar of Illinois,* I (Chicago: Lewis Publishing Co., 1899), 875.

16. Moses, *Illinois Historical,* I, 496.

17. Bateman, *Historical Encyclopedia of Illinois,* 327; Linder, *Reminiscences,* 259.

18. Snyder, "Forgotten Statesman," 321-27.

19. Ford, *History of Illinois,* 360; also see Linder, *Reminiscences,* 106.

✑ Religious Persuasion of Jurors ✑

Handwritten lists of the names of persons chosen for jury service during five different terms of court in 1844 and 1845 were located in the files of the Clerk of the Circuit Court in Carthage, Illinois. There were 426 names on 18 different panels of grand jurors or petit jurors during this period. All 426 names were compared with the comprehensive alphabetical index of the 1850 Illinois Census on card files in the Illinois State Archives in Springfield, and with other sources, as described below.

A prospective juror was classified as non-Mormon if his name appeared in the 1850 Census of Hancock County. Persons still in Hancock County in 1850 were assumed to be non-Mormons since most of the Mormons left Hancock County on their western migration by the fall of 1846, or shortly thereafter. Few remained by 1850. A person was also classified as non-Mormon if he resided in Illinois prior to 1839, the year when the Mormons commenced their settlement. This was determined with respect to a small number of names by use of the alphabetical list of official appointments to local and state offices in the Illinois State Archives.

A prospective juror was classified as Mormon if his religious persuasion could be determined from Mormon sources or from his presence in the 1850 Census of the Utah Territory, and if his name did not appear in the 1850 Census of Illinois. The Mormon sources used to establish religious persuasion included Smith, *History of the Church, Index*, comp. and ed. E. Keith Howick (Salt Lake City: Deseret Book Co., 1970); Frank Esshom, *Pioneers and Prominent Men of Utah* (Salt Lake City: Western Epics, 1966); "Journal History"; membership records in the Church Historian's Office; records of members, Nauvoo, Illinois, 1841-45, in the Genealogical Society; and the alphabetical card indexes of Nauvoo inhabitants and of the 1850 Census of the Utah Territory in the office of Nauvoo Restoration, Inc., Salt Lake City.

A person was classified as unknown if his name did not appear in the 1850 Census of Hancock County and if there was no other evidence of religious affiliation. The "unknown" characterization was also applied to persons whose names were too uncertain to classify — for example, where only initials were used or where the name was illegible on the handwritten jury lists. This classification was also used where available records referred to two persons with the same name, one apparently Mormon and the other apparently non-Mormon, with no way to determine which was the juror.

The worksheets showing the detail of these classifications are on deposit with the Mormon Manuscript Collection in the Harold B. Lee Library at Brigham Young University.

RELIGIOUS PERSUASION OF PERSONS ON JURY PANELS IN HANCOCK COUNTY, ILLINOIS, 1844 AND 1845

Term of Circuit Court	Religion of Prospective Jurors		
	MORMON	NON-MORMON	UNKNOWN
May Term, 1844 — Chosen by County Commissioners[a]			
Grand Jury	5	17	1
Petit Jury, First Panel	6	14	4
Petit Jury, Second Panel	7	14	3
October Term, 1844 — Chosen by County Commissioners[b]			
Grand Jury [Returned indictment in			
People v. *Levi Williams*]	0	23	0
Petit Jury, First Panel	2	20	2
Petit Jury, Second Panel	7	16	1
May Term, 1845 — Chosen by County Commissioners[b]			
Grand Jury	9	13	1
Petit Jury, First Panel [Scheduled for			
trial in *People* v. *Levi Williams*]	10	14	0
Petit Jury, Second Panel	11	11	2
Substitute Petit Jury Panels — Chosen by Elisors[c]			
First Panel [Used in trial of *People* v.			
Levi Williams]	0	22	2
Second Panel [same]	2	17	5
Third Panel [same]	1	20	3
Fourth Panel [same]	1	20	3
Special June Term, 1845 — Chosen by County Commissioners[b]			
Petit Jury, First Panel	0	24	0

Term of Circuit Court	*Religion of Prospective Jurors*		
	MORMON	NON-MORMON	UNKNOWN
October Term, 1845 — Chosen by County Commissioners[d]			
Grand Jury	8	12	3
Petit Jury, First Panel	6	12	6
Petit Jury, Second Panel	6	14	3
Substitute Grand Jury Panel — Chosen by Elisors[e]			
	4	19	0

Note: A grand jury panel contains 23; a petit jury panel contains 24.

[a] John T. Barnett (Non-**LDS** — friendly); Robert Miller (Non-**LDS** — anti); Andrew H. Perkins (**LDS**)

[b] John T. Barnett (Non-**LDS** — friendly); George Coulson (**LDS**); Andrew H. Perkins (**LDS**)

[c] William Abernethy (Non-**LDS** — anti); Thomas H. Owen (Non-**LDS** — friendly)

[d] George Coulson (**LDS**); Andrew H. Perkins (**LDS**); George Walker (Non-**LDS**)

[e] James D. Morgan (Non-**LDS**); Thomas H. Owen (Non-**LDS** — friendly)

∞ Bibliographical Note ∞

Documentary sources on the trial of the accused assassins of Joseph Smith are surprisingly diverse and richly detailed. Biographical and historical materials on the participants and related events are also abundant. Described here are the principal sources we used.

Footnote citations to "Documents" refer to "Documents Relating to the Mormon Troubles," a manuscript of brief handwritten notes on the testimony of witnesses at the trial, located in the Chicago Historical Society Library and used here by permission. These notes appear to have been made at the trial by counsel for the defendants or their partners or clerks.

Footnote citations to "Minutes of Trial" refer to "Minutes of Trial of Members of Mob Who Helped Kill Joseph Smith, the Prophet," a typewritten copy of a handwritten manuscript of trial proceedings purchased from Frank C. Baum of Quincy, Illinois, over thirty years ago and now in the possession of the Wilford C. Wood Museum in Bountiful, Utah. The typewritten copy was prepared by Wilford C. Wood and presented to the Historical Archives of the Church of Jesus Christ of Latter-day Saints in Salt Lake City, Utah. The typewritten copy is cited here because it is more legible and more accessible to scholars. Its accuracy has been verified by careful comparison with the original. The pages in the typewritten copy are unnumbered; the references noted in this book represent the sequence in the original. The original manuscript is written in at least two different hands, one apparently the same as in the "Documents" described above. This account was probably prepared by counsel for the defendants or their partners or clerks. This authorship is suggested by the manuscript's inclusion (on p. 102) of a letter dated June 20, 1845, from O. C. Skinner, one of the defense counsel, to his law partner, Almeron Wheat, concerning the text of Skinner's closing argument. The manuscript's professional origin is further suggested by the fact that the account of the trial is very detailed and shows preoccupation with legal terms and rulings, and also by the fact that it was discovered in Quincy, where defense counsel had their offices.

The "Minutes of Trial" provides the most complete single account of the trial and has been used frequently in the text of this book. In addition to a detailed narrative summary of each witness's testimony, it includes a memorandum on testimony before the grand jury, the indictment, a list of some ninety-six potential jurors with notations on those dismissed by challenges of opposing counsel and those ultimately chosen for service, notes on the closing arguments of prosecution and defense, and other less important matters pertaining to the trial. It also includes a parallel, shorter version of the testimony at the trial that only carries the narrative through the conclusion of the prosecution's case. This version is not cited in this book since it is invariably consistent with the complete and more detailed account.

Footnote citations to "Watt Manuscript" refer to a manuscript copy of George D. Watt's original minutes of the trial, which was probably made about 1858 by Daniel Mackintish, a clerk in Brigham Young's office, and is now located in the Historical Archives of the Church. The pages are unnumbered; the page references noted here represent the sequence in the original. This source covers some of the preliminaries at the trial and gives a detailed account of the trial testimony in question-answer form. The Church assigned George D. Watt, an expert in shorthand, to make an official record of the proceedings. He attended all sessions, passing his notes out of the courtroom hourly as insurance against threats that they would never reach Nauvoo. Watt later became the official reporter for the Church. See Smith, *History of the Church,* VII, 394, 404, 414, 421-22, 425; *Journal of Discourses,* I, v, vii.

Footnote citations to Sharp, *Trial of the Persons,* refer to *Trial of the Persons Indicted in the Hancock Circuit Court for the Murder of Joseph Smith,* a pamphlet published by defendant Thomas C. Sharp, apparently by enlarging and selectively editing the notes referred to above as "Documents."

All four sources on the trial have been meticulously studied and compared to construct the most reliable account of the trial testimony. All four versions generally agree in substance and thus mutually reinforce each other. Especially significant is the consistency between the "Minutes of Trial," which were apparently prepared by counsel for the defense, and the Watt Manuscript, which was prepared by a scribe representing the Mormons. The authenticity of our sources is further established by their invariable agreement with details that were also mentioned in contemporary press accounts or in documents preserved in official court records. Such differences as exist among the sources other than the Sharp pamphlet are usually merely differences in the thoroughness of the account or the precise form of expression. Where there are important discrepancies among the various versions, that fact is noted in the footnotes.

Other major sources on the events at the trial are the original file in the case of *People* v. *Levi Williams et al.,* discovered in the Hancock County Courthouse, and the *Circuit Court Record,* which contains official docket entries covering this period. Many of these original papers were photocopied, and extensive notes were made on the rest. The court files included the names of persons serving on various panels of juries, which permitted a reconstruction of the religious affiliations of jurors as shown in the Appendix. The original case file included the affidavit of prejudice and the motion to replace the juries chosen by the county commissioners, the original arrest warrant and the com plaint for the murders of the Mormon leaders (signed by John Taylor), the bond signed by the defendants to obtain their release prior to trial, the verdict of the jury, subpoenas and attachments requested by counsel for the prosecution and defense, and the judge's instructions to the jury. Also located in the Hancock County Courthouse were the original papers on the proceedings against Benjamin Brackenbury, a key prosecution witness, and non-Mormon John Elliott, a potential defendant, and the record of the prosecution of about a dozen Mormons charged with the suppression of the *Nauvoo Expositor.*

Other important sources have been located in various libraries. The Chicago Historical Society has the "muster roll" of the Warsaw Militia during its days of service at the time of the murder and a variety of other valuable documents, including an extensive collection of anti-Mormon manuscripts. The Illinois State Archives has the minutes of the county commissioners, election returns, legislative documents, and the executive records of Governor Thomas Ford. Columbia University and the Illinois Historical Library each have notes on the closing arguments of one of the defense counsel, Calvin A. Warren and Onias C. Skinner, respectively. The Archives of the United States in Washington and the Federal Records Center in Chicago both have government documents pertaining to the Mormon controversies. Census reports have also yielded valuable information. The Illinois Historical Survey at Urbana includes the letters of Minor Deming. Yale University has a manuscript history by Thomas C. Sharp. Many letters and manuscripts of importance to Mormon history are available on microfilm in the library of Southern Illinois University at Edwardsville. Brigham Young University has a large collection of sources, both Mormon and anti-Mormon, mostly on film but including some significant originals. This library's collection of typewritten diaries is perhaps the best in the world outside the Church Archives.

The study of Mormon history has been enriched in the last ten years by the greater availability to serious scholars of materials in the Archives of the Church of Jesus Christ of Latter-day Saints. We have drawn upon the journals of Joseph Smith kept by several of his scribes, and the manuscript of his history, which we have compared carefully with the published version. We have found the published version accurate in matters pertaining to our subject, and have therefore used it extensively since it is accessible to all scholars. The "Journal History of the Church," a typewritten manuscript compiled after the turn of the century by Andrew Jensen from miscellaneous original sources, has been helpful in adding to the details of our narrative. Other original sources consulted through the Archives are the journals of close associates of the Mormon prophet, such as Wilford Woodruff, William Clayton, Willard Richards, and Brigham Young, which have given us a better understanding of Mormon intentions and activities. We have also read the letters of numerous Mormon leaders. Those of Brigham Young, Almon W. Babbitt, Orson Spencer, and Willard Richards were especially helpful. The Archives also has some papers of non-Mormons, including Thomas Ford, Jacob Backenstos, and Edward Bedell. We have also benefitted by use of the collection of books and biographical material in the Genealogical Library of the Church of Jesus Christ of Latter-day Saints, and by access to the indexes of inhabitants of Nauvoo and the Utah Territory, prepared by Rowena J. Miller of Nauvoo Restoration, Inc. All of these sources are located in Salt Lake City.

Many excellent Ph.D. dissertations have informed us on early history, including Robert Kent Fielding's "Growth of the Mormon Church in Kirtland, Ohio" (University of Indiana, 1957); George R. Gaylor, "A Social, Economic, and Political Study of the Mormons in Western Illinois, 1839-1846: A Re-Evaluation" (University of Indiana, 1955); Warren Abner Jennings, "Zion Is Fled: The Expulsion of the Mormons from Jackson County Missouri" (University of Florida, 1962), and Marvin S. Hill, "Role of Christian Primitivism in the Origin and Development of the Mormon Kingdom, 1830-1844" (University of Chicago, 1968).

Two compilations of Mormon history materials have been of vital assistance in our location of original sources. Stanley B. Kimball's *Sources of Mormon History in Illinois, 1839-48: An Annotated Catalog of the Microfilm Collection at Southern Illinois University,* 2nd ed. rev. and enl. (Carbondale-Edwardsville, Ill., 1966), which catalogs Mormon sources in almost a hundred different locations, is unusually helpful to anyone who would do original research in this period of Mormon history. LaMar C. Berrett, *The Wilford C. Wood Collection* (Wilford C. Wood Foundation: printed by Brigham Young University, 1972), is an annotated catalog of the remarkable collection of Mormon documents and artifacts in this private museum in Bountiful, Utah.

Publications that give insight into this period of Mormon history are many. These include two contemporary accounts of the murder: George T. M. Davis, *An Authentic Account of the Massacre of Joseph Smith,* and William M. Daniels, *A Correct Account of the Murder of Generals Joseph and Hyrum Smith.* Also informative are John Hay's "The Mormon Prophet's Tragedy"; David S. Miller and Della S. Miller, *Nauvoo: The City of Joseph* (Salt Lake City: Peregrine Press, 1974); Reed Blake, *24 Hours to Martyrdom* (Salt Lake City: Bookcraft, 1973). The best scholarly study is Robert Bruce Flanders, *Nauvoo: Kingdom on the Mississippi.* Klaus Hansen's *Quest for Empire* traces the activities of the Council of Fifty in Nauvoo and beyond and is indispensable for an understanding of this period. Fawn Brodie's biography of Joseph Smith, *No Man Knows My History* (New York: Alfred A. Knopf, 1945), is generally outdated and has been criticized by Marvin S. Hill in "Secular or Sectarian History: A Critique of *No Man Knows My History,*" *Church History,* Vol. 43 (March, 1974), 78-96.

Many important articles by scholars such as James B. Allen, Richard L. Anderson, Leonard J. Arrington, Milton V. Backman, Richard L. Bushman, William A. Clebsch, Mario S. DePillis, Robert B. Flanders, Klaus Hansen, Dallin H. Oaks, and Marvin S. Hill have appeared in *Church History, B.Y.U. Studies, Dialogue: A Journal of Mormon Thought, The University of Utah Law Review,* and the *Utah Historical Quarterly.* All have been helpful in expanding our understanding of the Mormons and their history in Illinois.

Mormon and non-Mormon newspapers have been utilized throughout this book and have illuminated much of the story. Brigham Young

University probably has the largest microfilm collection of newspapers pertaining to Mormonism, including the Snider Collection, while the Church Archives also has many. Other libraries with important newspapers containing information on the Mormon controversies include the Library of Congress, the New York Public Library, the St. Louis Public Library, Huntington Library, and the libraries of Yale University and the University of Chicago.

This book has benefitted from heavy use of several local and state histories, including particularly the *History of Hancock County* by the anti-Mormon Thomas Gregg, and the more recent *History of Hancock County* by Charles J. Scofield. Biographies of several of the participating lawyers in such sources as the *Journal of the Illinois State Historical Society,* and some lectures published during the nineteenth century by the Chicago Bar Association, have provided information about early Illinois courts and their participants during the time of this narrative.

Accounts of the trial of the accused assassins of Joseph Smith have appeared in several publications. The first published account was Thomas Sharp's pamphlet, printed in Warsaw in 1845. Governor Ford devotes two pages to the trial in his *History of Illinois* (pp. 367-68). The earliest book including an attempted full description of the trial is Gregg's *History of Hancock County* (pp. 328-31, 755-56), published in 1880. Gregg's account is reproduced with some expansion in Scofield's *History of Hancock County* (pp. 850-53), published in 1921. The accuracy of these accounts on such matters as the identity of participants, the selection of the jury, and the judge's instructions to the jury suggests that their authors used the original papers in the Hancock County Courthouse. However, these accounts contain no summary of the trial testimony. Joseph Smith's *History of the Church* (VII, 420-23) contains a brief account of the trial drawn from the report of the Mormon scribe, George D. Watt. These three accounts are the basic printed sources on the trial and seem to be the principal source for all other published references up to this time. These references include Henry A. Smith, *The Day They Murdered the Prophet* (Salt Lake City: Bookcraft, 1963), 249-62; and B. H. Roberts, *The Rise and Fall of Nauvoo* (Salt Lake City: Bookcraft, 1965), 344-51. Some of the original sources pertaining to the murder of Joseph Smith and the trial of his accused assassins are published in N. B. Lundwall, ed., *The Fate of the Persecutors,* 268-79; and Keith Huntress, *Murder of an American Prophet.*

There are many works by students of American thought and legal institutions that have deepened our understanding of the roles of law and higher law in American life. Those to which we gave special attention include Perry Miller, *Life of the Mind in America;* Clinton Rossiter, *Political Thought of the American Revolution;* R. R. Palmer's first volume of *The Age of the Democratic Revolution;* William Blackstone's *Commentaries;* and Harry Kalven and Hans Zeisel, *The American Jury.*

Index

stos quartered in, 196-97; Backenstos ousted from, 198; convention of anti-Mormons, 199; mentioned, 4

Carthage Greys: hostility toward Joseph Smith, 18; guard Carthage jail, 20; flee Carthage, 21; involvement in murder rumored, 119; march to jail, 121, 144, 176; member carries message to mob, 130-31, 151, 152, 153, 156, 163-64; mentioned, 129

Cartwright, Peter: comments on Lamborn, 85

Chittenden, Abraham: testimony, 169

Christianity: and common law, xii

Circuit Court: fifth judicial circuit in Carthage, 1; October (1844) term, 48; May (1845) term, 75-79; civil business, 80-81; judges exchange assignments, 109n14; June (1845) term, 191; October (1845) term, 200

Circuit riders: arrival, 2

Civil disobedience, xi, 211

Civil rights, 212

Clay County, Mo.: Mormons in, 8, 9-10

Clayton, William: comments on anti-Mormon strategy, 72

Cole, Calvin: potential juror, 79

Commerce, Ill.: see Nauvoo

Communitarianism: Mormon, 8

Community: opinion of, 211. See also Higher law

Complaint for murder: signed by John Taylor, 38

Conspiracy: governor warned of, 19; theory explained, 52-114, 116-17; evidence evaluated, 155-57; denied, 180-81; mentioned, 143, 175

Constitution: Mormons' living, xii; guarantees insufficient for Mormons, 214

Coroner: performs sheriff's duties, 46; selects jury, 98; selects grand jury, 193

Coulson, George: candidate, 34; elected county commissioner, 46; biography, 59n1; resignation demanded, 199; abandons office, 204; mentioned, 200

Council of Fifty: described, xii, 13; seeks to avoid conflict, 71; advises Mormons to avoid Carthage, 72

County commission: key to control of

county, 46; legal duties in juror selection, 47; selects grand jurors, 48, 68, 200; abandons policy of not choosing Mormon jurors, 67-68, 77; selects potential jurors, 68, 78-79, 191, 200; disqualification sought, 97-98; significance of exclusion from jury selection, 102; no Mormon candidate for, 193

Court: rumored violence against, 49, 50; Mormons told to avoid, 72; public attendance at, 75-76

Courthouse: of Hancock County described, 3; militia camped near, 121; lookouts on, 122

Courtroom: use and description, 2, 76, 77

Crimes: in Hancock County, 3

Crooked Creek: Nauvoo Legion camps on, 50

Daniels, William M.: grand jury witness, 61n18; testimony, 125-36; testimony evaluated, 155-56, 180; similarity of grand jury and trial testimony, 164; testimony impeached, 164-68, 180, 183; accused of bribery, 166-68, 183; testimony excluded, 172-73; jury instructed to disregard testimony, 190n95; mentioned, 66, 176, 177

— booklet: contents of, 87-89; discounted by historians, 90; authorship, 127, 129-30; compensation received, 168; arrangement with Littlefield, 168; admitted as evidence, 171; described, 172

Daviess County, Mo.: Mormons in, 10

Davis, George T. M.: reports of rumors at Carthage, 19; says vigilantes planned murder, 22; threatens to implicate governor, 35; justifies murders, 35

Davis, Jacob C.: subpoenaed, 49; indicted, 51; biography, 55-56; officer in militia, 55-56, 86; arrested at Springfield, 65; Mason, 66; defendant at trial, 79; refuses to kill prisoner, 119; militia calls coward, 126; not at jail, 126, 153; heard agreeing to murder, 129; witness doesn't incriminate, 136, 153, 155, 173; returned to Warsaw, 145; says Smiths finished, 147, 148; witness incriminates, 149; en route to

∾ Illustration Sources ℘

Joseph Smith: Brigham Young University, photograph by Rick Nye.

Daniels, *Correct Account:* Illinois State Historical Library, Springfield.

Mark Aldrich: Arizona Historical Society, Tucson.

Thomas C. Sharp: Thomas Gregg, *History of Hancock County* (Chicago: Chas. C. Chapman & Co., 1880).

Thomas Ford: Illinois State Historical Library, Springfield.

Richard M. Young: J. F. Snyder, "Forgotten Statesman of Illinois, Richard M. Young," *Transactions of the Illinois State Historical Society* (1906), 302.

Orville H. Browning: A. J. Beveridge, *Abraham Lincoln, 1809-1858,* II (Boston: Houghton Mifflin, 1928).

William A. Richardson: John Moses, *Illinois Historical & Statistical,* II (2nd rev. ed., Chicago: Fergus Printing Co., 1895).

John Peyton, George Walker, James Gittings, and Frederick M. Walton: Thomas Gregg, *History of Hancock County* (Chicago: Chas. C. Chapman & Co., 1880).

Hamilton House: Church Library Archives Historical Department, Salt Lake City.

Hancock County Courthouse: Charles J. Scofield, *History of Hancock County* (Chicago: Munsell, 1921).

Mormon History from the University of Illinois Press

MORMONISM IN
TRANSITION
The Latter-day Saints and
Their Church, 1890-1930
THOMAS G. ALEXANDER

BRIGHAM YOUNG
American Moses
LEONARD J. ARRINGTON

JOSEPH SMITH AND
THE BEGINNINGS
OF MORMONISM
RICHARD L. BUSHMAN

NAUVOO
Kingdom on the Mississippi
ROBERT BRUCE FLANDERS

RELIGION AND SEXUALITY
The Shakers, the Mormons, and
the Oneida Community
LAWRENCE FOSTER

THE OCCULT IN AMERICA
New Historical Perspectives
HOWARD KERR AND
CHARLES L. CROW

HEBER C. KIMBALL
Mormon Patriarch and Pioneer
STANLEY B. KIMBALL

THE SAINTS AND
THE UNION
The Utah Territory during
the Civil War
E. B. LONG

POLITICAL DELIVERANCE
The Mormon Quest for
Utah Statehood
EDWARD LEO LYMAN

CARTHAGE CONSPIRACY
The Trial of the Accused
Assassins of Joseph Smith
DALLIN H. OAKS AND
MARVIN S. HILL

STUDIES OF THE BOOK
OF MORMON
B. H. ROBERTS
Edited with an introduction by
Brigham D. Madsen, with a
biographical essay by Sterling
M. McMurrin

MORMON THUNDER
A Documentary History
of Jedediah Morgan Grant
GENE A. SESSIONS

MORMONISM
The Story of a New Religious
Tradition
JAN SHIPPS

THE PLAINS ACROSS
The Overland Emigrants and
the Trans-Mississippi West,
1840-60
JOHN D. UNRUH, JR.